1872

STORIES OF RANGERS PLAYERS
OF YESTERYEAR

1872

STORIES OF RANGERS PLAYERS OF YESTERYEAR

DAVID HERD

First published 2022 by DB Publishing, an imprint of JMD Media Ltd,

Nottingham, United Kingdom.

ISBN 9781780916286

Printed in the UK

CONTENTS

DEDICATION

To my wife Diane, son Graeme and granddaughter Lily.
But most of all to the man who gave me my lifetime love of Rangers FC, my dad.
To Harry Herd, 1939–2014.

FOREWORD

'THERE'S NOT a team like the Glasgow Rangers' is a line from a song I was taught when not old enough to read or write. Like countless others, I was brought up in a family steeped in the tradition of following the club, and in my early years that was a time when our rivals from across the city were dominating. One of my most treasured possessions is an old colour photograph of me when four years old in my full Rangers strip, the iconic 1960s v-neck jersey.

Just before my fifth birthday, my first match was on 3 August 1968, a pre-season friendly against English giants Arsenal that finished 2-2. For years, my favourite bedtime reading was *Rangers – The New Era* by William Allison, a gift from my dad, and at primary school I was the wee guy who could tell you all about Moses McNeil, Alan Morton and George Young. Fast forward to 2022, and I'm now the guy on internet message boards posting articles about games and players from bygone years, with my season ticket in the Main Stand next to my son and my best pal my most prized possession.

Rangers inject that kind of passion into your soul, and once it is in there it stays for life. My club is about to celebrate its 150th birthday, a historic occasion that will rightly be marked the world over. Those internet articles seemed to be well received by other supporters who read them, with a few suggesting I should turn them into a book. The club's birthday seems a fitting time to do just that.

'Four lads had a dream' in 1872, and 1872 is the inspiration for this book. Ours is a football club with an unrivalled history of humble beginnings, hard work, cherished traditions, spectacular success, and some terrible tragedies. And at the centre of every football club are the men who represent the team, and the supporters, on the pitch. Football is nothing without fans, but success is impossible without great footballers.

In 150 years, Rangers have had more great players than most, with the very best inducted into the club's Hall of Fame. But are enough of those heroes celebrated as widely as they deserve to be? Every fan can talk of John Greig, Brian Laudrup, Jim Baxter, Davie Cooper, Sandy Jardine or Ally McCoist. They, and many other modern legends, need no new books repeating the same tales of their achievements. The '18' in the book's title refers to 18 Rangers greats from the Hall of Fame who mostly starred before even the oldest living supporters can remember. This section of the book looks to bring to life some names who feature in the Hall of Fame board at the top of the marble staircase and are long gone. Few, if any, will have seen them play.

But in 150 years there are so many other players who have stories that deserve telling and are not in that illustrious Hall of Fame. The '72' in the book title gives the total number of players whose stories are covered. The remaining 54 players are not in the Hall of Fame but some deserve to be for outstanding Rangers careers. Some provided landmark moments in the 150 years of the club. Some had brief careers at Ibrox, but found fame elsewhere. The second chapter of the book tells all kinds of individual stories, with each one having one thing in common: they played for Rangers.

I hope you find the book informative and entertaining.

ACKNOWLEDGEMENTS

MY HEARTFELT thanks go to many great people.

Firstly, Iain McColl and Gordon Bell at The Founders Trail, who do such a magnificent job of keeping alive the stories of the pioneers who created Rangers Football Club. Not only did they inspire me to research deeper into the club's incredible history, but they agreed to supply me with many photographs from their collection, allowing readers to picture many of the men featured who are now long gone. To show my gratitude, 50 per cent of any money I make from this book will be donated to their Restoration of Rangers Graves Project.

Another wonderful source of pictures came from Jim Lepick, who I got to know online but who lives within a couple of miles of my house. His amazing collection of Rangers memorabilia was invaluable in unearthing photographs from many years ago, and he has my eternal gratitude for supplying them freely.

Although the book is about players who wore the colours of Rangers, many of them also enjoyed great success at other clubs. I am indebted to the images provided by fans of these teams. In particular, Paul Days at Ryehill Football kindly allowed the use of a number of photographs from his huge collection from the history of Sunderland FC.

Also, my gratitude to my niece Shannon Watson, who helped proofread the book, spotting too many mistakes for me to admit to.

Finally, a big thank you to Michelle Grainger at JMD Media. Thank you for believing in my idea and in the advice given to allow me to turn it into a published work.

THE EIGHTEEN

1 ALEC SMITH

The first, but little-known, great Rangers left-winger

THERE WILL never be a definitive answer on who has been the greatest player to wear the Rangers colours; it is an impossible task to choose just one. But whenever the debate arises, one name that rarely get mentioned as part of the discussion is that of the first superstar winger to wear the shirt, Alec Smith.

Rangers have been blessed over the years to have had some truly outstanding wingers. The first in that illustrious long line was born in Darvel, Ayrshire, on 7 November 1875. As a teenager he starred for his local junior side, and was spotted by another son of the town, Rangers full-back Nicol Smith, who was no relation. Nicol saw a young player of speed, agility, instant ball control, and an eye for a pass, and he mentioned this to the club, recommending they offer Alec a trial. In early 1894, Rangers had just won the Scottish Cup for the first time in their history, and the club was celebrating the achievement as well as casting an eye out for potential talent to join the following season. A match was organised against FA Cup holders Notts County, and Rangers fielded Smith as a trialist to see if the recommendation of his better known Darvel namesake was worth pursuing.

Alec Smith was sensational. Undaunted by the exalted company he was suddenly playing in, he terrorised the County defence in a 3-1 victory. Rangers immediately offered him a contract, and at the age of just 18, Alec Smith became a Ger. Incredibly, he would still be wearing the Royal Blue over 20 years later, during the early days of World War One.

Rangers already had a highly effective goalscoring outside-left in John Barker, the first man ever to score a hat-trick for the club in a competitive Old Firm match. He started season 1894/95 still the man in possession of the jersey, but Smith was in brilliant form for the reserve team, and within the club it was accepted as a matter of time before he was given his chance in the first team. On 27 October 1894 the 18-year-old made his debut in a Glasgow Cup semi-final against Partick Thistle. His league bow came a few days later, and he made it a day to remember by scoring twice in an emphatic 5-1 home win over Leith Athletic. On 18 November he took to the field against Celtic for the first time, in the Glasgow Cup Final, but had to settle for a second prize in a 2-0 loss.

Smith wasn't yet an automatic choice, but in that first season he played 11 times, scoring three goals. As well as being a runner-up in the Glasgow Cup, he also played in a losing Charity Cup Final to Celtic. He ended the season as the first-choice left-winger in a Rangers team who finished third in the league behind winners Hearts, and in 1895/96 he nailed the place down by having a brilliant season.

Rangers didn't win any trophies, although they improved their league placing to second behind Celtic, but the young Ayrshire winger had done all he could to land a prize. He started in 17 of the 18 league games, scoring a hugely impressive 13 times. This included a four-goal haul against St Mirren, and strikes home and away against Celtic. Sadly, both those derby matches ended in heavy defeats. He scored in the Scottish Cup loss to Hibs and in the Glasgow Cup defeat to Queen's Park; the only competition he failed to score was the Charity Cup, which saw another big defeat to Celtic. Although he was a great creator for others, Smith was also proving to be a goalscoring match-winner in his own right, his 22 goals in all competitions in 1895/96 remaining his highest scoring season for the rest of his career.

Season 1896/97 saw Smith claim his first of many medals at the club. Rangers struggled again for the consistency to mount a serious league title challenge and Smith started 17 league games, scoring five times in another campaign that ended in third place. But Rangers kept their best for the cup competitions, and completed a memorable clean sweep for the first time. Smith scored in the Glasgow Cup semi-final thumping of Linthouse, then lined up in a familiar final against Celtic. After a 1-1 draw, he was part of the team who triumphed 2-1 in the replay on 21 November 1896 thanks to a double by centre-forward Peter Turnbull. Partick, Hibs and Dundee were all beaten in the Scottish Cup, setting up a semi-final with Morton. Smith scored one of Rangers' seven goals in a 7-2 rout, and it was old foes Dumbarton who were waiting in the final. On 20 March, Smith ran riot in the second half, scoring once in a 5-1 demolition that featured a four-goal blitz in just 16 minutes. Then in the end-of-season Charity Cup, Smith again scored in an emphatic 4-1 semi-final thumping of Celtic, and notched another in a 6-1 final victory over Third Lanark. Three winners' medals in the one season, scoring in all three semi-finals and two finals.

After their cup successes, Rangers started 1897/98 with high hopes they could mount a more successful league challenge, especially after signing the much-heralded R.C. Hamilton. But despite only two losses in the league all season, they finished second behind a Celtic team who lost none at all. Smith hit 12 goals in 17 league games, including a fine hat-trick against Clyde. He also helped defeat Celtic in the Glasgow Cup semi-final, being the tormentor in chief of their defence while Hamilton grabbed a double. Smith then scored one of the goals in the 4-0 win over Queen's Park in the final as Rangers retained their trophy. The Scottish Cup was also retained, Smith scoring six times in the competition, including a vital strike in a 1-1 semi-final draw with Third Lanark and the crucial opening goal in the final against Kilmarnock, which was won 2-0. Smith, incredibly, was one of seven Ayrshire players in the Rangers team that day. After defeating Celtic in the Charity Cup semi-final, Rangers looked odds on to win all three cups again, but Smith was shocked in the final when Third Lanark edged it by 1-0.

This was a Rangers team who hadn't been Scottish champions since 1891, but whose cup exploits had many neutrals calling the best team in the country. As well as Smith, the side was sprinkled with international-class footballers such as John McPherson, Neilly Gibson, Jock Drummond as well as Nicol Smith and R.C. Hamilton. And Alec Smith himself became an international player on 2 April 1898 when he lined up at Parkhead against England alongside club team-mates Drummond, Gibson and Jimmy Millar in a 3-1 defeat. Alec would go on to represent Scotland 20 times, a huge number of caps back in the days when there were often just three international matches per year. He played for Scotland in three different decades, his last appearance coming in April 1911, and he scored three times for his country. Probably his finest match for his country was in 1900 when he was superb in a 4-1 thrashing of England. At the time, when he won his 20th cap this was a record for any Scottish player. As well as those 20 full caps, he also played 14 times for the Scottish League.

Season 1898/99 was when Rangers finally brought back the title to Ibrox, and they did it in historic style with an incredible record of played 18, won 18. Smith played a huge role in it as one of five players who were ever present. He again scored 12 times in the league, his incredible consistency of performance being what helped make him such a special player. As well as weighing in with plenty goals for a winger, he was also the man whose ability to beat an opponent and to find his team-mates with a killer pass resulted in him being the main creative force for the other forwards. He had now built an almost telepathic understanding with Hamilton, the captain and centre-forward banging in 21 goals in those 18 games. Smith hit four goals in a record 10-0 win over Hibs to clinch the title on Christmas Eve, and he scored one of the goals against Clyde on the final weekend of the season to clinch the history-making 100 per cent record. With the focus all on the league, Rangers failed to win any of the cup competitions that season, but their championship record will mean Alec Smith and his 1898/99 team-mates are immortals.

Rangers had last lost a league game on 12 February 1898, and amazingly this would be their final league defeat of the 1800s. Smith started in 16 of the 18 league games in 1899/1900, and it would be match number 15 before they tasted defeat, a 3-2 loss at Parkhead on 1 January 1900, with Smith scoring the first Rangers goal and becoming the club's first goalscorer of the 20th century. Overall, he hit 13 goals in the league to maintain his excellent goals return. These included a hat-trick against Dundee, doubles against Clyde and Hibs, as well as an Ibrox Old Firm goal to go with his New Year's Day strike at Parkhead. Celtic ended hopes of adding the Scottish Cup, but Smith got his revenge in the other two competitions, playing in victories over them in both the Glasgow and Charity Cup Finals. The Charity Cup Final on 12 May saw the season rounded off in particular style with a 5-1 battering of their deadly rivals.

Smith enjoyed three-in-a-row title success in 1900/01. He again hit double figures with ten goals in all competitions, including one in a thrilling 3-3 Glasgow Cup semi-final against Celtic. He picked up yet another winners' medal in that competition to go along with that third league badge but the Scottish Cup was again a disappointment with a first-round loss at Parkhead.

Still only 25 years old, Smith was a fixture for club and country and was widely regarded as one of the finest players in Scotland. He enjoyed another ever-present league season in

1901/02 when Rangers made it four successive championships, scoring in the last-day win over Dundee that clinched the title. He also won another Glasgow Cup, but in strange circumstances when Celtic refused to play in a replayed final after being ordered to play the match at Ibrox after the original drawn match was also played there. But the entire season at the club was overshadowed by the awful events of 5 April 1902 when a stand collapse at Ibrox during a Scotland v England international caused 25 fatalities. Smith played in that fateful match, and also in the rearranged fixture played at Villa Park the following month. Other Rangers players on the field in the disaster match were Nicol Smith, Jock Drummond and Jacky Robertson.

Rangers immediately decided that their priority had to be raising funds to both rebuild Ibrox and to compensate the families of the victims. Numerous fundraising matches were played, with the Charity Cup being expanded to allow non-Glasgow clubs to enter, thus increasing the number of matches. Hibs were to win the cup, beating Celtic in the final. Several players were sold but Smith remained very much a Ranger, and like all his colleagues he was determined to win silverware in 1902/-3 as a memorial to those who had been killed. Perhaps unsurprisingly, Rangers lost three of their first five league games, and although regaining their form and focus later in the campaign the league was lost to Hibs. Smith played in all 22 league games, his six goals including getting on the score sheet in a 1-1 draw at Parkhead.

Neither the Glasgow Cup or Charity Cup saw Rangers challenge, with first-round exits in both, but it was the Scottish Cup that everyone at the club most wanted. Smith scored in an outstanding quarter-final win over Celtic away from home, opening the scoring in only four minutes as Rangers scored three times in the first half hour. The opponents in the final were to be Hearts, and it took three matches before a winner emerged. Smith was one of the heroes in the 2-0 replay victory, not scoring but playing in a more defensive role for much of the match after Rangers went down to ten men having lost Jock Drummond to injury. Little did Smith know at the time, but this would be his third and last winners' medal in the Scottish Cup, as the club then endured a competition jinx that was to last quarter of a century before the trophy was finally reclaimed in 1928.

The next seven seasons were the most barren spell of Smith's Rangers career, as the dominant team of the time broke up and manager Wilton searched for the right replacements. The constant over those years, though, was the magnificent Alec Smith. He started 32 games in 1903/04, although only scoring four times. Rangers ended the season in fourth but came so close to retaining the Scottish Cup after leading Celtic 2-0 in the final. Unfortunately, the match swung the other way and ended in a heartbreaking 3-2 reverse, but Smith did gain some revenge a few weeks later when he was outstanding in a 5-2 hammering of the same opponents at Hampden in the Charity Cup.

Season 1904/05 saw Smith play more games – 42 – than in any other season in his long Ibrox career. A much-improved goal tally of 11 wasn't enough to bring any trophies to the club. The league was particularly painful, Smith playing in the losing championship play-off against Celtic after both teams finished on the same points. If either goal difference or goal average had existed back then, Smith would have won a fifth title. To add to the pain, he scored in the Scottish Cup Final replay against Third Lanark, but his 81st-minute goal made little difference to a match that was lost 3-1.

By 1905/06, Rangers were virtually unrecognisable from the team who had won four successive titles. Smith now shared the forward line with the likes of Archie Kyle, Jimmy Speirs and R.S. McColl alongside the evergreen R.C. Hamilton, finishing the season a distant fourth behind Celtic. Smith scored seven times in 37 starts; the only trophy he won was the Charity Cup when he scored in the 5-3 semi-final win at Parkhead and played in the final victory over Queen's Park.

The Charity Cup was his only success again the following season, Smith starting in a 1-0 final win over Celtic with a goal by the ex-Celtic player and future Rangers director Bob Campbell. He scored a total of eight goals in 32 starts, with the only other real highlight being an unexpected but deserved new year win in the Old Firm derby. Celtic easily retained their title and also knocked Rangers out the Scottish Cup.

Things somewhat repeated in 1907/08 as Smith again started 32 games, once more finishing behind Celtic in the title race and suffering a Scottish Cup defeat to them. He played in the painful 1-0 loss to them at Ibrox on 25 April 1908 that meant Celtic won the title, he and ended the season with no more medals. The following season saw Smith rack up another 40 appearances and add nine more goals to his tally. Celtic were clear champions again, with Rangers losing eight league games over the season. But they did reach the Scottish Cup Final, and Smith played in both drawn matches before the cup was withheld after serious rioting by both sets of supporters when no extra time was played after the second draw. He did get his hands on some silverware, though, enjoying a fine game in a 4-2 defeat of Celtic in the Charity Cup Final in mid-May.

By 1909/10, Smith was now well into his 30s but as indispensable as ever. Manager Wilton had decided to look south for new players, and there was much excitement at the purchase of English international Billy Hogg, English goalkeeper Herbert Lock and free-scoring Scottish centre-forward Willie Reid, signed from Portsmouth. Along with ex-Celtic forward Alec Bennett, signed the previous year, Rangers now had what appeared to be a fearsome forward line. But the season was to be a big disappointment, both for Rangers and for Smith. He suffered some niggling injuries, restricting him to 25 appearances, and his goal tally of two was his lowest of his Rangers career. He was now, however, a different player to the explosive winger of his younger days, now a more measured and thoughtful footballer who relied more on craft than on pace. Rangers ended the season third and trophyless, losing to Bill Struth's Clyde team in the Scottish Cup, and losing to Celtic in a Glasgow Cup Final that Smith missed through injury.

But 1910/11 would see Smith finally be a champion again. Despite his advancing years, he remained the first-choice outside-left at the club, starting 29 times in the league. Although only scoring four league goals, these included important strikes in wins over Hibs and Third Lanark in the run-in as Rangers took the title by four points. Smith may not have been the goalscorer he once was, but he created plenty for the incredible Reid, who hit a scarcely believable 38 league goals in 33 games, and ended the season with 48 goals in all competitions. Apart from an unexpected defeat at Dundee in the Scottish Cup, Rangers dominated the season. Smith opened the scoring in the Glasgow Cup Final where Celtic were beaten 3-1, and he also started in the Charity Cup Final win over them, Reid scoring both in a 2-1 success.

This was to be the second period of league domination of Smith's long Rangers career, as the title was retained in 1911/12. Smith only scored twice in 34 games but he had a hand in many of the 39 plundered by the prolific Reid. Rangers could afford to lose three of the last five league matches and still cruise to the title, and Smith added another Glasgow Cup badge to his bulging personal trophy cabinet when he played in a final win over Partick. The annual Scottish Cup heartbreak was again provided by Clyde, who also ended the Rangers interest in the Charity Cup.

Smith was by the summer of 1912 heading towards his 37th birthday. He was determined to continue playing for as long as he could, and had no interest in wearing the colours of any other team. So he started his 19th season as a Rangers player and showed he was still a force to be reckoned with by hitting the net four times in his first seven starts of 1912/13. These included one in an amazing Glasgow Cup Final against Celtic on 12 October 1912. Rangers were a goal down at half-time, and lost defender John Robertson to a serious injury meaning they played the second half with ten men. Rather than accepting defeat, the team were inspired by their veteran winger, and Smith created an equaliser with a perfect cross for Hogg, then he scored one himself when knocking in a rebound after his initial shot was parried by the Celtic goalkeeper. The ten men clinched a memorable win with a third goal by Bennett, and Smith was named the best player on the field as he won yet another medal. He ended up playing 32 times that season, scoring seven goals, as the title was won for a third straight year. He was awarded a benefit match by the club, and such was his popularity that 35,000 paid to see him play for Rangers against an International Select team, who won the game 5-1.

Time was now catching up with Smith, and he missed the start of 1913/14 through injury then the great form of his replacement on the left wing, Jimmy Paterson. He did come back into the team in the second half of the season, but by then the title looked a forlorn hope as Rangers found themselves too far behind a very consistent Celtic team. He played in 11 league games after the turn of the year into 1914 and scored a creditable five times, including a last-day double in a 3-2 win over Hearts. He then started 1914/15 as first choice again, but after eight appearances, a combination of injuries, age and the excellence of Paterson meant that Smith played his last game for Rangers on 24 October 1914 at Ibrox in a disappointing 2-1 defeat to Raith Rovers. He was almost 39 years old, and it had been 20 years since his debut.

Smith retired from the game in early 1915. He was never booked or sent off in 624 first-team matches for Rangers, the only senior club he ever played for. Those 624 appearances put him in Rangers' all-time top five, and his 200 goals put him in the top ten scorers. After 21 seasons a Ranger, he was described in the publication *The Scottish Referee* in 1913 as being a player of 'magnificence, style and beauty' and a man of 'great character'.

After his playing career ended, he became a partner in Smith & Archibald Limited, a lace-making business in his home town of Darvel. He died on 12 November 1954, just a few days after his 79th birthday.

Alec Smith may or may not have been our greatest ever winger. But his place in our Hall of Fame is richly deserved, and his name should always be mentioned alongside the very best players in our unparalleled history. He is Rangers royalty.

- A Ranger for 21 seasons, and a one-club man
- 624 competitive appearances and 200 goals
- 87 competitive appearances against Celtic, more than any other Rangers player
- At the time, Scotland's record cap holder
- Seven league titles, including an ever present in the only ever 100 per cent league season
- Three Scottish Cups, and multiple medals in the Glasgow and Charity Cups
- League winner, Scotland international, and Old Firm goalscorer in three different decades
- A genuine footballing superstar of his era

2   ALEX VENTERS

The scorer of the winning goal in front of the record Ibrox crowd

IBROX HAS seen some famous occasions in front of huge crowds, but like any other club, Rangers have a record attendance for a match at their home ground. And just as there is only one match in Rangers' history that can boast the biggest ever crowd, there is only one player in Rangers' history who can boast of scoring the winning goal in front of more spectators than any other. This is his story.

Alex Venters was born in Cowdenbeath on 9 June 1913. Football was already a large part of life for the Venters family, his uncle Sandy being a player with Cowdenbeath and his mother Sarah coming from another well-known local footballing family, the Glancys. His father Peter did not share the love of football however; a dedicated Marxist, he was secretary of the local National Union of Mineworkers branch and spent his time in local politics.

Alex was an outstanding young player for his school, and joined Cowdenbeath as a part-timer at the age of 16 in 1930, while working in his first job at a local printing company. A quick, skilful inside-forward, Venters struck up an excellent partnership with Cowdenbeath's international centre-forward Jim Paterson, and had already been selected once for Scotland in 1933 against Ireland before his transfer to Ibrox. He notched 37 league goals for the Fifers in 95 appearances before Bill Struth paid £2,000 in November 1933 to beat off competition from Hibs and Blackburn Rovers and land his signature.

Venters made his Rangers debut on 25 November 1933 in a 3-1 home win over Falkirk and went on to play 15 league games in his debut season, not once tasting defeat. His first goal came in a six-goal thrashing of Hibs, but the highlight was his first goal against Celtic, in a 2-2 draw at Parkhead on New Year's Day 1934. Over his Rangers career, he developed a habit of scoring against our great rivals, something which really endeared him to the Rangers support. He also scored twice in the club's record victory, a 14-2 Scottish Cup win over Blairgowrie in his only Scottish Cup appearance of the season. Venters ended his first season with a championship medal, the first of four he would win, and he hit the net seven times in his 16 starts.

Over the next five years, Venters was a mainstay of the Rangers team who maintained their status under Struth as Scotland's most successful club. Season 1934/35 saw Rangers end as league champions and Scottish Cup winners. Venters scored ten times in 35 starts, including the first Rangers goal on New Year's Day at Ibrox in a 2-1 win over Celtic. He also played in every round of the Scottish Cup, winning his first final in Royal Blue when a Jimmy Smith double saw off a plucky Hamilton Accies team.

The following season saw Rangers win two cup competitions, but the league flag slipped away with too many drawn matches over the course of the campaign compared to a more consistent Celtic team. Venters won his first Glasgow Cup when he played in the October victory over Celtic, but roles were reversed in the Charity Cup when he picked up the runners-up prize. Venters had a fine season despite the disappointments, hitting the net 18 times which included league doubles against St Johnstone, Clyde and Airdrie. He scored just the once in the successful Scottish Cup run, in the first-round win over East Fife. His second winners' medal in the tournament came courtesy of a 1-0 final victory against Third Lanark, veteran Bob McPhail hitting the goal after just two minutes.

Season 1936/37 saw the league regained and Venters claiming a third championship medal. As in the last couple of seasons, he was an almost ever-present in the team at inside-right. He scored his first Rangers hat-trick on 12 September 1936, grabbing all three goals in a pulsating 3-2 win against Motherwell. A few weeks later he won another Glasgow Cup in a tense final against Partick, then he started 1937 in the best possible fashion, scoring the only goal in the Ibrox new year derby win in front of 95,000 spectators. A shock defeat at Queen of the South in the Scottish Cup didn't derail the title charge as Venters ended the season with 11 goals in 38 starts.

Several of the old guard at Ibrox had started reaching the end of the careers over the last year or two, and now new players such as Willie Thornton were being introduced into the team in 1937/38. Three draws in the first five games meant Rangers were chasing from the start, and despite a fine 3-1 win over Celtic in September featuring two Venters goals, the club's great rivals ended the season as champions. Venters also scored in a Glasgow Cup semi-final win over the Parkhead men that same month, and hit the net again in the final where Third Lanark were defeated. A Venters double was again not enough to prevent an incredible 4-3 Scottish Cup semi-final loss to Kilmarnock, meaning despite 19 goals over the campaign, it was only the Glasgow Cup that Venters won.

Season 1938/39 would be the most prolific season of Venters' career. He hit a red-hot scoring streak, notching 38 goals from just 36 appearances. These included 35 league goals, with hat-tricks against both Raith Rovers and Albion Rovers, and no fewer than seven matches where he scored a double. He hit the net in 25 of the 33 league games he started, and this included what turned out to be the winning goal in the 40th minute of the historic match against Celtic on 2 January 1939, when the all-time record attendance for a league match in Scotland saw Rangers defeat their rivals 2-1. Venters put Rangers 2-0 up that day before 118,567 people after winger David Kinnear had opened the scoring. Venters picked up an injury in February and missed four weeks of the season, and in his absence Rangers crashed out of the Scottish Cup in a dismal 4-1 reverse at Clyde. He did add a Charity Cup winners' medal to his collection at the end of the season, however, playing in a goalless final against Third Lanark that Rangers won by forcing seven corners to four.

His form earned him a third and final Scotland cap in the Hampden match with England, where he then played in front of Hampden's second-highest ever attendance of 149,269. Venters and goalkeeper Jerry Dawson shared the honour of playing before these combined crowds of almost 270,000 within the space of a few months.

There is no doubt that Venters would have gone on to greater honours. The following season he scored four in the first five league games before life changed for everyone in the world, as war was declared between the United Kingdom and Germany.

He continued to star for Rangers during the war years, playing over 180 times throughout the conflict. Included in this number was the famous 8-1 victory over Celtic on 1 January 1943, when incredibly for a man so prolific against them he didn't score. In 26 games against the team from Parkhead, Venters hit the net 16 times, putting him seventh in the all-time top scorers list in games between the clubs. During the war years he added four Southern League titles and four Southern League Cups to his medal collection. He also played four more times for Scotland.

Venters played his last game for Rangers on 24 September 1945, and scored his last Rangers goal in a 4-3 Glasgow Cup semi-final loss to Clyde at Shawfield. He joined Third Lanark after initially agreeing to rejoin his hometown club, and retired in 1948 after short spells at Cathkin followed by Blackburn Rovers and Raith Rovers.

For a time, he followed the traditional ex-player's route as mine host at the Railway Tavern, at Buckhaven. Prior to that he had owned a shop. Later, he returned to his original trade in the printing industry as a linotype operator in the Edinburgh office of the *Scottish Daily Mail*. In April 1959, Venters was preparing to leave his home in Park Street, Cowdenbeath, for night duty on the paper when he collapsed and died from a sudden heart attack. He was aged just 45.

In 2006, Venters was rightly inducted into the Rangers Hall of Fame.

- Rangers career: 1933–1945
- Scorer of over 200 Rangers goals4 Scottish league titles, plus four Southern Leagues
- 2 Scottish Cups
- Multiple Glasgow and Charity Cups
- 4 Southern League Cups
- 3 official Scotland caps and four wartime caps
- 16 goals against Celtic
- Scorer of the winning goal in front of the largest crowd Ibrox Stadium will ever see

3   ANDY CUNNINGHAM

The Rangers legend who became the oldest debutant in the English First Division

ANDY CUNNINGHAM was born in Galston in Ayrshire on 31 January 1890, and started his illustrious football career as a junior with Newmilns FC. An elegant and strong running inside-right, his ability was quickly apparent, appearing for the Scotland team at junior level before being signed by his local club Kilmarnock in 1909.

By the time he was snapped up by Rangers in April 1915, the club were getting a ready-made first team player who had scored over 70 goals for the Ayrshire side.

Cunningham's Rangers debut wasn't the most impressive start to an Ibrox career, a 1-0 home loss to Partick Thistle on 5 April 1915 as an inside-left coming just days after he signed. However, he quickly settled into life at Ibrox and scored his first Rangers goals in only his third appearance, a double in a 4-0 win over Queen's Park at Hampden on the final day of 1914/15. Coincidentally, this was the first time he had started at inside-right. His brief debut season ended when Rangers were knocked out of the Charity Cup 3-2 by Celtic in early May, although Cunningham did score his first Old Firm goal in the defeat.

The following season saw the name of Andrew Cunningham listed in 20 league starts, a season where inconsistency prevented Rangers from mounting a sustained challenge against title holders Celtic, despite Cunningham's hugely impressive 18 league goals. A highlight of these was the opening strike in the new year fixture at Parkhead, which ended 2-2. Over his time with Rangers, Cunningham enjoyed a great record against Celtic, scoring 12 times in 35 appearances.

Cunningham's Ibrox career went on hold in 1916 when he was called up for active service, one of many great Rangers players of the time to be active in the Great War. He served his country with distinction, rising to the rank of lieutenant in the Royal Field Artillery. Cunningham returned to the team briefly towards the end of 1917/18, his first game back against Third Lanark showing what the team had been missing as he notched a hat-trick. Rangers did win their league title back that season in a nail-biting finale, although Cunningham had played little part. The following season was also a stop-start affair for him as he completed his military commitments, but he did manage 20 appearances, mainly in the second half of the campaign, as the title was lost on the final day to Celtic. His total of five goals featured another hat-trick, this time against Queen's Park.

Cunningham was now back in civilian life, and back as a full-time Rangers player, and he was determined that 1919/20 would be a successful season. It proved to be precisely that as he started in 39 league matches, winning his first league medal as William Wilton's Rangers only lost two games all season. Cunningham had a spell at centre-forward in late 1919 when veteran goalscorer Willie Reid suffered an injury, and he proved a more than capable deputy by scoring an amazing 16 goals in a nine-game spell. This included four against Hibs, a hat-trick against Third Lanark, and doubles against Hamilton, Albion Rovers, Dundee and Celtic. It was the Celtic match at Ibrox on 18 October where he first moved to centre-forward, the 76,000 Ibrox crowd roaring their approval as war heroes Cunningham and Dr James Paterson shared the goals. By May, he was the club's top scorer for the season with 23 goals, and his right-wing partnership with Sandy Archibald was striking fear into every opponent. The only disappointment in an excellent season was the shock Scottish Cup semi-final loss to lowly Albion Rovers, meaning Cunningham had to wait for a chance to win a medal in the tournament. This was after knocking Celtic out in the previous round in front of a record Ibrox attendance.

That Scottish Cup heartache was to continue, with Cunningham playing in the 1920 and 1921 finals, both of which Rangers started as overwhelming favourites but lost, to Partick Thistle and then to Morton. The club seemed jinxed in the nation's premier cup tournament having last won it back in 1903. There was other more tragic news in the summer of 1920 when manager Wilton, who had been such a massive influence on Cunningham's career, died in a boating accident. This heralded the appointment of Bill Struth, and Rangers went on in the 1920s to totally dominate Scottish football (apart from the Scottish Cup), with Cunningham a key figure.

League titles, as well as the Glasgow and Charity Cups, were won with regularity. Struth's first season saw the league won with a record 76 points and only one defeat in 42 matches. Cunningham was again the top scorer, with 24 league goals, plus three more in other competitions. He scored in each of the opening nine league games, with Hibs in late September the first opposition to prevent him from hitting their net. He also scored in a revenge Scottish Cup win over the previous season's shock troops, Albion Rovers.

Despite being undefeated against Celtic in the following season, too many dropped points elsewhere saw the title relinquished. Cunningham did win a first Glasgow Cup Final when Davie Meiklejohn scored the only goal of the game, but he missed out on a first Charity Cup success through a broken jaw sustained at Hampden on 15 April 1922 in the first half of the surprise defeat to Morton.

He was back in the team for the start of 1922/23, and again started the season in goalscoring form with strikes in the club's first four matches. He won another Glasgow Cup, scoring in the first round and semi-final. He also got his hands on a first Charity Cup medal, scoring in a comfortable 4-0 final rout of Queen's Park, and he added a second league medal to his growing collection too, eventually hitting 11 goals in a campaign that saw Rangers regain the title, five points ahead of Airdrie. The only failure in the season was the Scottish Cup, Cunningham now enduring the same hoodoo that had befallen so many other great Ibrox servants in recent history as Ayr United provided what was now the annual shock result.

The pattern was almost identical in the next season. The title was secured convincingly again, and again it was Airdrie in second place. Cunningham contributed 13 goals this time from 30 appearances, including goals in the first five matches played. He won a Glasgow Cup Final, this time against Third Lanark, and he suffered another early exit in the Scottish Cup when Hibs prevailed 2-1 in the third round. The only real difference was a defeat in the Charity Cup Final, although Cunningham missed out after being injured.

Season 1924/25 was more of the same. Cunningham started 33 times in the league, scoring seven times as the title was retained easily from Airdrie, who finished second for the third successive year. No doubt the goal that gave him most satisfaction in the title race was Rangers' second goal in a 4-1 New Year hammering of Celtic. He also enjoyed a similar one-sided 4-1 win over them in the Glasgow Cup Final, where Rangers appeared to ease off in the later stages to preserve energy for upcoming matches. The Charity Cup was regained, but thoughts of a clean sweep were again dashed in the Scottish Cup where Cunningham endured a painful revenge from Celtic, who ran out shock 5-0 winners in the semi-final.

Season 1925/26 was one where Rangers suffered injuries to almost every key player at some stage. A miserable campaign saw the club end in sixth place, still the lowest placing ever for a Rangers team in the top division. Cunningham played more than most, and did what he could to salvage things by scoring 18 times in 31 starts. He scored against Celtic in a drawn Glasgow Cup semi-final, then again in another drawn replay, before Celtic won through at the third attempt. He also scored against them on New Year's Day at Parkhead, and he scored in each round of the cup to help the team to the semi-final, only to lose to St Mirren. Early defeat in the Charity Cup meant a bare trophy cabinet for the first time under Struth.

To demonstrate how important he was to Struth, Cunningham started more than 30 league games for Rangers in every season under his management through to 1926/27. And even then he played in 29 of the matches. He only hit seven goals this time, but the team were scoring freely without him having to contribute too often and the title was won back with ease as Cunningham had a sixth championship medal. He didn't add any cup medals, however, with Falkirk knocking Rangers out the Scottish Cup and Cunningham missed the 6-3 Charity Cup Final defeat to Partick as he was on international duty.

Six league medals became seven when the title was won in 1927/28. Cunningham scored in the Glasgow Cup Final loss to Celtic, but that wasn't the trophy he most desired. Despite the many triumphs and great personal performances, time appeared to be running out by now on adding that elusive Scottish Cup medal to his collection. The 1928 Scottish

Cup run to the final saw Cunningham net three times, the most important being the only goal at Cliftonhill to see off Albion Rovers in a very tight and nervous match. On 14 April 1928, just over 13 years after joining the club and at the age of 38, Cunningham finally won the medal he wanted most. In a famous and historic occasion, Rangers finally buried their Scottish Cup hoodoo in style, hammering four second-half goals into the Celtic net to win 4-0 and send the blue half of the 118,000 crowd into wild celebrations. Although not among the scorers, Cunningham was a vital player on the day, and he celebrated with as much passion and joy as any on the terraces. The season was rounded off the following weekend when Rangers secured their first league and Scottish Cup double, crushing Kilmarnock 5-1 at Ibrox. Man of the match Cunningham scored twice.

Cunningham played 12 times for the Scotland national team, scoring five times. Probably the most satisfying of these would have been a sweet strike at Hampden in a very impressive 3-0 win over England in 1921. Scotland only lost one match with Cunningham on the field.

Cunningham played just nine times in 1928/29, his final Rangers appearance being on 26 January 1929 when, typically, he signed off with a goal in a 2-0 win over Airdrie. This sounds like the end of an amazing career, but incredibly he went on to set more records. He left Ibrox for Newcastle United days after his final scoring appearance for Rangers, and became the oldest debutant in English top-division history at the age 39 when he started for Newcastle against Leicester City on 2 February 1929. The following season, he set another record when he became the first player-manager in top-flight English football when he took charge at St James' Park. The highlight of his managerial career came in 1932 when he guided Newcastle to victory in the FA Cup Final, beating the great Arsenal side of the time 2-1. He managed Newcastle until 1935 by which time they had suffered relegation from the top division, and made a return to Scottish football two years later when appointed manager at Dundee. After World War Two, he then enjoyed another successful career as a sports writer.

In 1973, just a few months after he carried out a ceremonial kick-off in the centenary celebrations match against the great Ajax Amsterdam side of the time, one of Rangers' great players and a man who made an indelible mark in the history of British football passed away at the age of 83. He died on Sunday, 6 May; perhaps it was fitting that the previous day Rangers had defeated Celtic in another classic Scottish Cup Final.

Greatness lives forever.

- Rangers career: 1915–1929
- Over 450 appearances, and 200 goals in all competitions
- 7 league championships and 1 very famous Scottish Cup12 Scotland caps
- Member of Rangers' Hall of Fame
- Oldest debutant in top-flight English football
- FA Cup winning manager

4 DOUGIE GRAY

The Rangers player who made more appearances for the club than any other

DOUGLAS HERBERT Gray was born in Alford in Aberdeenshire on 4 April 1905. A fine young junior footballer, he attracted the attention of Rangers while playing for local team Aberdeen Muggiemoss and signed for the Ibrox club in the summer of 1925. A quite incredible one-club career followed, which ended in Gray setting all kinds of records.

Manager Bill Struth was looking for a replacement right-back for the long-serving Ulsterman Bert Manderson, who had made the position his own for over a decade but was now well into his 30s. He hoped young Gray might be a player capable of filling such big shoes. Gray made his debut in a 3-0 home league victory over Kilmarnock on 3 October 1925 at right-back, fitting that his first match ended in a defensive clean sheet. It was a Rangers team who were missing several of their star players in a season that saw the squad decimated through injuries, with the forward line containing lesser names John McGregor and Robert McKay.

A few days later Gray made the first of many appearances against Celtic, when he kept his place in the team for the Glasgow Cup semi-final. It wasn't at right-back, however, as Manderson was back in his usual position. Such was the injury crisis now at the club, the manager selected Gray as a winger. Maybe unsurprisingly, and unlike much of his subsequent Rangers career, he tasted defeat as Celtic won 2-0. Manderson kept him out of the side again for a brief time, before Gray was recalled in December, and he stayed there for the majority of his long career.

Rangers had a dismal 1925/26 season, enduring their lowest ever league position and seeing no trophies won. But the form of Gray was a bright light among the darkness, his incredible consistency of performance at just 21 years of age attracting great praise. He was not particularly tall or strong, but he made up for lack of physical size by possessing great game intelligence. His positional play and ability to cover for his other team-mates was particularly impressive, and over the years Rangers fans lost count of the number of goal-line clearances he made when the ball seemed destined for the net.

He won no trophies in his first season, but it wasn't long before he went about putting that right. He started 30 times in the league in 1926/27 as Rangers comfortably regained the title. Gray's stalwart defending meant he rarely posed any threat to the opposition, and he still waited for his first Rangers goal. He was unsuccessful in the cup competitions, joining the club as it endured a long and painful period without a Scottish Cup success. But Rangers and Gray didn't have much longer to wait.

Gray started all 38 league games the following season as the title was retained. He played in his first Glasgow Cup Final in October 1927, but was on the wrong end of a 2-1 scoreline against Celtic. But the triumph he enjoyed in the Scottish Cup more than made up for that disappointment. Gray played in every round of the competition, including the iconic 4-0 triumph in the final on 14 April 1928 that saw the cup return to Ibrox for the first time since 1903. And the season ended with more final joy when he started in the Charity Cup win over Queen's Park.

Later in 1928, Gray was picked for the Scotland national team for the first time for the Home International match at Hampden against Wales. Lining up alongside team-mates Bob McPhail, Tommy Muirhead and Alan Morton, Gray helped Scotland to a 4-2 win. He went on to represent Scotland in ten official internationals between 1928 and 1932, and had a decent record of six wins, two draws and just two defeats. He also appeared in an unofficial international against Holland in 1929, as well as representing the Scottish League six times.

Up until the outbreak of World War Two, a Rangers team without Dougie Gray was something of a rare sight. He started in at least 34 league matches every season from 1927/28 to 1938/39, being ever present in three of these campaigns. And that meant he amassed a significant number of league titles, as Rangers dominated Scottish football for the majority of those years. He added seven more league titles in the 1930s to the three he won in the 1920s, becoming one of the most decorated players in the history of both the club and the Scottish game.

His medal collection wasn't confined to the league championship. He added five further Scottish Cup Final successes to that memorable day in 1928, playing in the right-back position he made his own in wins over Partick in 1930, Kilmarnock in 1932, St Mirren in 1934, Hamilton in 1935 and Third Lanark in 1936. Those last three successes were the first time the club had ever won the trophy for three successive seasons. He also won multiple Glasgow and Charity Cups, with 1929/30 and 1931/32 particularly special as in both seasons Gray helped Rangers to a clean sweep of all four domestic trophies.

Season 1930/31 was a unique one for Gray as it was the only one in his entire career that his name appeared on the scoresheet. On 4 October 1930 he scored with a penalty at Broomfield in a 3-3 draw with Airdrie. And the following month, he converted another penalty in a 7-1 win over Morton at Ibrox. These were the only two goals he scored in his long career, which meant that he never scored from open play in his 22 seasons as a Rangers player. But Struth had a dependable, consistent, resolute defender who was a great reader of the game and who never accepted defeat until the final whistle. Gray wasn't there as a goal threat. Gray was also an excellent sportsman, demonstrated by him completing his lengthy career without a single booking or sending off.

During wartime, Gray continued to play for the club in the revised competitions then taking place. He picked up another seven 'unofficial' titles during this time as Rangers were champions in every season of the conflict. As well as league titles, Glasgow and Charity Cups, he also collected winners' medals in some of the unique cup competitions that were only seen during the war years. He played in front of 90,000 at Hampden in May 1940 when Rangers beat Dundee United to lift the Emergency War Cup. The following year, he lifted the Scottish Southern League Cup by defeating Hearts. He won it again the following season and added the Summer Cup, where Hibs were the runners-up.

And on 1 January 1943, Gray played in the historic 8-1 defeat of Celtic at Ibrox, still to this day the biggest competitive win in an Old Firm match.

By the time normal competitions resumed in 1946, time had caught up with him, and it was time to pass on the right-back jersey to another legend, the great George Young. Gray did play his final two matches in post-war football, both in the 1946/47 Glasgow Cup, with his last appearance being against Clyde in a semi-final replay defeat on 25 September 1946. He officially retired at the end of that season aged of 42, an amazing 22 years after signing for the club. He went on to coach at Clyde to remain part of the game he loved.

Perhaps the greatest compliment to Dougie Gray came from the only manager who ever selected him in senior club football. Bill Struth considered Gray his best signing and said that he followed the ball more intently than anyone he had ever known. This was a manager whose first recruit had been Alan Morton, and who had assembled multiple teams to dominate Scotland, and who had brought in some of the greatest players ever to represent Rangers.

Dougie Gray died in 1972 at the age of 67 and holds some records that are highly unlikely ever to be broken: the longest serving Rangers player; if you include wartime competition, the most Rangers appearances and most championship medals. He is, of course, a member of the Hall of Fame, and deserves a place in any conversation about our greatest servants.

- Rangers career: 1925–1947
- 940 appearances (all competitions)
- 2 goals
- 10 official league titles
- 7 unofficial league titles
- 6 Scottish Cups
- 10 Scotland caps
- Hall of Fame member

5   GEORGE BROWN

The teacher who served Rangers as player and director

RANGERS HAVE had many great defensive units that laid the foundations for trophy successes. The dominant team of the 1930s was no exception, and a massive reason for that decade of silverware was a cultured wing-half named George Brown.

George Clark Phillips Brown was born in Glasgow on 7 January 1907. He was academically bright as well as outstanding on the sports field, and it was apparent from a young age that he was destined to do well in life. After his school years he trained to become a teacher, combining this with playing at both half-back and inside-forward at junior level with Ashfield Juniors. In September 1929, he was signed by Rangers and would go on to have a wonderful career at the club, even though he retained his job as an English teacher at the nearby Bellahouston Academy by day.

It didn't take long for the 22-year-old to make his first-team debut, when Bill Struth picked him at inside-right on 16 November 1929 at Ibrox against Ayr United in a league match. With Bob McPhail missing, the usual inside-right Dr James Marshall switched to the left and Brown filled the vacated position. Rarely could a debut have been easier, Rangers winning 9-0 with Jimmy Fleming hitting four and Brown marking his debut by getting on the score sheet. Brown kept his place in the side for most of the next three months and made an instant goalscoring impression by hitting the target in seven of his first eight starts. These included the winning goal at Parkhead on New Year's Day 1930, Rangers triumphing 2-1 in their first game of the new decade.

McPhail and Marshall remained the first-choice pair for the manager, however, and despite his hugely impressive introduction to the team, Brown was back on the sidelines for much of the run-in, not selected for the Scottish Cup semi-final or final victories after picking up a knock. He did return to the league team for the last few fixtures, ending his first season at the club with 17 league starts, 11 league goals, and a first title medal as Rangers won a clean sweep of trophies for the first time. That haul was completed on 10 May 1930 when the Charity Cup Final against Celtic was won by a coin toss after a thrilling 2-2 draw. Brown played at right-half in the match, moving back to more defensive role in the absence of regulars Jock Buchanan, Tommy Muirhead and Whitey McDonald.

By the start of the following season, Struth had decided wing-half suited the composure, intelligence, accurate passing and sharp tackling that Brown possessed, and the vast majority of his 31 appearances came at the back. He did occasionally move back to inside-forward, scoring against Hamilton and Falkirk from the more advanced role. He made 29 league starts in a successful title defence, making it two league medals in two seasons at Ibrox. Brown also played in another winning Charity Cup Final, this time against Queen's Park.

Although neither the Scottish or Glasgow Cups were retained, Brown would see this as a massively successful season. Not only was he now firmly established in the first team at Ibrox, but on 25 October 1930 he became an international footballer when starting at inside-forward for Scotland in a 1-1 draw at Ibrox.

Brown would become a mainstay of the Scotland team over the coming years, earning 19 caps, with the last of these in 1938. His final two caps, against England at Wembley and away to the Netherlands, were as team captain. The Wembley triumph was also memorable as the Scotland debut of the great Bill Shankly and the first home appearance for England by Stanley Matthews. Brown played six times in the annual clash with the English, winning four of them. These included the incredible 1937 match at Hampden when a British record attendance of 149,547 crammed into the stadium to see Brown's defensive partner Jimmy Simpson captain Scotland to a 3-1 win.

Although his third season in Royal Blue saw the title lost to an excellent Motherwell team, Brown managed to finally get his hands on the Scottish Cup when he played in both final matches against Kilmarnock in April 1932. Rangers won the replay 3-0. He also won his first Glasgow Cup when Queen's Park were defeated by the same scoreline, and rounded the season off with another Charity Cup winners' medal. By now, he was the undisputed first pick for the left-half position in a back line that the Rangers support of the time regarded as one of the finest the club ever had. Meiklejohn, Simpson and Brown were a combination that got the better of many a forward line. Brown started 45 games over the season, and he would continue to be virtually ever present for the next few seasons. Of that famous half-back line, he was the player most naturally gifted with the ball at his feet, with a former team-mate describing his passes as 'like full cream in their smoothness'.

He was ever present in the league in 1932/33 as the title was regained. He added both the Glasgow and Charity Cups to his medal collection again, the clean sweep was prevented by a surprise 1-0 loss at Rugby Park in February. But it was merely delayed by a year as in 1933/34 Rangers repeated the feat of Brown's debut season, and this time he picked up all four medals. He only missed three league games over the entire campaign, managing one goal in a topsy-turvy clash with Partick Thistle that was eventually won by the odd goal in seven. The Scottish Cup was reclaimed after a thumping 5-0 win in the final over St Mirren, the unfortunate Paisley goalkeeper on the receiving end being James McCloy, whose son Peter is immortal in the Rangers Hall of Fame by winning the 1972 European Cup Winners' Cup. The finale to the season in May saw Brown in his usual place, snuffing out the Celtic forwards to allow a Bobby Main goal to take the Charity Cup.

Brown was now an integral part of a team that was simply untouchable in the Scottish game. Over the next few seasons, it was regarded as highly surprising when Rangers failed to win a competition.

Another league and Scottish Cup double followed in 1934/35, with Brown at left-half in over 90 per cent of the matches. He scored just the once again, this time at Dens Park. He then picked up a third successive Scottish Cup in 1936, a final against Third Lanark mostly remembered as the last major final appearance of the magnificent Davie Meiklejohn before he retired. But the league was lost to Celtic thanks to some uncharacteristic inconsistency, a Glasgow Cup win over them earlier in the season giving Brown a medal but little consolation.

As he approached 30 years of age, Brown knew he was now the experienced wing-half who would play the role of mentor to a younger replacement for Meiklejohn, and he hoped he could do half as well at the job. He did pretty well as Rangers cruised to the title with weeks to spare. Brown's composed and level-headed leadership played a massive part in helping younger players like Tom McKillop and Jim Kennedy to settle into the right-half spot. A Glasgow Cup was also won in 1936/37, but the three-year reign as Scottish Cup holders ended when Queen of the South surprised Brown and his team-mates in the first round.

Season 1937/38 could be described as the only campaign in Brown's career that was unsuccessful. Manager Struth had to replace more of his previously dominant team, and although youngsters like Willie Thornton, Davie Kinnear and Willie Woodburn would all go on to future success, this was just a year too early. Old heads like Brown, Dougie Gray and Bob McPhail were still there to lend their experience, but the blend wasn't quite right and Celtic took the title, with Kilmarnock ending the Scottish Cup run at the semi-final stage.

Like all at the club, Brown was determined to put things right in 1938/39, little knowing this would be the last normal football season for some years. Unfortunately injury prevented him from starting as many times as the manager would have wanted, but he did make 19 league appearances and scored twice to help clinch the title and earn a seventh championship medal. He scored his last 'official' goal for Rangers on 3 September 1938 against the same team as he scored his first, Ayr United.

The outbreak of war made Brown's decision to wind down his football career all the easier. He had always been part-time anyway, but he did still appear occasionally. He scored against Celtic at Parkhead on 6 April 1940 in a Western League win, and hit his only Rangers hat-trick the following March when making a rare inside-forward appearance against Dumbarton. Brown started his last match for the club on 26 April 1941 in a defeat to Third Lanark in the Southern League. He also played one last time for Scotland in an 'unofficial' international against England in February 1941.

Brown had played 417 competitive times for Rangers, scored 28 goals, and had amassed seven league titles, four Scottish Cups, 19 Scotland caps, and several Glasgow and Charity Cups. He was never booked or sent off in his entire career, which saw him only represent one club.

Although he was now able to totally devote himself to his teaching, Rangers was in his veins, and not long after his playing career ended Brown was invited to join the board of directors at the club. He had no hesitation in accepting the honour, joining his old team-mate Alan Morton in the boardroom.

Brown became headmaster at Bellahouston, and was also given duties at Rangers that included introducing the club to new signings. One such signing was future Hall of Fame centre-forward Billy Simpson, and it was Brown who travelled across to Northern Ireland to help complete his move to Ibrox.

Brown remained a director into the early 1970s, being part of the club during the dark days of the terrible 1971 disaster. Although he had retired from the board by 1979, he was asked by the club to cut the ribbon to officially open the new Copland Road stand, the new stadium a lasting legacy to those who perished on that tragic day.

Brown was one of the greatest footballers of his generation. He was a one-club man, and one of the few to represent Rangers on the pitch and in the boardroom. He passed away in 1988, aged 81. He is inducted in the Rangers Hall of Fame, and deserves his place at the top of the marble staircase alongside other giants of our past.

- Rangers career: 1929–1941
- 417 appearances and 28 goals
- 7 league titles

- 4 Scottish Cups, including 3 in succession
- 19 Scotland caps
- A Rangers director for over 30 years

6   JERRY DAWSON

The Rangers prince named after an Englishman called Jeremiah

JAMES DAWSON was born in Falkirk on 30 October 1909, although after a magnificent football career this would be a name very few fans of the game would recognise. He began playing at local club Camelon Juniors, who at the time played in the outlawed Scottish Intermediate League, which had been formed in 1926 after a dispute among several clubs forced a breakaway from the recognised Junior Association. The 62 clubs that created the Intermediate League were exiled from the game in Scotland, meaning their players were barred from turning senior by the SFA. This meant that despite his consistently excellent displays in goal for Camelon, no senior club was able to sign Dawson until the dispute could be settled. In the early part of 1929/30, Camelon resigned from the Intermediate League and returned to the recognised junior league setup. This allowed senior clubs to then enquire about their players. In November 1929, Dawson signed for Rangers.

Manager Bill Struth saw Dawson as a deputy to Tom Hamilton, the long-serving number one, but with the potential to take over the goalkeeping position as he gained experience. Over the coming months Dawson would watch and learn from Hamilton in training and hone his skills, waiting for his chance to stake a first team claim. In 1930/31 he finally made his debut on 24 January at Ibrox against St Mirren in a league match when Hamilton was injured. An early Bob McPhail goal earned Rangers a draw in a patchy performance, but Struth saw enough from the young goalkeeper to be confident he was on the right track. However, Hamilton returned to the team for the next match and this would be Dawson's only start of the campaign.

Dawson's patience was soon to pay off, however, and he made his breakthrough near the start of the following season when he held the number one jersey from August through to early November before Hamilton came back into the side. He played 17 times in that spell, and four of those games were against Celtic. His baptism in the fixture came at Ibrox in early September in the league, and he kept a clean sheet in a fiercely contested goalless draw. He then started against the Parkhead men three times in just over a week as a Glasgow Cup semi-final needed two replays before being settled. The replays were held on successive days, on 6 and 7 October, with Dawson making several important saves as Jimmy Smith settled the third tie with the only goal. Dawson then won his first medal at the club in the final, where he kept another clean sheet in a 3-0 victory over Queen's Park.

Although not yet regarded as the club's first choice, his agility and fantastic reflexes had earned him a reputation as a potential future international, and by now to the world he was known as Jerry Dawson, a name given to him by his Ibrox team-mates who likened him to famous England and Burnley goalkeeper Jeremiah Dawson. The nickname stuck, and it was to be how he was known for the rest of his life. Rangers ended up losing their title to Motherwell that season, and by halfway through the following 1932/33 season Dawson was back as the first-choice goalkeeper, and from then on he made the position his own.

Over the following seasons, he would gain an even greater reputation than his English namesake, earning the nickname 'The Prince of Goalkeepers' as he became the reliable and spectacular last line of defence for the remainder of the decade and beyond. As well as his shot-saving ability, Dawson had a positional sense that often saw him somehow in the right place at the right time to snuff out danger and intercept crosses before his goal was threatened.

Rangers ruled Scottish football for much of the 1930s, which meant Dawson would build a formidable medal collection. He started in 20 league games in 1932/33 as the title was regained, with his clean sheets including a new year shut-out of Celtic at Ibrox. He added a first Charity Cup winners' medal to his first league badge when keeping goal in a 1-0 final success over Queen's Park in May.

Season 1933/34 was the perfect demonstration of the dominance Struth's Rangers had over their rivals, Dawson being the last line of a formidable defensive unit that played a huge part in securing all four available trophies. Rangers only lost twice in 38 league games that season, with Dawson in goal for 30 of them. He was unbeatable in both the Glasgow and Charity finals, beating Clyde 2-0 and Celtic 1-0. But injury forced him to miss the showpiece of the season in April, veteran Tom Hamilton taking over for the Scottish Cup Final triumph over St Mirren.

The next season saw Dawson selected for the first time by Scotland, starting behind his club centre-half Jimmy Simpson against Northern Ireland at Windsor Park. The match ended in a narrow defeat but it started a long Scotland career for Dawson, who soon became the almost automatic choice in the Scotland goal. He would go on to represent his country in 14 official international matches prior to the start of World War Two, including in front of the all-time record Hampden attendance against England in April 1937 when two Bob McPhail goals gave Scotland a 3-1 win before 149,547 spectators. He also played in nine unofficial wartime internationals, and six Scottish League XI matches.

As well as his first Scotland cap, 1934/35 also brought Dawson his first Scottish Cup winners' medal when he started in every round of Rangers' successful defence of the trophy, ending in a final victory over Hamilton. He missed only one league game all season in winning his third successive league title as well. These included another new year win over Celtic, this time 2-1 in a game where Celtic's Peter McGonagle was ordered off near the end for throwing the ball violently at Bob McPhail, and Dawson had to make two good late saves to prevent them from snatching an unlikely point. He also helped the team to a fine Glasgow Cup semi-final win over their old rivals, but Partick Thistle provided a surprise in the final.

Season 1935/36 was the last time Dawson had the imperious Davie Meiklejohn playing in front of him, the legendary trophy-laden captain retiring after the Scottish Cup Final. Dawson played in every round of the competition again, taking home his second medal in the tournament when Third Lanark were defeated at Hampden, with Dawson keeping a clean sheet after a very early McPhail goal. He went one better than the previous season in league appearances, starting all 38 games, but five points were dropped in the last five matches, allowing Celtic to win the title back by that very margin. The team in green were defeated in the Glasgow Cup Final, Dawson keeping another clean sheet in an impressive 2-0 success, but two late goals in the Charity Cup Final gave them revenge, meaning Dawson had to settle for 'just' two winners' medals in the season.

Dawson's consistency was now remarkable. He started all 38 league games again the following season, meaning he had missed just one league match in three years. And it was a season where he would earn a fourth championship medal; despite several early season draws Rangers pulled away to coast to a seven-point winning margin. One of those draws was thanks to a very controversial offside flag ruling out a late Davie Kinnear strike at Parkhead. This made the team all the more determined to win the new year match at Ibrox, which they did, 1-0, despite being down to ten players for much of the contest after winger Bobby Main was injured. In horrendous conditions, Dawson handled the ball faultlessly.

Season 1937/38 saw Dawson in his regular place until an injury suffered in a first league defeat of the season against Hearts forced him to miss almost three months. He had won another Glasgow Cup before this, and another two wins over Celtic, but his injury seemed to throw Rangers' season off track. Heavy defeats were suffered to Celtic, Partick and Dundee in his absence and there was no way back in the league challenge. Dawson was back in goal when Kilmarnock ended Scottish Cup hopes, and also for the Charity Cup Final loss to Celtic which saw a much-weakened Rangers side lose 2-0.

Dawson had played in front of the record Hampden crowd in 1937, and on 2 January 1939 he then also played in front of the largest ever Ibrox attendance of 118,567. He was heroic in a second half Celtic onslaught after Rangers had gone down to 10 fit players, ensuring the majority of the vast crowd went home happy after a 2-1 win. That was one of 33 league appearances as Rangers swept to another title, his fifth for the club. That was the only medal he won that season, with his long-time deputy George Jenkins in goal for the Charity Cup Final, and early defeats in the other two knockout competitions.

This was the last season of normal league football before the horrors of war revisited Europe. During the conflict, Dawson remained a Rangers regular, playing in the first team right up until the end of 1945. He added six more wartime league titles to the five he won during the 1930s, with an undoubted highlight being on 1 January 1943 when he kept goal in a scarcely believable Old Firm match that Rangers won 8-1, the record winning margin in the fixture. As well as multiple wartime titles, he also claimed several wartime cup competitions, with more wins in the Glasgow and Charity Cups to add to unique trophy successes such as the War Emergency Cup, the Southern League Cup and the Summer Cup. He also played in the famous friendly in 1945 against the touring Moscow Dynamo team.

Dawson played his last competitive match for the club on 24 November 1945, and fittingly it was a victory as Rangers defeated Motherwell 2-1 at Fir Park. He played in over 500 competitive matches for Rangers, when wartime appearances are included, in a career that lasted the best part of 16 years. He left in May 1956 to join his hometown club Falkirk, the same month as his successor in the Rangers goal was making his Ibrox bow. Bobby Brown would go on to be another wonderful servant to Rangers.

Dawson's Falkirk debut came in a Victory Cup tie a few days after signing, and his league debut was three months later at Tynecastle. Dawson was to play at Brockville for three seasons, racking up over 100 appearances for them despite nearing his 40th birthday. He was reunited with an old Ibrox team-mate in manager Tully Craig, who created a fine Falkirk team, with another former Ranger Jimmy Fiddes a key player. In October 1947 he played in a League Cup semi-final for Falkirk against hot favourites and cup holders Rangers, and proceeded to keep out everything that Willie Thornton, Jimmy Duncanson and Torry Gillick could throw at him to help the Bairns to a shock 1-0 win. He wasn't to add yet another winners' medal to his vast collection, however, as East Fife, managed by future Ibrox boss Scot Symon, defeated Craig's side 4-1 in a replay.

On retiring from the game in 1949, Dawson then started another successful career as a sports writer for the *Daily Record*, before returning to the game to become manager of East Fife in August 1953. He made an instant impact, leading East Fife to League Cup Final glory. In the final they beat a Partick Thistle team who were managed by yet another former Ibrox colleague, his old captain Davie Meiklejohn. Incredibly, this was East Fife's third League Cup Final win in just seven years. Things gradually went downhill from then on, however, and he left the club in 1958 after they suffered relegation.

But no matter what he achieved after playing, he would always be remembered as a truly great Rangers goalkeeper; for many he perhaps was the best ever to play for the club.

Dawson passed away in his beloved home town on 19 January 1977 at the age of 67, and was inducted into the Rangers Hall of Fame. The Prince of Goalkeepers' name lives on forever.

- Rangers career: 1929–1946
- Over 500 appearances
- 5 Scottish league championships
- 6 wartime championships
- 2 Scottish Cups
- 14 Scotland caps
- 9 wartime Scotland appearances
- Hall of Fame member
- A cup-winning manager with an unfashionable club

7 JIMMY GORDON

The war hero who could play anywhere and captained his country

THE 25 year 'hoodoo' Rangers endured between 1903 and 1928 in the Scottish Cup meant there were some all-time great players in Royal Blue who went through an illustrious career at Ibrox without winning the national cup competition. One of these great players was Jimmy Gordon.

James Eadie Gordon was born in Saltcoats on 23 July 1888, and was viewed as something of a footballing prodigy when a juvenile player at Thornwood Athletic, then a Junior with Renfrew Victoria. Gordon joined William Wilton's Rangers as a teenager and made his debut in a 3-0 home league win over Kilmarnock in April 1907 at the age of 19. That was his only appearance in the league that season, but he started in the Charity Cup semi-final and final in May, winning his first medal in only his third competitive start as he played at right-half against Celtic in the final at Cathkin Park. The blue half of the 38,000 crowd were highly impressed by the calm and determined youngster as Rangers upset league champions Celtic 1-0.

Gordon established himself at right-half in the Rangers team the following season, playing in 30 matches, including 22 in the league. He scored his first goal for the club near the end of the season in a 2-0 win against Clyde, which was a rare bright spot in a campaign of much disappointment. Celtic won all four available trophies, the first time the feat had been achieved, Gordon suffering at their hands especially in the Glasgow Cup Final which needed three games to separate the teams.

A versatile player, Gordon would feature in virtually every position over his long Rangers career (including one match in goal), and in 1908/09 he was briefly a very effective centre-forward. He scored a league hat-trick against Hamilton, and ended the season in real style by scoring seven goals in three Charity Cup matches, including a double in another winning final against Celtic, this time at Parkhead.

That season was probably best remembered for the infamous Hampden riot, when both sets of fans invaded the pitch at the end of a drawn Scottish Cup Final replay when it became apparent there would be no extra time as had been expected, resulting in the trophy being withheld for the season. Gordon had missed the initial 2-2 draw, but was at right-half in the replay, and he scored Rangers' goal in the 20th minute of the infamous 1-1 draw. Unbelievably, for a player who played in the Rangers first team for over a decade, this was to be Gordon's only appearance in the final.

The Charity Cup was the only silverware won that season, but there were high hopes at Ibrox for 1909/10 after some significant signings, especially Englishmen Billy Hogg and Herbert Lock. But things didn't go initially to plan, Gordon missing several games through injury at the start of the season, during which Rangers lost twice. Celtic were champions for the sixth successive year, and they compounded the misery at Ibrox by winning the Old Firm Glasgow Cup Final. Gordon's injury interrupted season saw him miss Scottish Cup and Charity Cup defeats to an excellent Clyde team, and by the summer, he was happy to see the back of 1909/10 and looked forward to a healthier and more successful 1910/11.

Gordon filled in at inside-right for the opening-day clash with St Mirren and scored the only goal. He kept the position the following week and scored again against Raith Rovers. He started a total of 28 times, mainly at right-half, as the team mounted a significant title challenge, which was to be successful in bringing the championship back to the club for the first time since 1902. Rangers had now fully bedded in their newer players to fit alongside their more established stars. In attack, Willie Reid's amazing goalscoring exploits were ably supported by the skill and goals of Alec Bennett, Alec Smith and Billy Hogg, while in defence the brave and agile Herbert Lock had the highly effective James Galt, Jimmy Gordon and Joe Hendry in front of him. Their status as the best team in the country was demonstrated by a convincing 3-1 Glasgow Cup Final success over Celtic in October followed by an end-of-season 2-1 Charity Cup Final win over the same opponents.

Rangers only failed in the Scottish Cup that season in a loss to Dundee, and it was Clyde who ended the run in 1911/12. Gordon also suffered Charity Cup defeat to them later in the season. But he claimed second winners' medals in both the Glasgow Cup and the league championship, scoring a rare goal in the league win over Celtic at Ibrox in October. He started every time he was fit, manager Wilton knowing he could rely on Gordon no matter the opposition and no matter the position he was asked to play.

Gordon earned his first Scotland cap in March 1912 in a 4-1 win over Ireland, and represented his country ten times, the last being in 1920. No doubt he would have added to that tally had international matches not been suspended during the Great War. Just prior to conflict breaking out, he enjoyed his greatest moment in Scotland's blue when captain of the team who beat England 3-1 in April 1914 at Hampden before 105,000 spectators.

Season 1912/13 saw Gordon remain a key man in the side as Rangers clinched a third successive title. He started the season as the previous year, scoring on the opening day. That was to be his only league goal all season from 28 appearances, however, with his only other goals in the campaign being a double in a Charity Cup tie against Partick the following May. He suffered defeat to Celtic in that competition, but enjoyed another Glasgow Cup win over them in a sensational final where Rangers were a goal behind and down to ten fit players in the second half, then came back to win 3-1.

This would be the last title-winning season Gordon would enjoy for a few years, Celtic regaining the crown in season 1913/14 despite Gordon's improved goal return of four from 36 starts. These goals included his first penalties for the club, scoring from the spot in successive weeks against Dumbarton and Airdrie. He had to make do with just another Glasgow Cup success in the campaign, the team's inconsistency in contrast to Gordon's sustained excellence.

This was the last season unaffected by war, although he did remain a regular in the team in the unsuccessful campaign of 1914/15. He scored eight times that season, his best for some time.

Gordon's career was put briefly on hold in 1916 when he enlisted with the Highland Light Infantry, reaching the rank of sergeant. While serving his country he lost his place in the Rangers team to a new right-half, Peter Pursell, signed from Queen's Park.

Gordon played more of a utility role in Rangers' title-winning team of 1917/18, amassing 16 league appearances without settling in a particular position, but filling in as a forward and also as a defender. He played centre-forward a few times, and showed he hadn't lost his ability to lead the line when hitting all four goals against Morton on 2 February 1918, and a crucial double against Motherwell on the penultimate weekend of the season as the race with Celtic went to the last day. This Rangers team was the beginning of the great side who would go on to dominate Scottish football by the early 1920s, as the likes of Tommy Muirhead and Sandy Archibald now wore the famous colours.

After he played in only half the league games in 1918/19, the departure of Peter Pursell for Port Vale allowed one more glory season for the veteran Gordon in 1919/20, which was to be the last Rangers played under the legendary William Wilton. Rangers raced to title glory in a season they dominated, with Gordon playing 40 games and scoring seven goals in all competitions, including seven in the league. His fifth championship medal had been won at the age of 32. Typically, he started the shock defeat in the Scottish Cup semi-finals to Albion Rovers, as the dominant team of the year flopped in the national cup tournament yet again.

Gordon scored his last Rangers goal on 24 April 1920, 13 years after his club debut, in a 6-1 home win against Dundee, and made his final competitive appearance at Dumbarton four days later. By this time a young right-half by the name of Davie Meiklejohn had made his debut, and the youngster was to take over that position and serve the club with incredible distinction for many years.

The tragic events prior to season 1920/21 that saw the untimely death of Wilton and the beginning of the Bill Struth era also coincided with the end of a glorious Rangers career for Gordon. He only played one match under Struth, a benefit fixture on 30 August 1920 for the magnificent servant Bert Manderson, when Rangers beat Celtic 2-1 in front of 20,000 spectators.

He left soon after, heading to the Kingdom of Fife to briefly play for Dunfermline, before he hung up his boots and enjoyed life after football as the owner of several billiard halls along with his old Rangers team-mate Jimmy Galt, as well as a director in Galt's motor business.

Gordon died in November 1954 at the age of 66, and he deservedly was inducted into the Rangers Hall of Fame. In what could be regarded as the ultimate accolade, it was reported that Bill Struth described him as, 'The greatest Ranger who ever lived.'

- Rangers career: 1907–1920
- 79 goals from 388 competitive appearances
- An international-class defender and goalscoring attacker
- 5 league titles
- 10 Scotland caps

- 6 Glasgow Cups
- 4 Charity Cups
- Rangers Hall of Fame member
- World War One veteran

8   JIMMY SIMPSON

The Rangers hall of fame star whose son is a Celtic legend

JAMES MCMILLAN Simpson was born in the small Fife village of Ladybank on 29 October 1908. A highly rated footballer in his schooldays, he represented Scotland at school international level while also playing for local Junior side Newburgh West End. Able to play as a defender or a forward, it was his calm versatility that quickly attracted the attention of senior clubs, and on Thursday, 13 August 1925 at the age of just 16 he was signed by manager Jimmy Brownlie for Dundee United of the First Division.

Simpson was clearly a player Brownlie rated, as just two days later he made his debut for United in the league away to Raith Rovers, which ended in a 4-2 defeat. The youngster started two more league games in August, both defeats, before Brownlie took him out of the firing line for a time to allow him to better adjust to the demands of the senior professional game. When he returned to the team the week after his 17th birthday in November, Simpson was there to stay. United were in a relegation battle right from the start of the season, and it would be December before Simpson enjoyed the feeling of a win when they beat Partick Thistle. Then, on Saturday, 19 December at Tannadice, he faced champions Rangers for the first time, playing in an inside-right role against a team badly struggling with injuries and loss of form. United held out for a shock 2-1 win, with the performance of young Simpson no doubt impressing Ibrox boss Bill Struth.

Simpson scored his first senior goal the following week, a Boxing Day winner at title-chasing Airdrie. In all, he started 24 games in his debut season on Tayside, adding one more goal on the final day in a heavy defeat to newly crowned champions Celtic. United survived relegation, ending the season just two points above the drop zone in 17th of the 20 teams.

They weren't as lucky in Simpson's second season. Despite the virtual ever-present's excellent displays, United were soon in the bottom two. They suffered several heavy defeats, conceding five to Dundee, Falkirk, Partick and Queen's Park and seven to Airdrie and Celtic. Simpson was mainly utilised in an inside-forward position, and he managed five goals in 36 games, but none came in matches that were won. Somehow, they did beat eventual champions Rangers again at Tannadice, this time 2-0. United were relegation certainties with weeks left of the season, and despite picking up two wins and a draw in their last four games they finished last and were consigned to the drop.

But Second Division football wasn't for Simpson. Hugely popular with the Tannadice fans, they realised it would be impossible to hold on to their prized asset, and a close-season transfer war started with several clubs interested in his signature. Struth was one of the managers determined to land Simpson, and a fee reported in different newspapers as £1,000 and £2,500 was enough to bring the 18-year-old to Ibrox in the summer of 1927. Most sources had the lower figure as the more accurate one.

Simpson had joined the undisputed number one club in the country, and at 18 years old he knew he would need to be patient before getting his first team chance. Struth saw the player as a natural centre-half, commanding on the ball and competitive off it. He was a regular in the reserve team in that position, learning his new trade, when in early October captain Tommy Muirhead picked up an injury just before an Old Firm Glasgow Cup Final. With Jock Buchanan also missing, Struth decided to move stand-in skipper Davie Meiklejohn from centre-half to right-half for the final, giving young Simpson a baptism of fire debut at Hampden Park. He acquitted himself well before a massive 84,000 crowd, but two quick first-half goals by the Parkhead team were enough to hold out for a 2-1 win. Simpson started seven league games in the title-winning season of 1927/28, scoring his first Rangers goal on 10 December 1927 against Dundee. He also started one Scottish Cup match, the semi-final against Hibs, and he scored that day too in a comfortable 3-0 victory.

Simpson remained mainly a deputy for the next three seasons, Rangers winning the title in all of them. In 1928/29 he appeared in five league matches and one Scottish Cup tie, the 11-1 demolition of Edinburgh City. And the following season he started in eight league games, most notably with a fine performance on 26 October at Ibrox as Celtic were beaten 1-0 by a Rangers team heavily depleted by international call-ups and injuries, thanks to a Willie Nicholson goal. Rangers won all four available trophies that year, but despite the massive collection the club was gathering Simpson had yet to win any medals himself.

Season 1930/31 changed that, however. While still not a first choice, Simpson was called upon a dozen times in the successful title defence. He made his first appearance in the new year derby game, a 1-0 Ibrox win in front of over 83,000 spectators decided by an Alan Morton strike. That would prove to be a decisive victory, as the league was won by just two points from Celtic. Simpson had a league medal at last.

The rest of his Rangers career was spent as a first-team regular. After a handful of games at the start of 1931/32, Simpson was drafted into a half-back line including himself, Davie Meiklejohn, and George Brown. This was to become a defensive line revered by fans of the day in the same way as the mighty Iron Curtain some years later. Simpson was a mainstay of the team by the time the Glasgow Cup semi-final against Celtic was played, and he was on the winning side after a replay. On 10 October 1931 he collected his first winners' medal in the tournament when Queen's Park were brushed aside 3-0 in the final. He started in every round of the Scottish Cup, appearing in his first final in April 1932 against Kilmarnock. A replay was needed before the Ayrshire team were beaten 3-0. He then completed the set of all four medals in the Charity Cup when Third Lanark were thrashed 6-1. The league title was the one competition Rangers didn't win that season, ending the season second behind the best Motherwell team in their history.

The rest of the 1930s were a golden era for the club, and Simpson was a key man in triumph after triumph. He started 32 times in the league in 1932/33 as the title was regained, and added winners' medals in the Glasgow and Charity Cups. Twenty-nine starts in the league the following season meant another title was won. He played in the Glasgow Cup Final win over Clyde, and was widely regarded as the man of the match in the end-of-season Charity Cup success against Celtic. A clean sweep of all competitions was completed in the Scottish Cup with Simpson again ever present, including a 5-0 hammering of St Mirren in the Hampden final in April 1934.

Season 1934/35 saw 'only' a double won; neither of the Glasgow or Charity Cups were retained, but Simpson only missed one league game all season as the champions kept their firm grip on Scottish football. He scored once, a decisive strike in a tight match at Airdrie. And Simpson was in his usual place at the heart of Rangers' defence in the Scottish Cup Final against Hamilton, a match Davie Meiklejohn missed and the team was captained by Bob McPhail. Two Jimmy Smith goals gave Simpson his third win in the competition.

Season 1935/36 was to be the last for the legendary Meiklejohn before his retirement. Simpson started 35 league games but the title slipped away due to too many drawn matches allowing Celtic to claim the crown. The Parkhead team were beaten 2-0 in the Glasgow Cup Final, Simpson featuring, but the Parkhead men gained revenge with two late goals in the Charity Cup Final to win it 4-2. Meiklejohn's last winning final had been the previous month at Hampden in the Scottish Cup, when with Simpson and Brown in that trusted defensive unit, he lifted the trophy after defeating Third Lanark 1-0.

Manager Struth had little hesitation in deciding the new club captain to fill the massive void left by one of the club's greatest ever servants. The new captain was Simpson, which was no surprise to any Rangers fan as he had deputised on several occasions in the preceding season.

By now Simpson was an international footballer. He had made his Scotland debut in October 1934 against Ireland, and he would go on to represent his country 14 times between then and November 1937. On no fewer than 13 of those appearances he was also the captain. He scored one international goal, in a friendly away to Czechoslovakia.

The new captain was determined to bring the league title back to Ibrox in his first full season in the role. He led from the front, starting 29 times in the league and scoring twice. His first cup tie as skipper was against Celtic in late September 1936 in the Glasgow Cup semi-final, and it was won 2-1 thanks to goals by McPhail and Smith. Simpson went on to captain the team in the final, where he lifted the trophy after a 6-1 replay romp over Partick. A surprise Scottish Cup defeat at Queen of the South didn't derail the title challenge, and Simpson was a championship-winning captain when the league was won by a comfortable seven-point margin.

His second season as captain wasn't as successful, the league campaign suffering from a poor start with four draws in the first six matches, and the 13 draws proving fatal to any realistic challenge. A third-place finish was not what either Simpson or the Rangers support was used to. A bitter 4-3 Scottish Cup semi-final defeat to Kilmarnock and a dismal 2-0 loss to Celtic in the Charity Cup gave the end of the season a depressing feel, Simpson's earlier lifting of the Glasgow Cup being little consolation.

Rangers were now a team in transition, Simpson leading a side with several new faces. Young centre-forward Willie Thornton had made his debut that season, and 1938/39 would see debuts for Jock Shaw, Scot Symon and Willie Woodburn. The blending in of younger players needed old heads around them, and it didn't help that Simpson missed the first Old Firm league game at Parkhead in early September 1938. Woodburn started at centre-half and endured a torrid afternoon as Celtic won 6-2. Many newspaper headlines were predicting the end of the Struth dominance of the game in Scotland. Not for the first time, they got it totally wrong. Woodburn kept his place and Rangers scored five in their next two games. When Simpson returned, results were already improving, and his influence on the team helped them go on a run that took them top of the table for the turn of the year.

Simpson was at centre-half on 2 January 1939 when the record Ibrox attendance of 118,567 saw Celtic defeated 2-1 thanks to goals by Davie Kinnear and Alex Venters. A shock defeat by Clyde in the Scottish Cup apart, Rangers cruised through the remainder of the season with Simpson's side finishing a massive 11 points clear. Simpson was rested for the Charity Cup Final at the end of the season against Third Lanark, allowing young Woodburn to get his first winners' medal in the competition.

The 1938/39 league title would be the last trophy won by Simpson at Ibrox. The following season was curtailed early on by the declaration of war and he played his last game for the club in the Western League on 24 April 1940, a 3-2 away win against Dumbarton. By now the centre-half baton had been passed to a worthy successor in Willie Woodburn, and in 1941 Simpson left Rangers and returned to Dundee United. His Ibrox career was one of success after success. He won six league titles and four Scottish Cups, along with multiple wins in the other cup competitions of the time. He scored six goals in almost 370 first team appearances. He captained club and country.

His second Dundee United spell lasted just a few months, with 17 wartime competition starts and one goal. In early 1942 he briefly moved to St Mirren where he played 16 times. In 1943, at the age of 34, he retired from the game.

Simpson was tempted back into football after the war, first as a player-manager at non-league Buckie Thistle then in December 1947 as the manager of Alloa Athletic. He left the club after just 14 months and worked as an engineer, a qualification he had gained while playing at Ibrox.

Simpson passed away on 15 March 1972 at the age of 63. He is a member of the Rangers Hall of Fame. His son Ronnie became a famous Scotland international goalkeeper who won two FA Cups with Newcastle and was a member of the 1967 Celtic team who won the European Cup. He is a member of the Celtic Hall of Fame, surely a family double that is very unlikely ever to be repeated.

- Rangers career: 1927–1941
- Over 370 appearances
- 6 league titles
- 4 Scottish Cups
- 6 Glasgow Cups
- 3 Charity Cups
- Scotland captain
- A true great, and half of a unique Hall of Fame family double.

9 JIMMY SMITH

381 goals for Rangers, but only two international caps

THE TINY village of Slamannan can't have many claims to fame, but it was there on 24 September 1911 that the greatest goalscorer in the history of Rangers was born. During his career at the club he was given many unflattering descriptions: battering ram; bludgeoning; aggressive; uncultured; basic. But there is one word that described the career of Jimmy Smith better than any other: goals.

His football career didn't get off to the most promising of starts. At 14 the Airdrie Academy pupil joined local side Denny Hibs, where he played alongside Matt Busby, but they decided he would never make the grade and allowed him to leave for local rivals Longriggend. At 15 he was given a trial by Middlesbrough but was unsuccessful, and was picked up finally by a senior team when signing for East Stirling. Smith would only play 12 games for them before manager Bill Struth yet again showed his instincts in seeing the potential in young centre-forwards and he joined Rangers in August 1928 at the age of 17.

At such a young age, and with Rangers dominating Scottish football, it was no surprise he had to wait to make his first-team debut. Season 1928/29 saw double winners Rangers look invincible. After 30 league games unbeaten and reaching the Scottish Cup Final again, Struth decided to throw in young Smith on 27 March 1929 at Douglas Park during a hectic spell of fixtures. It wasn't the debut Smith would have wanted as Hamilton upset the odds, winning 3-1 to end Rangers' long unbeaten record. Smith's only other appearance that season wasn't much better; a disappointing goalless draw at Ibrox against relegation-threatened Ayr United. The following season, Jimmy Fleming remained the undisputed centre-forward at Ibrox, his 27 league goals ensuring another title won. Smith only started one match all season, but it saw him score his first league goal for the club in a 3-1 away win over Dundee.

But his career would suddenly change when Rangers undertook a close-season tour of Canada. Young Smith suddenly found an incredible scoring streak while in North America, firing in 18 goals in just seven games. As a result, Struth decided that Smith would start the following season as his first-choice number nine.

The manager had his confidence in Smith rewarded as he scored doubles in the opening two matches, then recorded his first goal against Celtic, albeit in a losing Glasgow Cup Final. And after losing his place in the team during mid-season, Smith returned on Valentine's Day 1931 to score five goals in a massacre of Clyde. He kept his place in the run-in, eventually scoring 21 goals in 21 games, including the only goal in crucial 1-0 wins over both Falkirk and Hibs. The league was retained by just two points from Celtic. The first of Smith's nine championship medals had been won and he rounded off the season in style, scoring a crucial equaliser in a tight Charity Cup Final against Queen's Park at Hampden that was eventually won 2-1 after extra time.

Smith had become a real favourite with the Ibrox fans for his no-nonsense and fully committed approach, as well as his uncanny ability to be in the right place in the penalty box at the right time. At 6ft 1in tall and 14st in weight, he was the biggest regular centre-forward the Rangers support had watched up to that time.

Amazingly, 1931/32 saw him lose his place again as an even younger and more prolific striker called Sam English broke all kinds of records. His tragic story is well known, but it meant Smith saw far fewer first team starts than he must have expected. He did manage to win a first Glasgow Cup Final, scoring the only goal of the semi-final against Celtic as well as one of the three Rangers goals in the final against Queen's Park. Despite the amazing goal feats of English, who scored 44 goals in just 32 league matches, the title was lost to Motherwell. Smith also showed his scoring power when called upon, hitting the net five times in just eight appearances. He played no part in the winning Scottish Cup run as both English and Fleming starting the final victory against Kilmarnock.

The tragic incident involving English and Celtic goalkeeper John Thomson cast a huge shadow over English, and 1932/33 saw Smith resume his role as the main attacking force. He started in 33 league games, hitting 34 goals as the title was regained. Kilmarnock, Cowdenbeath and his old club East Stirling all were on the receiving end of a Smith hat-trick, and he also scored six doubles. Smith played in the Glasgow Cup Final win over Partick but missed out on Scottish Cup glory when Kilmarnock gained revenge for the final of the previous year by knocking Rangers out in the third round.

If Smith's scoring exploits were impressive that season, in 1933/34 they were even better. He hit a career best 41 league goals from just 32 appearances, starting the season in almost unbelievable fashion by hitting four on the opening day against Airdrie and then scoring six against Ayr the following week. He hit four more hat-tricks during the season, three in the league and one against Third Lanark in the Scottish Cup. In among this blitz of goals he suffered an injury after scoring in a 1-1 Glasgow Cup semi-final draw with Celtic, forcing him to miss almost a month of action, which included the replay win and the final victory over Clyde. But he did finally get his hands on the Scottish Cup, scoring the only goal of a tense quarter-final win over Aberdeen and another in the final where St Mirren were humbled 5-0. Smith missed the record 14-2 first-round win against lowly Blairgowrie, his deputy Jimmy Fleming hitting a club record nine goals. Who knows how many the regular centre-forward might have scored that day. Fleming scored five more the following Saturday against Dundee, making it 14 goals in a week. Not bad for a veteran stand-in.

Rangers won all four trophies that season to complete a clean sweep, Smith leading the line in the Charity Cup Final win over Celtic that was decided by a Bobby Main goal.

The league title and Scottish Cup were both retained the next season, and Smith again scored at a rate of better than a goal a game. He showed how much he enjoyed the opening day when hitting the Dunfermline net six times in a 7-1 romp. They must have hated the sight of Smith as he scored four in the return fixture later in the season. He also hit four in a brilliant Scottish Cup fourth round win away to an excellent Motherwell team as well as two league hat-tricks in a fortnight at Cliftonville and Hampden. Overall, Smith scored 44 times in all competitions, with the highlight being both goals on 20 April 1935 at Hampden to defeat Hamilton in the Scottish Cup Final.

Season 1935/36 saw Rangers win a third successive Scottish Cup for the first time in their history. Smith scored six times in a cup run that ended in a 1-0 final win against Third Lanark, with the goal scored by Bob McPhail. That final may never have been won, however, if it wasn't for a Smith hat-trick in a 3-1 away win over Albion Rovers in the second round.

It was a mixed season for Smith against old rivals Celtic. He played in a 2-0 win over them in the Glasgow Cup Final and scored twice in a thrilling new year win at Parkhead that ended 4-3. But Celtic showed greater consistency over the campaign to win the title, and ended the season defeating Rangers 4-2 in the Charity Cup Final, Smith not among the scorers. Despite it being a season Struth's Rangers did not see as a great success, Smith had still scored 38 goals including three hat-tricks and a five-goal haul at Somerset Park.

He hit 37 more goals in 1936/37, 31 of these in the league as the flag was comfortably brought back again to Ibrox. He hit a vital equaliser against Celtic in late September in a Glasgow Cup semi-final at Ibrox won 2-1 thanks to a late McPhail winner. This was a match that saw 11 people taken to hospital after a crushing incident at its conclusion. He also scored in the final against Partick as Rangers retained the trophy. But there wouldn't be an unprecedented fourth successive Scottish Cup as Smith hit a rare blank away in the first round to Queen of the South, who sneaked through 1-0.

His strike rate in 1937/38 slowed slightly, although most forwards would be proud of a season with 22 league goals in 32 matches. He scored in ten successive games between mid-September and late November, including a winner in the Glasgow Cup semi-final over Celtic, the winner in the final against Third Lanark, and four goals in a 6-0 thrashing of Dundee. But it was a season that saw the team lose their way from the turn of the year onwards, and the Glasgow Cup was to be the only trophy that was won. Smith endured a dismal end to the season when playing in a comprehensive 2-0 defeat to Celtic in the Charity Cup Final, and there were some supporters and journalists asking if this was the end of Struth's dominance of Scottish football.

Nobody was asking this at the end of 1938/39, however, as Rangers romped to the title by a massive 11 points. Smith didn't add a sixth league medal to his collection as the centre-forward position became the property of a youngster destined for great things, the legendary Willie Thornton. Smith only started seven league games in the season, scoring four times. He didn't play in the unsuccessful Scottish Cup or Glasgow Cup runs, and wasn't selected for the Charity Cup Final success against Third Lanark.

By the time war was declared a few months later, Smith had five league medals, three Scottish Cups, and 23 Rangers hat-tricks or better. He then picked up plenty more silverware, and plenty more goals, during wartime. He added over 100 more goals to his incredible haul between October 1939 and May 1946 at an average of around nine goals in every ten games.

In 1939/40 he scored 17 times in 19 Western League games, including two hat-tricks. The league was won, and he also scored the only goal of the only War Emergency Cup Final against Dundee United. By the following season he was back to being the main Rangers centre-forward, with Thornton serving his country in Europe. This time he scored an amazing 35 goals in 29 appearances, including three hat-tricks and a five-goal spree at Albion Rovers. He collected a Southern League medal and also won the Southern League Cup, scoring in the final against Hearts.

Season 1941/42 saw him win another Southern League title, again scoring better than a goal a game. Smith started that season in blistering form, scoring ten times in the first four matches. But by now, a combination of age, injuries and strong competition for places had started to restrict his first-team appearances. In 1942/43 he played just six games, scoring just once. He did, however, win another medal when starting in the Glasgow Cup Final success against Third Lanark. Season 1943/44 was similar, with three league starts, but this time he scored in each one of them. He also scored a double in an exciting 4-2 Southern League Cup semi-final win at Hampden against Celtic but had to settle for a runners-up badge when playing in a goalless final against Hibs that was lost on the number of corners for each team.

The 33-year-old Smith enjoyed something of an Indian summer in 1944/45, starting in 18 matches of the successful Southern League campaign. His 11 goals helped the team to yet another title, making this Smith's ninth league medal at the club. He also scored six times in the run to the Southern League Cup Final, and started as Motherwell were defeated at Hampden to win the trophy.

Season 1945/46 was the last of wartime competition, Smith scoring six goals in nine Southern League games. His last famous appearance at Ibrox was in November 1945, the legendary 2-2 draw with Russian superstars Moscow Dynamo in front of an enormous attendance. Needless to say that Smith, now aged of 34, managed a goal that day, a typical effort. A high cross was floated into the box and Smith collided with Dynamo goalkeeper Khomich before, ever alert, sticking out a foot while on the ground to divert the ball into goal.

Smith, despite his incredible goals record, only won two Scotland caps, both against Ireland. His only Scotland goal was scored in the second of these games, at Pittodrie in 1937. He did also play in three unofficial wartime internationals, and always spoke afterwards of a particular career highlight when meeting Sir Winston Churchill at Wembley.

He retired in May 1946, days after playing his final game for Rangers. Typically, it was a 4-0 Victory Cup win over Airdrie that saw him also score his 381st and last Rangers goal. Smith continued serving the club for many years after this, first as club trainer until 1954, then as chief scout on the appointment of Scot Symon, a position he filled until retiring in 1967. From then until failing health in his later years, he kept close ties with the club and was a regular on matchday.

He died on 5 December 2003 at the age of 92, and was buried in Craigton cemetery, not far from Ibrox. A member of the Rangers Hall of Fame, Smith has a place in our history that is likely never to be bettered. A goals to games ratio over a lengthy career that warrants the title of our 'Greatest Ever Goalscorer'. Goals make heroes – over 380 make a legend.

- Rangers career: 1929–1946
- 420 competitive games, including wartime competitions
- 381 goals, including wartime matches (more than any other player in Rangers' history)
- 5 Scottish league titles
- 4 wartime titles
- 3 Scottish Cups
- Multiple other trophies
- 2 Scotland caps

10 JOHN MCPHERSON

Player, captain, director, and maybe the greatest player of the club's first 50 years

VERSATILITY IS a useful skill in a footballer, and Rangers have had many great players over the years capable of playing in different positions in the team. Possibly the best of them all starred for Rangers for over a decade, set all kinds of 'firsts' at the club, and served as a director after his playing days were over. His name was John McPherson.

McPherson was born on 19 June 1868 in Grange Street, Kilmarnock, before Rangers FC was founded. One of three brothers, he was given the nickname 'Kitey' as a youngster and the name stuck for the rest of his life. His football career started at his local club Kilmarnock, and by the age of just 18 he had represented Ayrshire against Lancashire in a match at Preston and also helped Kilmarnock to win the Ayrshire Cup Final by beating Hurlford 2-0. His skill and reading of the game marked him out from this early age as a potential star, and it wasn't long before he was approached by a bigger club, and he was invited to train with Everton in 1887 along with several other Scottish players.

At this time, McPherson did not occupy one particular position, turning out at full-back, half-back, inside-forward, centre-forward, or on the left wing as the occasion merited. On 8 April 1887 he made his Everton debut in a friendly against FA Cup holders Aston Villa, starting as a half-back in a 2-2 draw in front of a club record crowd of 8,000. He made a further ten appearances for the Merseyside club before returning to Kilmarnock where he had a job as an engine fitter. By then, his registration was with Cowlairs, a senior club in the Springburn area of Glasgow, and he starred in a hard-fought Scottish Cup 2-1 win over the mighty Third Lanark. He returned south to appear in two more Everton matches before being called back to Glasgow in September 1887 to go before an SFA enquiry as Third Lanark had protested that Cowlairs had fielded several ineligible players, McPherson being one of them. At this time, football in Scotland was strictly amateur, unlike in England, and any players deemed to have been paid to play could be subject to severe penalties. McPherson was given a letter from the Everton club secretary, Alex Nesbit, who confirmed that McPherson had retained his amateur status during his entire spell with them, and the charge of professionalism against the player was dismissed. One other Cowlairs player was found to have taken payment from Bootle FC, however, and Robert Calderwood was banned from all football for two years and the Third Lanark match was ordered to be replayed. McPherson played in the new fixture, with Cowlairs winning again, this time 4-1.

McPherson was never tempted to move south again, and was selected to play in a Scottish international trial at Ibrox in early 1888, where he lined up at inside-left and was universally regarded as the best player on the field. His display for the 'possibles' against the 'probables' earned him a first cap on 10 March 1888, in a 5-1 win over Wales at Easter Road. From then on, his usual position became inside-left, although he was regularly seen filling in elsewhere for club and country. He won three more caps while at Cowlairs, scoring against Ireland and England in 1890, as well as starting in an unofficial international match against Canada at the Glasgow Exhibition Ground in September 1888. In spring 1890, the first Scottish league was confirmed, and before it started, McPherson made the move from Cowlairs to Rangers. He would go on to have an incredible career in Royal Blue.

McPherson was a massive capture for the club, widely regarded as the best player in the Scotland team, and was probably the first 'superstar' signing Rangers had made. His impact in the blue shirt was both instant and unforgettable. His debut came on 16 August 1890 at home to Hearts, the very first league match Rangers ever played. He scored in a 5-2 victory, but this was something of a warm-up. He scored four times the following weekend at Cambuslang, and within a month had added a Glasgow Cup hat-trick against minnows Carrington and a five-goal haul in the league against St Mirren. In his first four league games for the club, he had scored ten goals.

His strike rate settled down after this, but he still managed to find the opposition net 21 times in all competitions in his debut season, which saw McPherson start in every league match as Rangers and Dumbarton tied at the top of the table after the fixtures were completed. He also played in the championship play-off match between the teams on 21 May 1891, which ended 2-2, meaning the first Scottish championship was shared between the clubs.

McPherson remained a virtual ever present in the league in both 1891/92 and 1892/93, scoring 14 times in all competitions in each season. Despite this, he couldn't help bring any silverware to Rangers in that first season, the closest being a 2-0 Charity Cup Final loss to Celtic in May 1892, the first competitive final between the clubs. The next season was different, however, when on 18 February 1893 he starred in the first Glasgow Cup Final win by the club, scoring the decisive third goal in a 3-1 win over Celtic. That was his first goal against the Parkhead men, but it certainly wasn't his last as by the time he finished his Ibrox career McPherson had racked up 17 strikes into the Celtic net.

McPherson started 1893/94 with another historic high, the first league win over Celtic, on 2 September. He scored once and John Barker hit the club's first Old Firm hat-trick as Celtic were humbled 5-0. McPherson kept his happy habit of scoring against them in November by scoring the only goal of a Glasgow Cup semi-final, and then repeated the feat in the final with the only goal to defeat his old club Cowlairs. Rangers had retained a trophy for the first time, thanks to 'Kitey'.

But the season was to get even better, despite the league challenge ending in fourth place. Rangers had never won the Scottish Cup and McPherson was determined that record had to end. He scored in every round as Rangers reached the final, where inevitably Celtic were to be the opposition. After a goalless first half in front of 17,000 fans at Hampden, Rangers hit their opponents with three quick-fire goals, McPherson keeping up his goal a round record by notching the third. A late Celtic consolation was a mere annoyance as Rangers cruised to a 3-1 win, history was made, and McPherson and his team-mates celebrated their first win in the country's biggest cup competition.

The next two seasons were frustrating for McPherson and for the team. He had now been made captain, but despite a nucleus of a team capable of dominating the game in Scotland, with players such as McPherson, Nicol Smith, Jock Drummond, Neilly Gibson and Alec Smith, they failed to win any silverware, losing in Glasgow and Charity Cup Finals to Celtic and finishing third then second in the league. Nevertheless, McPherson maintained his amazing consistency with 31 goals in just over 50 starts across 1894/95 and 1895/96, including one in a losing Charity Cup Final against Celtic when playing at inside-right.

Season 1896/97 saw another frustrating league campaign, with inexplicable defeats by Dundee and St Bernard's in the run-in meaning a third-place finish, but just three points behind winners Hearts. Rangers lost four times in the league that season, with McPherson only starting in one of them; he missed the others due to injury. He hit 11 goals in just ten league starts and it was a story, perhaps, of what might have been. But in the cup competitions that season, Rangers were kings.

Rangers reached the Glasgow Cup Final against Celtic. It took two attempts to find a winner, McPherson playing an important part in both games, with Rangers coming out on top 2-1 in the replay thanks to a double by Peter Turnbull. McPherson scored in an impressive Scottish Cup win over Hibs, and hit two more in the semi-final hammering of Morton, before he scored the third goal in the final, a 5-1 rout of Dumbarton that earned him his second winners' medal in the competition. The season was rounded off by winning the Charity Cup, meaning all three knockout trophies were won for the first time, with McPherson scoring once in the semi-final win over Celtic and twice in the 6-1 win over Third Lanark in the final. McPherson had lifted his first three trophies as captain in the space of just a few months.

McPherson played his tenth and final official match for Scotland in March 1897, and marked the occasion by scoring twice in a 5-2 win over Ireland at his home patch of Ibrox alongside fellow club-mates Matt Dickie, Jock Drummond and Neilly Gibson. Overall, he scored six times for his country. He also scored twice in his five Scottish League XI appearances.

Despite looking on the verge of total dominance in Scotland, McPherson didn't add a second league title to his collection the following season, when Celtic won the 1897/98 championship with a first unbeaten league season of 15 wins and three draws. But there was silverware still won in a season when Kitey hit the opposition net 23 times. He scored against Celtic in the Glasgow Cup semi-final and in the final win over Queen's Park, both from inside-right. He also scored a crucial Scottish Cup semi-final clincher against Third Lanark, and lifted the old trophy after leading the team out in the final against his hometown club Kilmarnock when goals by Alec Smith and R.C. Hamilton saw it retained for the first time. He was back at inside-left when Rangers defeated champions Celtic again in the Charity Cup semi-final, but a second cup clean sweep was denied when Third Lanark won the final.

By the start of 1898/99 the captaincy had passed to Hamilton, but McPherson was still a vital part of the team, who made history by winning all 18 league games in the season, a unique 100 per cent record. McPherson played in 15 of the 18 matches, scoring seven times, including one on the day the title was clinched against Hibs in an unbelievable 10-0 win.

Rangers went on to win the next three league championship, cementing their status as the best team in the land. McPherson hit nine league goals in 13 starts in 1899/1900 including one hat-trick. He also enjoyed two cup final wins over Celtic, a narrow 1-0 win in the Glasgow Cup and a thumping 5-1 success in the end-of-season Charity Cup. Unfortunately, there was a Scottish Cup exit to them sandwiched between, a replay defeat after Kitey had scored in the drawn first match.

By 1900/01 he was approaching the veteran stage of his distinguished career, but he still earned his fourth league medal with seven goals from 18 starts. Easily the highlight of these came on New Year's Day 1901 when he scored the winner in the Old Firm derby, his goal being somewhat controversial as Celtic claimed in vain he had handled the ball.

That goal clinched the title for the team who were supreme at the beginning of the turn of the 20th century. McPherson added another Glasgow Cup to his medal haul that season, scoring in the final win against Partick.

Season 1901/02 would prove to be McPherson's last as a Rangers player. A combination of injuries, age and competition for places meaning he only played in five of the matches that brought the club a fourth successive title. He scored his last competitive goals for Rangers in a 3-2 away win against Morton in mid-November, and played his last league game on 18 January 1902 against St Mirren. And what a bizarre final match it was, as regular goalkeeper Matt Dickie had to call off injured shortly before kick-off, meaning a stand-in was required. So the ever-versatile McPherson started his last league game for Rangers in goal, and he played well in a 3-2 win that was crucial in a tight title run-in that saw the league won by a margin of just two points. It was fitting he made an appearance in goal, as that meant the incredible career of McPherson included a start in every position from goalkeeper to left wing. Sadly, his last competitive match was a disappointing one, a 2-0 loss to Hibs in the 1902 Scottish Cup semi-final. His last recorded appearance for Rangers was in a friendly at Glentoran on 2 April that year.

McPherson retired from the game at the end of the season, his magnificent 12-year Rangers career ending after 322 appearances, 173 goals, and a huge haul of medals.

In 1907, McPherson returned to the club he loved as a director, and he remained on the board until his death. During this time, he played a prominent role in the 1923 golden anniversary celebrations, which included a dinner for former players. There were many attendees of the opinion that the best player the club had seen in those first 50 years was John McPherson.

He passed away suddenly on 31 July 1926, collapsing at the Clyde Sports at Shawfield stadium. He was just 58 years old. His funeral saw a huge attendance from both Rangers and the world of Scottish football, with several Rangers greats walking alongside the horse-drawn hearse.

Kitey was the star of a footballing family. His younger brother David was also a Scotland international and briefly a team-mate at Rangers, and he played against his sibling for Kilmarnock in the 1898 Scottish Cup Final. Older brother James didn't reach the same heights, but he did turn out for two of his brother's old teams, Cowlairs and Kilmarnock. Kitey had a son, Robert, who played junior football, and a grandson, Johnny, who played very briefly for Rangers before scoring in the Scottish Junior Cup final for Irvine Meadow.

- Rangers career: 1890–1902 (player); 1907–1926 (director)
- 322 competitive appearances
- 173 competitive goals
- Scored in Rangers' first league game
- Played in the first Rangers teams to win the league and the Scottish and Glasgow Cups
- Scored in the first Old Firm league win, and the first Scottish Cup Final win

- Captain of the team who won all three knockout trophies in the one season
- An 1898/99 'invincible'
- 5 league titles
- 3 Scottish Cups
- 9 Scotland caps
- 17 goals against Celtic
- Member of the Hall of Fame

11   NEILLY GIBSON

The Victorian era's 'Jim Baxter'

RANGERS FANS of all ages can talk of the genius that was Jim Baxter. As much an artist as a footballer, his elegance, self-confidence and skill were at the centre of the dominant team of the time. And it's not just Rangers supporters, as Baxter's legendary performances in great Scotland victories over England made him a national hero too. But decades before Baxter was strutting on the Wembley turf, Rangers had another magnificent wing-half who also possessed many of the same attributes and who enjoyed as much success for club and country. The 'original Baxter' was called Neilly Gibson.

Gibson was born in Larkhall on 23 February 1873. His career started the same way as a great many others in the late 19th century, in the junior game. He starred for Larkhall Thistle and Larkhall Juniors as a teenager before moving to local senior non-league side Royal Albert where he helped them to some successes in minor competitions. The fair-haired youngster was too good for this level of football, dominating games from the right-half position where he dictated play and demonstrated wonderful close control. At the age of just 20, he signed for Scottish Cup holders Rangers in November 1894.

Despite manager William Wilton having an impressive group of players to choose from, Rangers were struggling when Gibson arrived. The Glasgow Cup which had been won in the previous two seasons had been lost to Celtic, the league challenge was already looking forlorn, and league leaders Hearts had ended the Scottish Cup defence a few days earlier in the first round. Gibson was pitched straight into the team, making his debut on 1 December 1894 in a league match away to Dumbarton. It wasn't the start he hoped for, a 1-0 defeat in a poor match. But young Gibson impressed even in a team struggling for form, and he played in eight of the remaining league games, including a first Old Firm start in March 1895 that ended in a 1-1 draw. He suffered a dismal 4-0 loss to them in the Charity Cup at the end of May, meaning a trophyless season. But all Ibrox onlookers agreed that manager Wilton had unearthed a real gem, Gibson displaying a level of skill and confidence that had rarely, if ever, been seen in the Scottish game.

He had been so impressive that just a few months into his career in the top division, Gibson was capped by Scotland, playing in a win over Ireland at Parkhead on 30 March

1895, and an away defeat to England a week later. His style of play was unique at the time, preferring to hold possession and beat players and wait for the right moment to pick a pass rather than launch the ball forward. He also was one of the first footballers to perfect the back-heel, and had a famous trick that had spectators gasping in excitement, when he perfected the skill of allowing a ball to go over his head then back-heel it back over his own head to wrong foot an opponent. He was supremely confident in his ability, some opponents regarding his outrageous skills as bordering on arrogance.

Despite his brilliance, Gibson suffered another trophyless season in 1895/96. He played in all but one league match as Rangers were runners-up to Celtic. He scored just the once, one of seven the team ran in against Hearts at Ibrox. This was a Rangers team who seemed to have much better individual players than the results being achieved, but when they conceded six goals to Celtic for the second time in the season in the Charity Cup Final in May 1896, Wilton determined that new blood was required. Probably the two most important captures were international forward Jimmy Millar from Sunderland and goalkeeper Matthew Dickie from Renton.

His club season was a definite disappointment, but Gibson again shone in a Scotland shirt. After a fine display in a high scoring draw with Ireland in Belfast, he enjoyed his first win over England in April 1896 before a record crowd at Parkhead, with several of the opposition side saying after the match that Gibson was as fine a player as they had ever encountered. This was the first defeat England had suffered in 20 internationals. In the report of the match in *The Times*, the importance of right-half-back Gibson was explained, even if he wasn't named,

'The secret of England's loss was to be found in the important position of half-back. Here, England were weak, and the Scottish in the same line were fast and strong.' Gibson was a virtual ever present again in 1896/97, a year when the balance of power in Scottish football started moving towards Ibrox. He started in 17 of the 18 league matches, scoring twice in the first half a dozen, but a couple of surprise defeats in the run-in meant a third-place finish, just three points behind champions Hearts, who Rangers had defeated 5-0 in September with Gibson running the show. Third would probably have been second if not for the fact seven regulars, including Gibson, were missing for a 0-0 draw with Third Lanark as they were representing the Scottish League against the English on the same afternoon. But the league was the only significant competition that Gibson failed to win during the season.

He played in both the initial draw and the 2-1 replay win over Celtic in the Glasgow Cup Final to win his first medal as a professional. He was instrumental in the club bringing the Scottish Cup to Ibrox for only the second time, scoring in the first-round win against Partick, the third-round win over Dundee, and the semi-final defeat of Morton, before helping the team dominate the final against Dumbarton in a 5-1 scoreline. Then he ended the season on a high, inspiring a comfortable 4-1 Charity Cup semi-final success against Celtic before scoring in a 6-1 thumping of Third Lanark in the final. For the first time, all three cups belonged to Rangers in the same season, and Gibson was a huge reason why.

Gibson proved his worth that season for club and country. He played in seven Old Firm games in all competitions, and was undefeated. He also starred again for Scotland, scoring his only international goal in March 1897 in a win over Ireland, before being majestic in a famous 2-1 win over England at Crystal Palace, the Scotland goals scored by his Ibrox team-mates Tom Hyslop and Jimmy Millar.

Gibson continued his rich vein of form in 1897/98, although it again wasn't enough to see the league title arrive at Ibrox. He scored once in 15 league starts as Rangers finished second to Celtic. But he claimed another Glasgow Cup medal after seeing off Celtic in the semi-final and then Queen's Park in the final, before the club successfully retained the Scottish Cup for the first time, Gibson hitting home a crucial penalty in a tight semi-final replay win over Third Lanark before starting in the 2-0 final win over Kilmarnock. He saw his winning run against England end that season, playing in a 3-1 defeat to them at Parkhead in his only international start of the campaign.

Season 1898/99 saw Gibson play in all 18 league matches, and what a campaign it was. The immortal 100 per cent season was achieved, the team not dropping a single point as they dominated in a way never done before or since. Gibson hit the net three times in the league, one of them a penalty in the 10-0 humbling of Hibs that clinched the title with three games left to play. His clever passing and creative genius helped create countless chances and goals, however, for a potent forward line that contained the likes of R.C. Hamilton, Alec Smith, Johnny Campbell, Jimmy Millar and John McPherson. He is one of just five players who played in all 18 games that season, giving him a unique place not just in Scottish football but in the game worldwide.

Gibson equalled his best goals tally for the club over the season, with seven to his name. These included three in the Scottish Cup, but the tournament ended in disappointment when the final was lost 2-0 to Celtic.

That had been the first time Rangers had won outright the Scottish title (the previous success was a joint win with Dumbarton), and they weren't happy with just one. Season 1899/1900 saw the team continue their domination, Gibson starting in 16 of the 18 matches as the championship was retained by a clear margin of seven points. It threatened to be a season where all four trophies might be won, with the league already in the bag before a new year defeat at Parkhead, and the Glasgow Cup regained when Gibson played in his third winning final in the competition against the bitter rivals. But the team, including Gibson, chose the worst possible occasion for their worst display of the season against Celtic in the Scottish Cup semi-final, slumping to a horrible 4-0 loss. There was to be one last meeting of the giants in the Charity Cup Final on 12 May 1900, and the Scottish Cup demons were swept away in an incredible 5-1 win, Gibson scoring his only Old Firm goal that day in front of 15,000 fans at Hampden.

Season 1899/1900 saw Gibson win three trophies with Rangers, but perhaps his greatest performance, and the day he rose to even greater fame, came on 7 April 1900 before 63,000 at Parkhead when he inspired an unforgettable 4-1 win for Scotland over England.

Scotland wore the famous pink and yellow racing colours of the former Prime Minister Lord Rosebery in his honour as he was a guest of honour at the match, and future Rangers centre-forward Robert 'RS' McColl scored a hat-trick. As well McColl, Gibson had four current Ibrox team-mates alongside him that day – Nicol Smith, Jock Drummond, Jacky Robertson and Alec Smith. All played well in a match England were two down within the first ten minutes, but it was the genius of Gibson that stood out. He gave a masterclass in tackling, ball control and artistry that had the watching English press looking up the dictionary for superlatives. But probably the biggest compliment Gibson was paid after the match came from the great England goalscorer Steve Bloomer, who scored their consolation goal on the day. He simply said that Gibson was 'the best player I have ever seen'. This was the Victorian era version of Baxter in 1967.

Gibson only played once more for Scotland as a Rangers player, a 1-1 draw against Wales in 1901. In that season of 1900/01, Gibson claimed his third successive league medal as Rangers cruised to the title, not dropping a point at home all season. The only match he missed was the 20th and last fixture of the season against Morton as he was away on international duty. He scored on the opening day against Third Lanark, which was his only strike the whole campaign. Gibson was particularly impressive in the Glasgow Cup wins over Celtic and Partick Thistle that saw him claim yet another winners' medal in the competition, but he was again frustrated in the Scottish Cup by Celtic, who eliminated Rangers for the third year running.

His season in 1901/02 was interrupted by injury, Gibson now heading towards his 30th birthday. He scored a Glasgow Cup semi-final goal to help beat Partick, before playing in a drawn final with Celtic that was never replayed due to the Parkhead club's refusal to take part in a second match at Ibrox. But the main excitement in the season was the championship race, with Celtic threatening to deny Rangers a fourth straight success. Rangers had suffered a terrible form slump in November, losing four successive league matches. Gibson missed three of these matches through injury. When he returned to the team, the deficit was five points to Celtic with just five matches remaining; the title looked lost. But Celtic then lost to Hearts and Queen's Park in successive games, then drew with Hibs, and suddenly the new year fixture on 1 January 1902 had massive significance.

It was Celtic's final match, and they had 26 points. Rangers still had three more games after the derby to play and stood on 20 points. If Celtic won, the title was theirs. If Rangers won, the gap was four points with six still available. Parkhead was crammed to see the decisive match, and Gibson was now back to full fitness. He shrugged off an early Celtic goal to pull the strings in an impressive Rangers performance as Nicol Smith equalised, then Johnny Campbell made it 2-1. Celtic had complained the first goal was illegal, then protested again about this goal, saying Campbell had handled. The referee was manhandled, and Celtic's McMahon was sent off. After initially refusing to restart the game, Celtic did play on, and went 3-1 down to a goal by Jacky Robertson. Gibson was the one man still trying to play football as tempers flared all around him, Celtic pulling a goal back with 20 minutes remaining. Then Gibson sent R.C. Hamilton through for a decisive fourth goal, which ended the contest and also saw yet another Celtic protest claiming offside. Rangers won, Celtic had lost the plot, and there was an SFA enquiry held later on the day's events. In the meantime, Gibson inspired his team to three more victories over Queen's Park, St Mirren and Dundee. Rangers had won an unlikely title.

That season ended in sorrow rather than delight, however, with all at Ibrox devastated by the loss of life at the Scotland versus England international in April. Gibson wasn't on the field that day, but four of his team-mates were, and he shared the grief of all involved.

That was the last league title Gibson won, but he remained at the club for a further two years. Season 1902/03 saw the title surrendered early on with several defeats as the club was still dealing with the aftermath of the disaster, and all eyes turned to the Scottish Cup, a prize Rangers hadn't won in five years. Gibson scored in an easy first-round win over lowly Auchterarder, and stood out in a brilliant quarter-final win over Celtic at Parkhead. He lined up on 11 April 1903 against Hearts in the final, looking for a third winners' medal in the competition, but a very good Hearts team were worth their 1-1 draw. A goalless replay followed, Gibson suffering an injury near the end. He was forced to sit out the third match, and watched his team-mates battle to a magnificent 2-0 win despite playing for around an hour with just ten players after an injury to Jock Drummond.

Injury was becoming a recurring problem for Gibson, with his 1903/04 season disrupted early on. His last league campaign at Ibrox saw the team finish fourth, five points behind Third Lanark. He scored his last Rangers goal on 13 February 1904 against Port Glasgow, then played his 283rd and last competitive game for Rangers on 10 May in a 4-1 win over Third Lanark in the Inter-City League.

Rangers were a team in transition now, many of the 'old guard' were either reaching the end of their careers or had already moved on, and in the summer of 1904 he agreed with manager Wilton that he would leave for a new challenge. Nobody could begrudge him this; Gibson had been a massive reason why Rangers had won so many honours during his Ibrox career. On 24 August he received a benefit match from the club, Celtic providing the opposition. An Alec Smith goal won the game 1-0. Then on Friday, 9 September 1904 he agreed to sign for Partick Thistle, who had lost 8-1 at Ibrox the previous weekend.

Most observers thought this was Gibson now winding down his career. But he soon put that notion to bed, making his debut in a Glasgow Cup win over Clyde. He was appointed team captain and immediately improved the side to such an extent they went on a run of eight successive wins. His sparkling form saw a Scotland recall for one last international appearance, against Ireland in a 4-0 win in March 1905. He was made captain for the day in recognition of his service to the game, an honour richly deserved.

He continued playing with Thistle until 1909, helping them to their best league placing of fifth in 1906. When he left, he wound down his football career with spells at his old club Royal Albert and then Wishaw Thistle, playing the game he loved until after his 40th birthday.

Neilly Gibson left more than a legacy of wonderful football. His three sons were all professional footballers. His eldest son William played left-half for Newcastle United, winning the FA Cup in 1924. His second son Neil played centre-half for Clyde, and scored the winning goal in the 1925 Glasgow Cup Final against Celtic. And perhaps the most famous son of all was the youngest James. He played at right-half for Partick Thistle and Aston Villa, was capped eight times by Scotland, and was one of the immortal 'Wembley Wizards' in 1928. His proud father was in the Wembley crowd that day to see England thrashed 5-1.

Gibson died at the age of 73 in his home town, Larkhall, in January 1947. As well as the compliment from the great Steve Bloomer, other football notables also spoke of Gibson's greatness. England international Harry Wood called him 'Pavlova in football boots', and legendary Scottish football referee and manager Willie McCartney said Gibson was 'the greatest player of my, and any, generation'. His name might not be as well known as Baxter, but to his generation he was every bit as much a hero.

- Rangers career: 1894–1904
- 29 goals in 322 competitive appearances
- 4 league titles, including the 'Invincible' season
- Also won 3 Scottish Cups, 5 Glasgow Cups and 2 Charity Cups
- Hall of Fame member
- The inspiration behind one of Scotland's greatest victories over England
- To many, the best footballer in the world at his peak

12 AND 13   NICOL SMITH AND JOCK DRUMMOND

The first great Rangers full-back partnership, but it ended in tragedy

RANGERS HAVE had many great full-back partnerships over the years. Manderson and McCandless, Young and Shaw, Shearer and Caldow or Jardine and Greig might all be put forward as the best of the best. But there's a decent argument that the full-back pairing who graced the Royal Blue jersey at the end of the 19th and beginning of the 20th centuries might have been the greatest of them all. They played in the first truly dominant Rangers team and their names were Nicol Smith and Jock Drummond.

Right-back Smith was born on Christmas Day 1873 in the Ayrshire town of Darvel, a small place but one that produced no fewer than three of the greatest players to play for the club in our early years, the others being the great John 'Kitey' McPherson and the legendary left-winger Alec Smith. It was Nicol, in fact, who recommended the non-related Alec to the club and helped organise him taking part in a trial match that led to his incredible 21-year career as a Rangers player.

Nicol Smith started out in junior football, playing full-back for Vale of Irvine and Royal Albert as well as his hometown team Darvel, during which time his performances earned him national recognition by being picked for the Scotland junior international side. It was no surprise that he then moved to the senior game, joining Rangers in early 1893, and he soon became a first-team regular after his debut in a 2-1 league victory against Hearts on 18 March of that year. A solid, hard-tackling defender first and foremost, Smith also possessed an excellent football brain, and started many a counter-attack from his right-back position with his range of passing. His debut marked the first time that a legendary full-back partnership was seen in Royal Blue, as on the left side of the defence was John 'Jock' Drummond.

Drummond was older than Smith, born in Alva, Clackmannanshire, on 13 April 1870, and he was already a full Scotland international before joining the club. He moved to Falkirk at an early age and attended the Liddle's School before becoming an apprentice at a local bank. He combined his job with football, joining Falkirk as a teenager and playing at left full-back or left-half in their reserves before graduating to the first team. His debut was against Alloa Athletic in a friendly on 16 April 1887, just days after his 17th birthday, and over the next few years he became an automatic choice. He helped Falkirk to local trophies such as the Stirlingshire Cup and the Falkirk District Charity Cup, and in 1892 he became the first Falkirk player to be capped when selected for a 3-2 win over Ireland in Belfast. Just a few weeks later, in March 1892, he joined Rangers, turning down a move to English football with Preston North End in the process. His Rangers debut came on 16 April in a 3-2 home win over Leith Athletic, and he had played in around 20 competitive matches for the club prior to the debut of his future defensive partner.

Drummond's first Rangers honour came exactly a month before Smith's debut, when he played at left-back in the unforgettable first Glasgow Cup Final win for the club, beating Celtic 3-1 with goals by John Barker, Neil Kerr and John McPherson. He was a menacing and uncompromising figure on the pitch, totally committed with a no-nonsense style that captured the hearts of the Rangers support. He wore a cloth cap while playing, something hard to imagine these days, pulling the peak down to add to his intimidating presence. Drummond would nowadays be regarded as a somewhat over aggressive player, but he wasn't without skill too. He knew his first job was to prevent the opposition scoring, and he took great pleasure from making sure they did not breach his iron defending.

By the start of the following season, 1893/94, Smith had settled into life at the club and became the undisputed first pick at right-back. It was to be a momentous season both for the new full-back pairing and for the club. The league campaign was a disappointment, awful inconsistency seeing a fourth-place finish despite both players starting all but one match each. There was one huge highlight, though, both players starring in a 5-0 thrashing of Celtic in September, which was the first league win over them. It was a season more remembered for the cup competitions. Both players started the Glasgow Cup semi-final win over Celtic and the 1-0 victory over Cowlairs in the final, the first time a Rangers team had successfully defended a trophy. But it was the Scottish Cup that everyone at the club craved most; it had never been won by Rangers, who were without even a final appearance in 15 years.

Rangers roared into the semi-finals, racking up 15 goals in the earlier rounds without reply. The draw saw them paired with Queen's Park, still a giant of the game, and after a 1-1 home draw the Hampden side were favourites with home advantage. Smith picked the replay to score his first goal for the club, the match ending in a 3-1 victory and setting up an Old Firm final the following weekend. Smith and Drummond were rocks at the back against Celtic in front of 17,000 spectators, and by the time Maley had scored for the Parkhead side late in the game it was already much too late as Rangers had cruised into a three-goal lead by then. The cup was won for the first time, and the full-back partners had their names forever etched into club history. The pairing also made the Charity Cup Final that season, where Queen's Park extracted some revenge for the Scottish Cup loss.

Drummond had by now been capped again by Scotland, this time as a Rangers player, and he would feature regularly in the international side over the coming years. At one time he gained the distinction of being the country's most capped player, and ended his international career in 1903 with 14 appearances, four of them as captain.

The following two seasons saw Rangers fail to build on that amazing cup season, with no trophies won. Smith and Drummond played whenever fit, but despite their continuing good form, the team overall struggled with a few heavy defeats along the way. This culminated in a horrific 6-1 drubbing by Celtic in the 1896 Charity Cup Final, which prompted manager William Wilton to bring in some new faces for the coming season. These included goalscoring forward Jimmy Millar from Sunderland and goalkeeper Matt Dickie, who would prove to be an inspired signing, providing extra defensive solidity behind the full-backs.

Smith missed a large proportion of the 1896/97 season with several injuries, only starting nine league games. He did start in the Glasgow Cup Final against Celtic, alongside Drummond, but picked up a knock in the 1-1 draw, forcing him to sit out the replay. Rangers won it 2-1, giving Drummond his third medal in the competition. Drummond only missed two league games, being paired with several different full-back partners during Smith's enforced absences, with Davie Crawford the deputy most often. The two players did start all five Scottish Cup ties and it was to be a second season of glory for them in the competition. Smith scored in the opening round win over Partick, and he and Drummond picked up their second winners' medals when helping the team to a resounding 5-1 final hammering of Dumbarton. Both players also started in the Charity Cup Final, and wrapped up the season in style with a 6-1 win against Third Lanark, meaning all three cup competitions were won for the first time in club history. A third-place league finish, just three points behind Hearts, was the only blemish on the season.

By now Smith was also a Scotland player, his first international match being a 2-1 win over England at Crystal Palace, London on 3 April 1897. Smith would go on to play 12 times for his country, twice chosen to captain the team. He and Drummond played together only three times for Scotland, most notably in the famous 4-1 thrashing of England in 1900.

In 1897/98 Rangers were favourites to finally win the league title again, something they had not done since the first league season in 1890/91. But old rivals Celtic proved too consistent over the campaign, their championship win achieved without suffering a defeat, winning 15 games and drawing three. But they were beaten in the Glasgow Cup semi-final by Rangers after a replay, Smith only starting the first drawn match and then suffering another injury. He also missed the final win over Queen's Park the next weekend. Drummond did claim another winners' medal, though, the semi-final and final wins both featuring goals by the prolific new centre-forward, R.C. Hamilton. And Hamilton also scored in the Scottish Cup Final against Kilmarnock, the trophy retained for the first time, which meant a third winners' medal for both the full-backs.

Smith and Drummond were now at the peak of their careers, the defensive wall that manager Wilton had now built a special team around. Both were Scotland regulars and both were desperate to add the one trophy to their collection that was still missing, the league title. That gap was to be filled in spectacular style in 1898/99, although injuries prevented both players from playing a full part in football history. Rangers won all 18 of their league games, the first time in world football that any team in a national top division had completed a 100 per cent season. Smith started 13 times but Drummond only made five appearances, a long-term injury disrupting his season. Dependable reserve player Davie Crawford ended up filling in for both players over the season and made more starts than either of them.

Smith missed the first five games, making his comeback into the team in a sensational match at Parkhead that Rangers won 4-0. He was an ever present from then on, enjoying the new year rout of Celtic which featured a hat-trick for Hamilton, and was on the pitch against Clyde in game number 18 when the invincible record was achieved. Strangely, Drummond's absence was a virtual mirror image as he started the season in the team, but then had to sit out the historic run-in. The pairing only started together once in the 18 fixtures, a 5-0 win over Partick.

They made up for it over the next three seasons, however, as the first truly dominant Rangers team racked up four successive league titles. Both players remained first choice in their positions throughout these years, with only injury or international duty seeing them absent. Smith scored on the opening day of 1899/1900 against Third Lanark, and it would be 1 January 1900 that the players would suffer a defeat in the league together for the first time since September 1897 when Celtic won 3-2. Celtic also ended their Scottish Cup hopes that season, but they would get some revenge over their rivals before the season ended as both starred in a Charity Cup Final masterclass that saw the Parkhead side humiliated 5-1.

Smith and Drummond were virtual ever presents in the 1900/01 title win, and both also claimed another Glasgow Cup after overcoming Celtic in a first-round replay then going on to beat Partick in the final. Season 1901/02 saw a title race that reached a satisfying ending when the flag was clinched by beating Celtic 4-2 at Parkhead in January. Both players started, and Smith enjoyed the occasion even more as he chipped in with a rare goal. Rangers also retained the Glasgow Cup, although in bizarre fashion after both players appeared in a 2-2 final draw with Celtic, who then refused to play in the replay after the venue was chosen again as Ibrox. The season ended in tragedy for the pair, however, as they were on the field at Ibrox representing Scotland against England on 5 April 1902 when a temporary stand collapsed, killing 25 spectators. The match, although completed, was declared unofficial and caps not awarded, although both players did play in the replayed game at Villa Park in May which ended 2-2. That match was Smith's last for his country, Drummond only starting once more.

The club was in mourning for those who perished, and the following season was totally overshadowed by fundraising for those affected and also rebuilding work at the stadium. Unsurprisingly, there would be no fifth successive title for the full-back pair in 1902/03, although the team did go on a winning Scottish Cup run. Smith missed virtually all of this, however, but Drummond started all three matches in the final against Hearts. The second replay was won 2-0 to give Rangers a highly emotional win, and one that would see them lift the cup for the last time in 25 long years. Drummond only played a small part in the victory as he was carried off injured after half an hour, the team still winning 2-0 despite the handicap of only ten players for so long.

Season 1903/04 would be the last of the great partnership. Smith was now back to full fitness and played in almost every match. Drummond, however, was now in the veteran stage of his career, and saw little action in the run-in after playing most of the games up to the new year. Both players scored during the season, the only time this happened in their decade together. Smith hit an important goal in a 2-2 draw at Kilmarnock while Drummond scored an equally vital one in a 3-2 win at Queen's Park. The league challenge ended in a fourth-place finish behind new champions Third Lanark, but the team reached another Scottish Cup Final where Celtic were waiting. Alex Fraser had played most of the previous few months at left-back, but Drummond returned to the team for an Inter-City League match and manager Wilton decided to go with the old head in the final against Celtic.

The cup final would be Drummond's last game for the club, and the 197th time that he lined up beside Smith in defence. Sadly it would not be a happy ending to his time in Royal Blue as Rangers lost 3-2 despite an early Finlay Speedie double giving them a two-goal lead. Fraser returned to the team beside Smith for the remaining games, including a thumping 5-2 Charity Cup win over Celtic.

Now aged 34, Drummond left Rangers to return to his hometown club Falkirk. He played there for another season and became a director while still registered on the playing staff. His last recorded match for Falkirk came on 7 May 1907 when he turned out in a friendly against a Morayshire XI at the age of 37. Drummond was a keen bowler, and won several prizes during his membership of the Falkirk Adrain bowling club. By 1915, he was a janitor at Falkirk Science and Art School, and he particularly enjoyed holidays in Millport, where he went as often as he could. In 1923 he attended Rangers' golden jubilee dinner as a former player, despite his association with Falkirk. He passed away on 23 January 1935 after a long illness, aged 65.

Smith started 1904/05 still as the right-back. He played in 12 of the first 14 league games but after starting in the home win over Third Lanark on 19 November 1904, he complained of feeling unwell. Smith was diagnosed with enteric fever, something which is easily treated in the 21st century, but was a serious condition in the days before antibiotics. His wife Annie nursed him during his illness, and sadly also became infected with the same condition, causing her untimely death on 20 December 1904. Rangers' players and staff were devastated for their popular colleague and a benefit match against Queen's Park was immediately arranged which raised the sum of £500 for their five children. Tragically, Smith did not see any of this money as he passed away just two days later aged just 31, a tragedy that was felt all over Scottish football. It is thought the cause of the enteric fever was drinking of contaminated water.

The loss of Smith was too much for many of his Rangers team-mates. It took some time for the club to recover from what was a heartbreaking loss.

With 197 Rangers appearances together over 11 years, these two great players are members of the Rangers Hall of Fame, and are remembered as much as a pair as they are as individuals.

Theirs is a story of a great partnership, glorious success on the pitch, but a tragic ending.

- Nicol Smith Rangers career: 1893–1905
- 304 competitive matches
- 5 goals
- 4 league titles
- 3 Scottish Cups
- 12 Scotland caps, twice Scotland captain.

- Jock Drummond Rangers career: 1892–1904
- 312 competitive matches
- 3 goals
- 4 league titles
- 4 Scottish Cups
- 14 Scotland caps, four times Scotland captain

14   ROBERT HAMILTON

The Lord Provost who holds the record for the most Old Firm goals

ROBERT CUMMING Hamilton was born in Elgin on 13 May 1877, and his football career started with the local Elgin City club of the Highland League. An intelligent young man who had excelled academically at school as well as on the sports fields, he accepted an offer from Glasgow University in 1896 to study teaching. This meant a move south to the big city, and it also meant he would need to find a new club if he wanted to continue his love of football. After a successful trial, he joined the famous amateurs of Queen's Park.

Hamilton, known as either 'R.C.' or Bob, was a centre-forward with a natural instinct for scoring goals. He was quick, two-footed and strong, and he quickly made an impact at Hampden. He only spent one season with Queen's Park, who already had another brilliant goalscoring talent in R.S. McColl, where he attracted the attention of scouts from the professional game. On 3 May 1897 he scored all four goals in a 4-0 win over Celtic in the Glasgow League at Parkhead, and shortly afterwards he was snapped up by Rangers. This was a Rangers side who had won all three cup competitions in 1896/97 and who were seen as the emerging force in Scottish football, but manager William Wilton felt that he still lacked an out-and-out centre-forward to lead the line. As there was no transfer fee due to Queen's Park's amateur status, this move must rank as one of the best signings ever made by the club.

Hamilton's competitive debut came on the opening day of the 1897/98 league season away to St Bernard's in Edinburgh. In a sign of things to come, he scored twice in a 4-2 win. Despite high hopes of a first Scottish league title in eight years, Rangers were to end the campaign in second place behind Celtic. But that didn't stop Hamilton from being prolific, scoring 17 goals in just 15 league appearances. He hit four against St Mirren in December, then three more the following week at Hibs, finding the net in ten of his 15 starts. In the Glasgow Cup, he scored his first Old Firm goals on 30 October in a 2-2 semi-final draw, before scoring twice in the 3-1 replay victory. Hamilton hit the Celtic net no fewer than six times in his debut season, adding to those three Glasgow Cup goals with strikes home and away in the Glasgow League before a crucial counter in a tight Charity Cup semi-final win. Hamilton would go on to enjoy astonishing success in fixtures against Celtic, eventually scoring an all-time record of 35 goals in matches between the clubs in all competitions.

He also scored in the Glasgow Cup Final, collecting his first winners' medal as a Rangers player against his old Queen's Park team-mates. In the Scottish Cup, he scored in each of the opening three rounds, including a four-goal haul in a 12-0 rout of hapless Cartvale, before scoring once in the semi-final matches against Third Lanark. Hamilton then won a first Scottish Cup, hitting the clinching second goal in a 2-0 final win over Kilmarnock as Rangers retained the trophy for the first time. Despite a surprise loss to Third Lanark in the Charity Cup, he could look back on a brilliant first season as a Rangers player, winning two cup finals and scoring 40 times in all competitions from just 35 starts.

Hamilton was the top scorer for the club that season, which he repeated for an incredible nine successive campaigns. As 1898/99 dawned all at Rangers were confident the team could finally bring the league title back to Ibrox, and Hamilton was appointed as the new club captain. He would go on to lead the team to a success unprecedented in the world of football.

Hamilton started all 18 league matches over the season, and continued his amazing goal ratio by scoring 21 times. He started the campaign off in style with a hat-trick on the opening day against Partick, before a crucial double against Hearts ensured a tight 3-2 win in early September. Much to everyone's surprise, he didn't score in a wonderful 4-0 win at Parkhead a few weeks later, a team performance that had the Rangers support in raptures and opposition teams fearing what lay in store for them. He did hit both goals against Celtic to win their Glasgow Cup semi-final, and then went one better on New Year's Day 1899 by scoring only the second Old Firm league hat-trick for Rangers in a comprehensive 4-1 win. He had also hit a treble a fortnight earlier, as Rangers crushed Dundee 7-0, then scored two more in a 10-0 thumping of Hibs to clinch the title with three matches still to play.

That new year win meant 17 wins from 17 games, with a last fixture to play away to Clyde. Hamilton led his team out in a 3-0 win to clinch immortality, the first captain of a team to go through an entire league season without dropping a single point. At the post-match tea party, Hamilton made a speech to mark this momentous occasion. He said,

'Our great success was due largely to the splendid esprit de corps that had animated the team. They were indeed the heart and soul of the club, prepared to fight out every match until the last second, and indeed, the story of their victories shows that without indomitable courage this wonderful record could never have been created.' He was undoubtedly referring to the nerve-shredding match at Easter Road in November, where the team found themselves 2-0 then 3-2 down, with time running out. Hamilton scored the equaliser before being fouled in the penalty area in the final minute, letting Bobby Neill coolly slot the spot-kick home to snatch the win and to keep the winning run intact.

Despite the league perfection, Hamilton was to suffer disappointment in all three cup competitions as Rangers were defeated in the final each time, no doubt their title heroics draining them. Overall he had scored 32 times in 31 starts, and his goalscoring form was impossible for the Scotland selectors to ignore any longer. Hamilton made his international debut against Wales on 18 March 1899 and played in all three of the Home International matches. He scored three times: a double in a 9-1 mauling of Ireland, then a consolation second-half goal against England in a 2-1 loss at Villa Park.

Rangers retained the league title in 1899/1900, the first time the club had achieved this feat. Hamilton played in 16 matches, and his 17 league goals included a run of seven in just four games in November into December to ensure the flag stayed at Ibrox. He also enjoyed cup final victories over Celtic in both the Glasgow and Charity Cups, scoring in the latter success, although the Scottish Cup ended in disappointment due to a heavy loss at Parkhead.

In 1900/01 he continued the pattern of collecting medals and hitting the Celtic net. Twenty league goals in 19 appearances meant he had averaged better than a goal a game for all four league seasons in Royal Blue, a quite astonishing record. His goals were a massive reason why a third successive league title was won; over the season he hit hat-tricks against Dundee, Partick and St Mirren as well as four goals in the other St Mirren fixture. There was one other hat-trick during the campaign, a second treble against Celtic in his career, at Ibrox on 8 April in a 4-3 Inter-City League win. He also scored in the Glasgow Cup Final win over Partick, although Celtic again ended his Scottish Cup hopes when winning a close first-round match at Parkhead.

Hamilton also continued his impressive goalscoring rate in Scotland colours. In February he hit four goals in a record 11-0 win over Ireland, then he scored a vital equaliser in the 70th minute against England in a 2-2 draw in London.

Season 1901/02 was overshadowed by the disaster at Ibrox during the Scotland v England match, which meant the club was in little mood to celebrate winning an unprecedented fourth successive league title. As ever, Hamilton was the top scorer, although he had only scored nine goals in his 16 starts. These did include the goal that effectively won the championship, the final nail in Celtic's coffin in a controversial 4-2 new year win at Parkhead. He also hit another international hat-trick in a 5-1 away win over Ireland in Belfast.

That was the last league title Hamilton won with the club, despite being a Rangers player in five more seasons. A combination of several key players reaching the end of their careers, the selling of players to help fund the victim compensation and stadium rebuilding after the disaster, and the emergence of an excellent Celtic team all playing a part.

Hamilton did start 1902/03 on fire, scoring seven times in the first three league games. But inconsistent results soon mounted up and the title was lost from early in the campaign. Nevertheless, the club were determined to bring the Scottish Cup back to Ibrox for the first time since Hamilton's debut season in 1898 as a tribute to all those impacted by the disaster, and Hamilton was to play his part in making that wish come true. He scored in a routine first-round win over little Auchterarder, then scored a much more important goal in the third round when Celtic were swept aside 3-0 on their own pitch. He hit a semi-final double against Stenhousemuir to help set up a final against Hearts. It took three tough and bruising encounters to settle the final, Hamilton's magnificent run and thumping finish settling the third match 2-0 in a game where Rangers battled with just ten players for an hour due to an injury to Jock Drummond. For such a feared penalty box forward, Hamilton was also a magnificent striker of the ball, and he scored many great long-range goals.

Despite Rangers no longer being the dominant force in the game, Hamilton showed he was still the deadliest marksman in Scottish football in 1903/04 when he scored a fantastic 29 league goals from just 24 starts. The team still only managed a fourth-place finish, even though they had the country's top goalscorer. In just the first six league games Hamilton registered 15 goals, with hat-tricks against Third Lanark, Hearts and Queen's Park as well as four goals against Motherwell, all before the end of September. He was to miss a significant part of the season's end through injury, missing two Old Firm finals, a defeat in the Scottish Cup and a win in the Charity Cup. He did play his tenth and last international match as a Rangers player in March, scoring the Scotland goal in a 1-1 draw in Dublin. He had also represented the Scottish League on seven occasions, scoring nine goals, including a hat-trick against the English League in 1901.

Nineteen league goals followed in 1904/05, this time from 17 appearances. He scored against Celtic in a 2-1 Glasgow Cup Final defeat, and against them in a 2-2 draw at Parkhead in the league. Unfortunately injury forced him to miss two other vital matches against them. First, he was out for a 4-1 loss in the league that eventually meant a play-off would be needed as the teams finished level on points. Then he had to sit out the play-off itself, and looked on in disappointment as Celtic won 2-1. He also missed the Scottish Cup Final replay defeat to Third Lanark after playing in the first drawn match.

Season 1905/06 would be Hamilton's lowest goals return in his Rangers career, but his ten still were more than anyone else at the club. After hitting an opening-day double to snatch a win over Kilmarnock, he and the team struggled to find any kind of fluency, ending the season a distant 4th behind Celtic. His goal at Ibrox against Hibs in a 1-1 draw on 3 March 1906 would prove to be his last for the club before a transfer was agreed to allow Hamilton to join English Southern League side Fulham. He had scored over 300 Rangers goals with minor competitions included, and as well as being top scorer in all nine seasons at Ibrox, he was the Scottish First Division top scorer six times.

Hamilton wanted the move mainly to secure a signing-on fee and higher wages to finance a Master's degree on his return to Scotland. Fulham had won the Southern League the previous season, but had failed to be elected to join the Football League. Hamilton was seen as a shrewd buy who was worth the outlay, a man whose experience and goals would hopefully retain the title and see the club win election next time. Known down south as Bobby Hamilton, his style of play wasn't at first appreciated by the London crowd; he was more studious in his approach than the battering ram centre-forwards they were accustomed to watching. He made his debut at Norwich on 1 September 1906, and scored his first goal for the club a fortnight later against Crystal Palace. When he scored his 11th and last Southern League goal of the season in April 1907, he had finished the campaign as top goalscorer, and had helped Fulham to a title win by just two points from Portsmouth. Fulham were then successful in their application to join the Football League.

He returned north after that one season in London and rejoined the club he still held dearest to his heart, Rangers. But despite high hopes the move might help rejuvenate a struggling side, his return proved to be disappointing. He started just 13 matches and scored only three times. Hamilton made one last cup final appearance for the club against Celtic in the Glasgow Cup in October 1907, but he failed to hit the net as it was lost 2-1. His last goal for Rangers came on 7 December 1907 at Tynecastle in a 2-1 win, and his last start came in a 3-2 win over Partick Thistle on 2 January 1908, a day after his last Old Firm appearance. Later that month, the 30-year-old Hamilton was transferred to Hearts, ending his magnificent Rangers career.

Hamilton was only at Hearts for a few months, starting just seven games for them. His debut was on 15 February in a draw against Morton, and his only goal for the club came against St Mirren a few weeks later. He did start a match for them against Rangers at Ibrox, receiving a rousing reception from the Rangers fans in a 2-1 win for the home side. Overall, however, his spell at Tynecastle was poor, and many felt Hamilton's career was over. But he was to prove them wrong.

He left Hearts in the summer of 1908 and agreed a contract to join Morton. At Greenock he rediscovered his love of the game, and rediscovered his scoring form. He spent two enjoyable seasons with Morton and despite spending most of his time at the wrong end of the table, he hit 27 goals in just 57 competitive appearances. This alerted Scottish Cup holders Dundee in the summer of 1910, and despite Hamilton now being well into his 30s, he signed for the Tayside club.

Although not winning any major honours with the Dens Park team, Hamilton impressed as both a centre-forward and wider attacker. His debut came against Hibs in August but he really hit the headlines in February when scoring in a 2-1 win over league leaders Rangers in the Scottish Cup. He scored 20 goals in his first Dundee season, and was sensationally recalled to the Scotland international team for the first time in seven years in March 1911 for the match against Wales in Cardiff. Typically, Hamilton scored both Scotland goals in a 2-2 draw, his second being a last-minute equaliser.

Hamilton finished as the top scorer for Dundee in both 1910/11 and 1911/12, and he played in the first Dundee derby when his team drew 2-2 with Dundee Hibernian in the Forfarshire Cup, going through on a toss of the coin. He hit eight goals in 1912/13, but age was catching up with him by this time, and he left Dundee with a record of 43 goals in 101 starts.

He briefly returned to where it all began at Elgin City before retiring from football in 1914 at the age of 37. By now, Hamilton had completed a Master of Arts degree, and he was first a teacher then a headmaster in his home town, where he also played an active role in the Moray and Nairn Education Board. He was also a successful businessman, running a family net manufacturing company. Hamilton also became active in local politics, serving on the Elgin Council for over 20 years, and holding the position of Lord Provost between 1931 and 1937. He died of stomach cancer in May 1948, just after his 71st birthday.

The boardroom at Elgin City contains a tribute to the town's greatest ever football son on its wall, and Robert Cumming Hamilton was inducted into the Rangers Hall of Fame in 2011.

- Rangers career: 1897–1906; 1907/08
- 312 goals in 367 games, including minor competitions
- 35 goals Old Firm goals in all matches, more than anyone else in the fixture
- 4 league titles, and the ever-present captain of the Invincibles
- 2 Scottish Cups, a scorer in both winning finals
- Rangers' top scorer in nine successive seasons
- Scottish league top scorer six times
- 15 goals in just 11 Scotland appearances
- A top footballer, but also an academic, a businessman and a politician

15 SANDY ARCHIBALD

The player who holds the record for most league title medals

IF EVER asked who holds the record for the most Scottish league championship medals, many would hazard a guess at one of the stalwarts of either the Rangers or Celtic nine in a row teams of the past 50 years. But the correct answer (if unofficial wartime titles are excluded) goes much further back, to a fiery, pacy, goalscoring right-winger who wore the Rangers shirt with great pride and distinction from 1917 to 1934. His name was Sandy Archibald.

A native of Crossgates in Fife, Alexander Archibald was born on 6 September 1897, and he joined local club Raith Rovers in 1915 from Dunfermline Juniors. Despite his young age, he became a regular in the Kirkaldy club's first team and it wasn't long before bigger clubs were monitoring his progress. In early May 1917 manager William Wilton brought the miner and part-time player to Rangers, and he made his debut in a Charity Cup Final defeat against Celtic at Ibrox on 12 May. Archibald would go on to avenge that initial defeat many times over, enjoying numerous great victories over Celtic in his long Ibrox career. His goals, creativity, and sheer determination to win for his beloved Rangers earning him a fearsome reputation in the Parkhead dressing room.

In fact, one of the most famous quotes about the player was spoken by long-serving Celtic manager Willie Maley, who said of Archibald, 'So long as he is on the pitch, we can never be sure of victory over Rangers, no matter the score.'

Season 1917/18 was his first full campaign with the club, and it was surely no coincidence that it coincided with Rangers regaining their league title after four successive years where Celtic were winners. Archibald played in all 34 league games, scoring eight goals, including a crucial double in a win over Kilmarnock in the title run-in. The championship was won by the narrowest of margins over our great rivals, a single point, with Archibald scoring the opening goal on the final day, a 2-1 win against Clyde. He also scored his first Old Firm goal in a 3-0 Glasgow Cup semi-final win at Parkhead, going on to collect his first winners' medal in the competition when starting in the defeat of Partick a few weeks later.

Incredibly, Archibald would only see four seasons during his long Ibrox career where Rangers didn't win the title; 1918/19 was the first of these and although Rangers had to do without Archibald for virtually all the first half of the campaign, he only started in 15 of the 34 matches. He was back for the end-of-season Charity Cup, and he collected his first winners' medal in that tournament when starting in the 2-1 defeat of Queen's Park at Hampden in front of a massive post-war crowd of over 50,000.

Season 1919/20 saw him back as a virtual ever present, and Wilton's team roared to a hugely impressive championship win, losing only twice in 42 matches. Archibald's 11 league goals included scoring in three successive games in October and also a last-day double against Morton. He was to experience the horrors of the Scottish Cup jinx, however, when playing superbly in the mammoth quarter-final win against Celtic at Ibrox in front of a record crowd, then watching on as Albion Rovers sensationally dumped Rangers out in the semi-final after three matches.

As the Wilton era tragically ended and the Bill Struth era began, one thing that did not change was the importance of Archibald to the team. His partnership with inside-right Andy Cunningham was almost telepathic, both players seemingly able to predict where the other would be, with countless goals and assists between the pair. Only one league match was lost all season as Rangers looked even more dominant than ever. Cunningham hit 24 league goals to end the season as top scorer, albeit thanks to a spell at centre-forward, with Archibald bagging 14. The cup continued its torture, though, Archibald scoring in the semi-final revenge win over Albion Rovers before suffering final agony when unfancied Partick Thistle shocked everyone with a 1-0 win thanks to a goal scored while Rangers were temporarily down to ten players as James Bowie had to leave the field to replace his torn shorts.

Archibald by now was an international regular. He had played in one unofficial wartime international against England in June 1918 when aged just 21, but it wasn't until February 1921 that he made his proper Scotland debut, starting in a 2-1 home win over Wales. He would play eight times for his country, the last being a full 11 years after his first appearance. He scored once for Scotland, and also once for the Scottish League, who he represented 12 times.

Archibald was to suffer the rare taste of missing out on silverware the following season as too many draws surrendered the title to Celtic, and he again fell foul of the Scottish Cup curse after scoring in a semi-final win. It was the turn of Morton to shock Scottish football in the final, winning 1-0 in a match Archibald had to play for an hour without his right-wing partner as Cunningham suffered a broken jaw and was forced off the field. He did enjoy success in the minor competitions, playing in the 1-0 Glasgow Cup Final win over Celtic in October before hitting a Charity Cup Final hat-trick to win the trophy against Queen's Park.

Normal service was resumed the next season, Rangers comfortably reclaiming the 1922/23 title even though Archibald's goal return was less than normal with just four goals in 34 starts. These did include a strike against Celtic, the first of an amazing five times he scored in the big Ne'erday clash. He picked up winners' medals again in both the Glasgow and Charity Cups, but the clean sweep was denied when Archibald and his team-mates slumped to a 2-0 Scottish Cup loss at Ayr.

Struth's Rangers were now imperious, and Archibald was soon collecting his fifth title as Rangers cruised to a nine-point winning margin the next season. The winger scored a crucial goal at Parkhead in a new year 2-2 thriller, and he also hit the net in another Glasgow Cup Final triumph as Third Lanark were brushed aside. He had to make do with a rare second prize in the Charity Cup, however, and the yearly Scottish Cup heartache was supplied at Ibrox by Hibs, in a game when a gale sprung up in the second half to favour the Edinburgh team after they had gone in at half-time a goal down.

Archibald suffered further agonies in the 1924/25 Scottish Cup, playing in a scarcely believable 5-0 loss to Celtic in the semi-final, which came after the Parkhead men had been easily defeated 4-1 in both the Glasgow Cup Final and the league. His ten league goals were crucial in securing a third successive championship, however, as an excellent Airdrie team pushed Rangers all the way.

The Scottish Cup jinx extended into the entirety of 1925/26, with several of the team's key players missing large stretches of the season through injury. Archibald was one of them, only playing in half the matches as Rangers finished a lowly sixth, their lowest placing ever. There were no cups won either, a very rare bare season for the winger.

Archibald missed only a handful of league games in the following season, Rangers back to normal business under Struth as they powered to the title. His goal on New Year's Day 1927 to defeat Celtic certainly felt normal to the watching 63,000 crowd. His ten goals during the season included one at Brockville in a hard-fought Scottish Cup tie that ended 2-2, before he endured yet more disappointment in the competition as the Bairns snatched an extra-time win at Ibrox after a muscle injury to full-back Billy McCandless reduced Rangers to ten fit players for the additional 30 minutes.

Archibald now had seven league medals, and in 1927/28 it looked a good bet from long before the last match that he was adding an eighth. He played in all 38 league games, his 16 league goals included vital points-saving efforts in draws with Hamilton and Kilmarnock, as well a double against Hamilton in the run-in that many saw as the day the title looked inevitable. But before the crown was officially clinched, Rangers had reached the Scottish Cup Final, Archibald scoring in the semi-final win over Hibs. On 14 April 1928 they were to play Celtic at Hampden to decide the destination of the famous trophy. Like so many of his team-mates, Archibald had suffered incredible misfortune in a competition that had somehow eluded Rangers for 25 long years. The wait would now end, as in front of a record 118,115 crowd, Rangers blitzed their rivals with four second-half goals.

Goals number three and four were long range thunderbolts from the right foot of the inspired Archibald. The normally exuberant Fifer was strangely quiet in the post-match celebrations, overcome by the emotion of finally achieving the goal that had so often been cruelly snatched from the grasp of the club he loved. The league and Scottish Cup double of 1928 was incredibly the first time Rangers had won both trophies in the same season. Archibald collected a Charity Cup win for good measure to round off an unforgettable season, scoring in the final.

Rangers were the undisputed trophy kings of Scotland, and Archibald was as important a player as any as the successes kept coming. He scored in home and away league wins over Celtic among 12 league strikes in 1928/29 as the title was won with weeks to spare. He terrorised the Celtic defence in the end-of-season Charity Cup Final where doubles from Tommy Muirhead and James Marshall clinched a 4-2 win. But the old Scottish Cup hoodoo seemed to return, as after he scored a crucial semi-final goal to beat St Mirren, Archibald played in a 2-0 final loss to Kilmarnock, in a game where Tully Craig missed a penalty and Jock Buchanan became the first player to be sent off in the national final.

This merely delayed more Archibald celebrations as in 1929/30 Rangers completed their first clean sweep of all four honours. He started in 34 league games and scored 12 times as the title was retained by a five-point margin. The Glasgow Cup was won by beating Celtic 4-0 in a final replay, Archibald scoring once in a game remembered for a brilliant hat-trick by Jimmy Fleming. Archibald scored one of the goals that helped knock out league runners-up Motherwell in the Scottish Cup, before starting both matches against Partick Thistle in the final; the replay won thanks to a late Tully Craig goal from long range. That just left the Charity Cup to complete the full set, Archibald and his team-mates jumping for joy when skipper Davie Meiklejohn guessed correctly to win the trophy on a coin toss after Celtic had scored a last-minute equaliser in a 2-2 thriller.

Now nearing his 33rd birthday, the irrepressible Archibald was showing no signs of slowing. His fiery competitive spirit and will to win shone as brightly as ever. Season 1930/31 saw Rangers win a fourth successive title, and bring the Archibald personal total to 11. He scored four times in the last nine league games to help the team over the line in a race with Celtic that was won by just two points. He missed the Scottish Cup exit to Dundee through injury, but was back in the team to pick up another Charity Cup badge against Queen's Park.

He missed part of 1931/32 as well, although he did score his customary new year goal in a win at Parkhead. His absence was felt as the team failed to win a sixth successive title when the best Motherwell team of all time took the championship for the only occasion. He missed the Glasgow Cup Final win over Queen's Park after having scored in the semi-final against Celtic. Archibald was back in the side for the Scottish Cup's latter stages, scoring another semi-final goal before earning a third winners' medal in the tournament that had eluded him for so long when playing in the final defeat of Kilmarnock.

Archibald still had two more league titles to win. Season 1932/33 saw him make 28 league starts and score four goals in a successful championship race won by three points from former champions Motherwell. And in his last season in Royal Blue, the veteran winger started 15 times, although now more of an understudy to the younger Bobby Main. Struth picked Archibald for the last time on the final league day of the season against Queen's Park at Hampden, ensuring he had played enough matches to qualify for a medal. After a Rangers career of 667 games, 162 goals, and an almost countless number of medals, Archibald left Rangers in the summer of 1934 at the age of almost 37 to rejoin his hometown club Raith Rovers as player-manager. His 513 league appearances for Rangers is still a record number to this day.

He only played a handful of games for Raith before hanging up his boots and concentrating on the managerial role, which he then combined with club secretary duties. Archibald then set another record, when Rovers scored 142 league goals in 1937/38 to set the British record for most goals in a title-winning season. He was approached the following year to join local rivals Dunfermline as their manager, and worked long hours to keep the club afloat during World War Two while juggling a second full-time job helping the war effort at Rosyth dockyard.

In among his shipyard work, he found time to scout players for East End Park, and discovered talents such as Willie Cunningham, Jimmy Baxter and Willie Kelly who were all sold for big transfer fees. He built a very useful side during the wartime competitions, and was looking forward to competing in post-war football when tragedy struck. In November 1946 the lifetime smoker took seriously ill with bronchitis. Although he tried to work on despite his illness, he died at home on 29 November, just a day after he was seen at East End Park still carrying out his job. Archibald was aged just 49.

- Rangers career: 1917–1934
- 667 appearances in all competitions
- 162 goals in all competitions
- Club record 513 league appearances
- 13 league titles
- 3 Scottish Cups
- 9 Glasgow Cups
- 10 Charity Cups
- 8 Scotland caps
- Rangers Hall of Fame member

16   TOMMY MUIRHEAD

The Rangers captain who briefly left Ibrox, and who suffered a Scottish Cup jinx

THOMAS ALLAN Muirhead was born in Cowdenbeath on 24 January 1897. A talented young player who was equally at home as a half-back or as an inside-forward, he briefly played for local junior team Hearts of Beath before joining Hibs at the age of 18 in 1915.

This was a period in history dominated by the Great War, and Muirhead joined the King's Own Scottish Borderers during the conflict, meaning his football career often took second place. His Hibs debut came on 1 April 1916, when he started as inside-left in a 3-1 defeat to St Mirren in Paisley, and he played a further five times before the season ended, grabbing one goal in another 3-1 defeat, this time to Hamilton. His second season in Edinburgh saw him nail down a more regular starting slot, albeit not always in the same position. He made 23 appearances in 1916/17, scoring twice. His first experience of playing at Ibrox was a particularly unhappy one, being on the receiving end of a 5-1 hammering just before Christmas. His last appearance in the green of Hibs was in April 1917, a dismal 2-0 loss to local rivals Hearts.

Despite Hibs going through a difficult spell at this time, Rangers had been watching Muirhead, and in May 1917 an offer of a mere £20 was enough to persuade the capital club to sell the player to William Wilton's men. Rarely can such a low transfer fee have proven to be so well spent.

Muirhead's Rangers debut came on 15 September 1917 at Ibrox, ironically against Hibs. A comfortable 3-0 win was a sign of things to come for him, with great Rangers players Jimmy Bowie and Tommy Cairns being among the scorers. Muirhead started in seven league games in his debut Ibrox season, scoring five times, including an important winner in a tight derby at Third Lanark. That would prove crucial come the end of the season as Rangers won the title by a single point from Celtic. He hadn't played enough times for a medal, but Muirhead had made his mark.

Wartime service meant he didn't appear at all in 1918/19, but on his return to the team in 1919 he made a starting place his own. Season 1919/20 saw both Rangers and Celtic dominate the rest of Scottish football, and Muirhead saved some special performances for the games against the Parkhead team. He was excellent in a commanding 3-0 Ibrox win in front of 80,000 fans in November, a match remembered for a brilliant performance by another war veteran, winger Dr Jimmy Paterson. Then, in the return league match at Parkhead on New Year's Day, he became the first Rangers goalscorer of the 1920s when his strike earned a valuable point in a 1-1 draw. The clubs were also paired together at Ibrox in the Scottish Cup quarter-finals, when a massive crowd which many observers estimated at over 100,000 packed the ground to see a Muirhead goal win the tie. Incredibly, Rangers went on to lose to lowly Albion Rovers in the semi-finals after two replays, Muirhead now suffering in the club's long-running Scottish Cup hoodoo which had lasted since 1903. He did, however, win his first league championship, a rampant Rangers losing only twice in 42 league games and scoring over 100 goals in the process. Muirhead scored ten of those league goals in 34 starts.

The close-season of 1920 saw the tragic death of manager Wilton and the beginning of a new era under Bill Struth began. Muirhead started at inside-right in Struth's first league match on 17 August 1920, an easy 4-1 win at home to Airdrie. Injury and fierce competition for the places in the forward line restricted him to 19 league starts, although he did play in the famous Parkhead encounter in October when Alan Morton's 30-yard strike in the dying minutes gave Rangers a 2-1 win. That goal that was immortalised in song on the Ibrox terraces in the months that followed. The song was known as 'the baw that Charlie Shaw never saw' and had the same tune as 'The Red Flag':

Oh Charlie Shaw he never saw
Where Alan Morton put the baw
He put the baw right in the net
And Charlie Shaw sat down and gret

Rangers won the title by a massive ten points and only lost once in 42 games, the first of the 18 won under Struth, meaning Muirhead was awarded his second championship medal. He never appeared at all in the Scottish Cup, a competition that still cruelly eluded the club as Rangers suffered a shock final defeat to unfancied Partick Thistle.

Season 1921/22 saw Muirhead restored as an automatic choice in the team, but in a less advanced position. He assumed the left-half role which had mainly been filled by either veteran Jimmy Bowie or by the now injured James 'Fister' Walls the previous season. This more defensive role meant Muirhead's goal threat significantly reduced and he didn't score at all during the season. It was a season where Rangers won more league games than anyone else, but lost the title by a single point to a highly consistent Celtic team, with both league games between the teams ending in draws. Muirhead played in his first Scottish Cup Final in April, and with Morton the opponents the whole country assumed that the jinx in the tournament was finally about to end. He and the Rangers support were to suffer crushing disappointment yet again, however, as Morton prevailed by the only goal of the game, a Gourlay free kick scored in the first half, and Rangers played for an hour with ten men due to an injury to Andy Cunningham. There was some consolation in the Glasgow and Charity Cups, which were both won and gave Muirhead his first winners' medals in both. Celtic were defeated 1-0 thanks to a Davie Meiklejohn goal in the Glasgow Cup, and Queen's Park defeated 3-1 in the Charity Cup thanks to a Sandy Archibald hat-trick.

By now Muirhead was an international player, making the first of his six Scottish League appearances against the Irish League in 1921, before his full international debut arrived in March 1922 at Parkhead in a 2-1 win over Ireland. In all he went on to gain eight Scotland caps, and was captain of his international team once.

Season 1922/23 saw Rangers return to the top as champions, Muirhead a regular with 31 league starts, chipping in with four goals too. He also won a second Glasgow Cup Final, this time against Clyde, although missing the Charity Cup Final success over Queen's Park. But his Scottish Cup torture continued when on 27 January 1923 mid-table Ayr United provided a huge upset with a 2-0 home win over the clear league leaders.

The following season threatened to be a carbon copy. Rangers eased to another convincing league championship win to earn Muirhead his fourth winners' medal in a season he made 27 league starts. He scored three goals that season, his two league strikes being joined by a Glasgow Cup Final goal against Third Lanark as Rangers, and Muirhead won the trophy for the third successive season. But yet again, the one prize all at the club wanted most was to prove elusive. This time it was Hibs who came to Ibrox and shocked the 53,000 crowd by winning 2-1. Muirhead also was disappointed in the Charity Cup when he played in the losing final against Celtic.

Season 1924/25 saw Rangers start the season without the services of Muirhead. He was offered big money by American Soccer League side Boston Soccer Club, who were also known as the 'Wonder Workers', to assume the role of player-manager, and given further incentive by the club signing another Scottish player he knew very well in Alex McNab of Morton, as well as recruiting Barney Battles, the son of the late former Celtic player from the early 20th century. It was an offer too lucrative to turn down, and Muirhead travelled across the Atlantic with the good wishes of all at Ibrox. He struggled to settle into life in the USA, however, and after only 14 games in charge he was given a lifeline by Bill Struth and allowed to return to Ibrox just before Christmas 1924. Ironically, he would take the field in Boston one more time in his career, as Rangers played the Wonder Workers in their North American tour in 1928, a game drawn 2-2.

Muirhead became the first Rangers player to leave Ibrox under Struth and then return to the club, and his second debut came on 27 December 1924 at Ibrox when he played at right-half in a 1-0 win. He moved to left-half for the next match, the New Year's Day date with Celtic at Ibrox, and he gave a solid display in a convincing 4-1 win where Rangers had scored three times in the opening 25 minutes. This was a season where Celtic weren't the main challengers to Rangers for the title; instead the best Airdrie team in their history was pushing hard for the league flag. Muirhead played in 12 league games in total, not enough for a medal, but he had played his part as Rangers held off the Airdrie challenge by just three points. He also missed the disastrous Scottish Cup semi-final against Celtic, which ended in a humbling 5-0 loss. The season did end on a higher note, however, when Clyde were defeated at Ibrox in the final of the Charity Cup.

The least said about Muirhead's first full campaign back at Ibrox the better. Season 1925/26 seemed to entail a catalogue of injuries to key players on a weekly basis, with disrupted team selections, some bad luck and some very poor performances combining to leave Rangers a dismal sixth in the table. The season was probably summed up in the Scottish Cup semi-final when yet again a shock defeat was suffered, this time to St Mirren. No trophies were won, the highlight of Muirhead's season being a goal in the 2-2 new year derby at Parkhead. Muirhead played more games than most that season with 33 starts in all competitions.

The remainder of Muirhead's Rangers career saw the league title won in each of four successive seasons. He made 24 starts in the league, which was won by five points from Motherwell. His three league goals came in successive games before Christmas against Falkirk, Clyde and Hamilton when he was pushed further forward due to injuries. There was again to be no cup glory, however, Falkirk this time being the club who knocked Rangers out the Scottish Cup. Muirhead suffered defeat also in the Glasgow Cup Final to Celtic, but missed the incredible Charity Cup Final where a weakened Rangers team were hammered 6-3 by Partick Thistle with their forward with the memorable name of Sandy Hair scoring five of their goals. While the game was being played Muirhead was sailing with a Scotland team to Canada along with usual Ibrox regulars Tully Craig, Sandy Archibald and Andy Cunningham.

Rangers' long-serving captain Tommy Cairns left at the end of the season, and Struth decided to award the captaincy to Muirhead, ahead of that other magnificent club servant Davie Meiklejohn. And his first season as captain started off brilliantly, Rangers going on an impressive unbeaten run in the league. Muirhead picked up an injury that forced him to miss the Glasgow Cup Final, which saw un unexpected Celtic victory, but he was back in the team the following weekend for a deserved home win over them in the league at Ibrox. The league title was rarely in doubt and again all eyes were on the Scottish Cup.

Muirhead was struggling with a persistent injury and didn't start in the semi-final win over Hibs, which set up a final showdown with Celtic on 14 April 1928. Struth gave him a chance to show his fitness in a home fixture against Dunfermline five days before the final at inside-right, but it was obvious that the final was too early for him and Muirhead knew he wasn't fit enough to start in such a titanic match, now 25 long years since Rangers' last victory in the national cup competition. Meiklejohn proved a more than adequate deputy captain when he opened the scoring with a nerveless penalty in the second half as Rangers then brushed Celtic aside by scoring three more goals to finally bring the cup back to Ibrox. Despite again missing out on a winners' medal, Muirhead was as delighted as anyone connected with the club and heartily joined in the celebrations. He missed the decisive league match a week later against Kilmarnock which clinched the title, before being fit enough to lead out the team in the last league game of the season against Bo'ness. Despite his injury problems, he played in 26 of the 38 league games, more than earning his sixth championship medal.

Muirhead started in 28 matches the following season as Rangers' stranglehold on the honours in Scottish football continued. The league title was won with weeks to spare, only losing one match from the 38 played, and cruising to a scarcely believable 16-point margin over the runners-up. And that defeat didn't come until game 31 against Hamilton, when Rangers had their eyes firmly on the following Saturday and another Scottish Cup Final date, this time with Kilmarnock. Muirhead had chipped in with a few goals over the season, ending it with eight, and these included an important opening goal at Shawfield in a tense Scottish Cup third round tie. Muirhead's versatility was very much in evidence during the season, playing as both right- and left-half as well as the two inside-forward positions. He led out the team at Hampden on 6 April 1929 as inside-right, this surely being the day this devoted club servant would finally get his hands on the trophy and a winners' medal that he craved.

The 90 minutes would sum up the luck Muirhead had in the competition. Rangers dominated the match for long spells, missed a penalty at a crucial time, and were hit by two counter-attacking goals by the Ayrshiremen. Then to round off a miserable afternoon, right-half Jock Buchanan was sent off by the referee in the dying minutes for dissent, becoming the first player ever dismissed in the final. Muirhead, typically, refused to let this latest setback keep him down, and he rounded off the season with two well-taken goals against Celtic in the Charity Cup Final against Celtic in a 4-2 success.

In 1929/30, Muirhead remained the club captain, but his appearances were now becoming fewer with Meiklejohn deputising as skipper when he was absent. Rangers were to make club history that season, winning all four main competitions for the first time, but it was only in the league that Muirhead won a medal, starting in just over half the 38 games. He scored his last Rangers goal on 29 March 1930 at Ibrox in a victory over Clyde, and collected his eighth league medal as the team eased to a straightforward title success. He watched on as Partick Thistle were defeated in the Scottish Cup Final after a replay, meaning that in his Rangers career the club had competed in four finals, winning two and losing two. Sadly, his only two appearances were on those losing occasions. When

Meiklejohn won a toss of a coin in the Charity Cup Final, it meant that the clean sweep was complete, and Muirhead left Rangers at a time the club were undisputedly Scotland's premier team. His last start came on 26 April 1930 in his home town of Cowdenbeath, a low-key meaningless end of season match that ended in a 3-2 defeat.

Overall, Muirhead had played 352 times Rangers over his two spells as a player, scoring 49 goals. He left Ibrox and took up a role as a sports journalist, but within a year the lure of the game was too strong and he accepted an offer from Second Division St Johnstone in June 1931 to become their manager. Muirhead was an instant success. He guided the club to promotion in his first season, and then built a team capable of challenging towards the top end of the First Division. The Perth club finished fifth twice in three seasons, and also reached a Scottish Cup semi-final, where they lost narrowly to his old club Rangers. Signings such as Jimmy Benson, Bobby Davidson and future Rangers star Jimmy Caskie had the Perth fans enjoying their football, and it was no great surprise when Muirhead was tempted south by a big money offer from Preston North End in May 1936. His record at St Johnstone is still second to none, winning almost 60 per cent of the points available in league matches, and an overall win percentage of 49 per cent from his 205 games in charge across all competitions.

His time at Preston wasn't as successful, and he left after a year to return to sports journalism. It was Muirhead, writing for the *Daily Express* in March 1940, who broke the story that the great English winger Stanley Matthews had signed for Rangers to play in a wartime match, quoting Matthews as saying, 'To play for Rangers has been one of my most cherished ambitions.' Muirhead retired and lived out his days in Helensburgh, where he passed away on 27 May 1979 at the age of 82. Ironically, Rangers won the Scottish Cup the next night.

- Rangers career: 1917–1930
- 352 competitive appearance
- 49 competitive goals
- Hall of Fame member
- Served his country in the Great War
- Twice a Ranger in a 13-year Ibrox career
- Club captain ahead of the legendary Davie Meiklejohn
- Captain of Scotland
- 8 league medals and multiple Glasgow and Charity Cups.

17 TORRY GILLICK

The only Rangers player to win the Scottish Cup before and after World War Two

TORRANCE 'TORRY' Gillick was born in Airdrie on 19 May 1915. A quick and skilful right-winger with Petershill Juniors, he was signed by Bill Struth in 1933 at the age of 18 as the club sought a successor to the wonderful servant Sandy Archibald.

He started his Rangers career out wide at Firhill on 30 September 1933 aged only 18 years and 134 days, his debut a thrilling match which Rangers defeated Partick by the odd goal in seven. But his first season was one almost exclusively spent in the reserves, learning his craft and the demands of being a Ranger. He only made one other league appearance although he also won his first medal, playing in the Glasgow Cup Final in a 2-0 defeat of Clyde.

It was to be the following season that Gillick made a starting position his own, still mainly as a winger. He scored a memorable first goal for the club, a decisive 80th-minute winner in a 2-1 victory over Celtic in a Glasgow Cup semi-final tie at Parkhead in September 1934. He quickly became a real favourite with the Ibrox support, and cemented that status when scoring the winner in the New Year's Day derby at Ibrox against the old enemy. Winning goals against Celtic at both Ibrox and Parkhead and still only 19 – not a bad start to a Rangers career.

In all Gillick made 27 league appearances in 1934/35, scoring 17 goals and earning his first championship medal. These involved a purple patch in front of goal at the turn of the year when he scored in eight games from ten. He added a Scottish Cup badge too, scoring a crucial semi-final goal against Hearts and playing his part in a hard-earned final victory over Hamilton Accies at Hampden.

Season 1935/36 started well with seven more goals in 17 league starts, as well as another Old Firm goal, this time in a 2-0 Glasgow Cup Final triumph. But in December 1935 Struth surprised the Rangers support by accepting an £8,000 bid from Everton for Gillick, a record fee for the Merseyside club. The manager never explained his reasons for selling such a talented and popular player, but some suspected the strict disciplinarian wasn't too fond of Gillick's carefree attitude to the game.

He remained at Goodison until 1939, won a league championship with them, and even played against Rangers at Ibrox in the 1938 Empire Exhibition tournament. The title was won in 1938/39 when Gillick and another former Rangers star, Alex Stevenson, were the creative force of a potent forward line. One man in no doubt of Gillick's importance to the team was inside-right Stan Bentham who described his style of play, 'Torry just stayed on the wing, not interested. But suddenly he'd tune in and go past three or four blokes as easy as anything, and either score or put over a great cross.' He scored 44 goals in his Everton career in 131 starts, and while at Goodison he won all five of his official Scotland caps.

He made his international debut in May 1937 in Austria, and scored three times for his country in his five appearances. Gillick also played in three wartime unofficial Scotland international matches when a Rangers player, all against England, and all defeats. These included an infamous 8-0 hiding at Maine Road in 1943.

But as war began, he returned to Scotland and briefly played as a guest player for hometown club Airdrie. He then returned to Ibrox in July 1940, some months after suffering serious burns to his lower arms when trying to rescue his car from a fire in his garage in Liverpool, making over 200 appearances for Rangers during these unofficial times. By now Gillick was no longer a winger, but a skilful and powerful inside-right, his previous knowledge of playing wide giving him an almost telepathic understanding with winger Willie Waddell. He won honours aplenty during these years as an unregistered Rangers player, with a highlight undoubtedly a hat-trick in the all-time record winning margin in an Old Firm match, the 8-1 new year destruction of Celtic in 1943.

During the war, as well as winning league medals every season, he gathered plenty cup prizes too. Gillick scored twice in the 1941 Charity Cup Final win over Partick. He also scored in the Glasgow Cup Final victory over Clyde later that year. He scored the only goal of the 1942 Southern League Cup Final at Hampden to beat Morton in front of 43,000 spectators. In 1942/43 he scored in a 5-2 rout of Third Lanard in the Glasgow Cup Final, and he hit the only Rangers goal in the Southern League Cup Final against Falkirk. And as the war years started to come to an end, he hit another Southern League Cup winner in 1945 to beat Motherwell before scoring in the 1946 Victory Cup Final against Hibs.

He also played in the famous friendly match against Moscow Dynamo at Ibrox in November 1945, an occasion memorable in many ways, not least for Gillick forcing the referee to briefly stop play when the wily inside-forward had realised the Russians had 12 players on the pitch. Struth had officially re-signed Gillick in 1945, and he would be a vital attacking cog in the post war Ibrox trophy machine. He opened the scoring in the 1946/47 and 1948/49 League Cup Final victories over Aberdeen and Raith Rovers, the goal against Aberdeen being the first scored in a Scottish League Cup Final. He scored in the drawn first Scottish Cup Final against Morton in 1948 and played in the replay win. He won another league championship medal in 1946/47, scoring Rangers' goal in the new year draw with Celtic. And even as a veteran who only appeared occasionally, he scored both Rangers goals against Clyde in the 1949 Glasgow Cup Final replay to lift the trophy yet again. His first and last medal at the club were the same scoreline against the same opponent in the final of the same competition, but 16 years apart.

His last league appearance was in November 1949, a win over St Mirren, just over 16 years after his debut. And his swansong came in the Old Firm Charity Cup Final the following May, when in front of a massive crowd that included famous American actor Danny Kaye, Gillick suddenly inspired Rangers from three goals down to almost force extra time, scoring once and creating another for Willie Thornton.

He left the club soon afterwards, and after retiring he made a one-season comeback with Partick Thistle before leaving the game to focus on running a Lanarkshire scrap metal company.

A real character on and off the park, there were multiple stories of his exploits. Gillick hated wearing the bowler hat that manager Struth insisted all his players must wear when travelling to and from Ibrox, and he would carry a paper bag with him for the journey. The bowler hat was inside it, and he would take off his preferred flat cap on arriving at Ibrox subway station and swap headwear so the eagle-eyed Struth always saw him arrive properly dressed. He wasn't the most dedicated trainer either, often trying to fool the manager by joining in with laps of the track part way through in the hope Struth didn't realise he had skipped the first few circuits. He rarely succeeded.

And the manager even got involved in his courtship. Struth grew impatient waiting on Gillick proposing to his long-term girlfriend, so deducted money from his weekly wage packet to save up for an engagement ring on his behalf. But given how long he wore the colours for the manager, and given the fact Struth brought him back to the club after selling him, it does suggest Gillick was seen more a loveable rogue by The Boss rather than a troublemaker.

There is one story that backs this up. Gillick was with a Scottish League squad who were staying overnight for an away match, and was told that breakfast was to be a minimal affair due to money constraints. The bold Gillick was having none of this, and ordered the works, tucking in while his team-mates looked on. He told the hotel to send the bill to the SFA. When that bill arrived, the SFA forwarded it on to Rangers, saying that they would need to pay for their player's extravagance. Struth politely sent it back with a note saying that Rangers players were always treated to the best, and that this would not stop if they played for Scotland. He added that if the SFA wanted Rangers players to represent them, then they had to be treated the same way as at their club. Neither Gillick or Struth heard about the bill again.

Gillick has multiple claims to fame as a Ranger, being the only player brought to the club twice by Struth, the only Rangers player to win a Scottish Cup medal both before and after World War Two, and the first goalscorer in a Scottish League Cup Final.

He also had another unusual claim to fame as a Rangers player mentioned in a debate in the House of Commons. In 1972, during a debate on Northern Ireland, the Scottish Labour MP Dick Douglas said this in response to a speech by the MP Bernadette Devlin,

'She does not speak for the Protestant workers, and I do not believe that she really speaks for the Catholic workers either, because they do not want a challenge to the established order in the way that she sees it. I dislike Tories as well. There is a saying, if I may be colloquial, that the only good Tory was Tory Gillick and he played for Glasgow Rangers.'

Gillick passed away on 15 December 1971, a doubly sad day for Rangers, as it was the same day as the death of the legendary Alan Morton. He was just 56 years old.

- Rangers career: 1933–1935; 1940–1950
- Over 200 goals from around 400 appearances when wartime football included
- 2 league titles
- 6 wartime championships
- 2 Scottish Cups
- 2 League Cups
- Multiple wartime competition wins
- Scorer of many cup final and Old Firm goals
- Member of the Hall of Fame

18 TULLY CRAIG

Discarded by Celtic, then won 14 winners' medals with Rangers

ON 18 July 1895, Thomas Breckenridge Craig was born in the small village of Laurieston near Falkirk. Although a very keen and talented footballer comfortable as a forward or a wing-half, he remained a Junior player well into his 20s. However, his life changed in June 1919 when Scottish champions Celtic plucked him from the obscurity of playing for the Grangemouth local team Grange United and gave him the chance to play in the national First Division.

By now known to friends and team-mates as Tully due to his residence in the town of Tullibody near Alloa, he was made to wait for his Celtic debut, which came on 17 January 1920 at Kilmarnock. Playing as a centre-forward, he scored twice in a 3-2 win. A defeat to Clydebank the following Saturday saw him dropped again, and Craig remained mainly a reserve player during his three years at Celtic. Utilised mainly as a centre or inside-forward, he played only eight league games across those three seasons, only adding one more goal to his debut double. Celtic manager Willie Maley regarded him as too lightweight and easily brushed off the ball by bigger defenders, and it came as no surprise to see him leave Parkhead in May 1922, when he was used as a make weight in a swap deal with Alloa that saw Craig and two other Parkhead players leave the newly crowned First Division champions in return for Alloa centre-forward Willie Crilly, who had fired them to the Second Division title.

Season 1922/23 remains the only full campaign Alloa were a top-division club, and they finished last as Rangers under Bill Struth reclaimed the title. But despite their league position, Craig, back in his home area and with a point to prove, stood out with several excellent displays. He scored seven goals, despite often not playing up front which to this day is the second most in the top league in Alloa's history, and in the summer of 1923 Struth paid the hefty sum of £750 to bring him back to Glasgow, this time at Ibrox.

Struth saw the benefit of having such a versatile player to call on, and Craig began repaying the faith shown in him straight away. Playing at inside-right, he made his Rangers debut on Monday, 24 September 1923 at Ibrox, and he scored in a 2-1 win over Clyde. He had to wait a few weeks for his next start, and again scored when replacing usual inside-right Andy Cunningham in victory over Ayr. Over the course of his first season Craig played 20 times and scored a very respectable 13 goals, the highlights being a hat-trick against Clydebank and a double against Motherwell when playing centre-forward. He won his first league medal as Rangers cruised to the title.

The following season was when Craig became an established first choice at Ibrox. With an embarrassment of riches to choose from up front, Struth deployed him now as a thoughtful and influential left-half, a position he made his own. He won his first Glasgow Cup medal in a 4-1 hammering of Celtic, a game where Rangers seemed to ease off to reserve their energy for big games ahead. He played 24 times that season, scoring just twice in successive January wins over Glasgow rivals Partick and Third Lanark. But despite another league medal, the season ended in bitter disappointment when losing 5-0 to Celtic in a shock Scottish Cup semi-final.

Craig was one of the few key players not to suffer significant injury in 1925/26, a dismal season for Rangers as they slumped to that record low of sixth. He was a virtual ever present while Struth had to constantly juggle his line up through what seemed to be an injury jinx. Things returned to some kind of normality the following season though, Craig again playing almost every week as the championship was won. His consistent excellence was rewarded in February 1927 with a first Scotland cap when he put on another assured display in a solid 2-0 win at Northern Ireland. He would go on to win eight Scotland caps, including three in a European tour in 1929 when Scotland beat Norway and Holland and drew with Germany. He scored his only international goal in the 7-3 rout of the Norwegians.

As 1927/28 started, it was to be the 25th season since Rangers last won the Scottish Cup. While enjoying league dominance, all at the club yearned for the national cup to be brought back to Ibrox. Tully Craig played another 34 league games that season, but no doubt it was his appearance at Hampden on 14 April 1928 that was his highlight. Rangers 4 Celtic 0 in the cup final meant a quarter of a century of failure was brushed away in one of the great afternoons of Rangers history in front of 118,00 fans. And after being rejected by Willie Maley six years before, it must have felt extra sweet for Craig. The following week, Rangers clinched their first league and Scottish Cup double with a 5-1 hammering of Kilmarnock to win him his fourth league medal.

A fifth came in 1928/29 as Rangers were now supreme in Scottish football, going through a league championship campaign with only one defeat and a massive 16-point winning margin. Craig lined up in his second Scottish Cup Final on 6 April 1929 against Kilmarnock surely expecting another glory day. It turned out to be the opposite. Rangers were awarded a 15th-minute penalty when Jock Buchanan was fouled. Despite Davie Meiklejohn having scored from the spot the previous year, the responsibility this time was given to Craig who saw his shot saved by goalkeeper Sam Clemie. This was the first penalty ever missed in a Scottish Cup Final. It was typical of the day and Rangers dominated but were hit by two breakaway goals, with the final insult a sending off for Buchanan in the 88th minute for foul language at the referee.

Season 1929/30 saw Rangers, with Craig still a regular well into his 30s, dominate even more. His sixth league medal was secured, and this time Partick Thistle were the opponents in the cup final. After a tense goalless draw, the replay looked to be heading for extra time as the minutes ticked away. Then in the 86th minute Craig scored the winner when he picked up a clearance fully 40 yards from goal and flighted in a lob that deceived the Thistle goalkeeper and floated into the net. What a difference a year made. Rangers won the clean sweep as they also added the Glasgow and Charity Cups too, both finals won against Celtic.

Now 35 years old, time was catching up with Craig. The great George Brown was emerging as a left-half of outstanding ability, and Craig accepted the role of reliable deputy. He stayed until the summer of 1935, preferring to be a Rangers backup rather than moving to another club. In all he wore the Royal Blue 293 times, the last being a win against Aberdeen in April 1935 just short of his 40th birthday. He scored 38 times, and won six league titles, two Scottish Cups, two Glasgow Cups and four Charity Cups. He also contributed in four other title-winning seasons where he didn't play enough for a medal.

Craig was still under contract to Rangers as a player when he became Falkirk manager. He wasn't allowed to play for Falkirk and nor could he formally take up the position until after the Scottish Cup Final on 20 April 1935, in case Rangers wanted to play him. He wasn't selected, so he took over at Brockville for the final match of the season. He remained Falkirk manager for 15 years, war robbing him of what looked to be a team capable of challenging for honours. He won the Second Division and reached the Scottish Cup semi-final in his first season, and took Falkirk to the 1947 League Cup Final with legendary former Rangers goalkeeper Jerry Dawson in goal. After beating Rangers in the semi-final at Hampden, he must have anticipated a famous trophy win, but they lost after a replay to East Fife.

Craig was something of an innovator, being instrumental in the creation of all-ticket matches, with the first ticket-only game in Scotland being the Scottish Cup quarter-final at Brockville on 19 March 1938, when 18,000 tickets were printed and sold. Rangers won 2-1.

He also had a short spell in Northern Ireland as Linfield manager in 1952/53, finishing second in the league to Glentoran and winning both the Irish Cup and the County Antrim Shield.

Craig saw out his days in England, passing away in Halifax, Yorkshire on 30 January 1963, aged 67.

- Rangers career: 1923–1935
- 6 league titles
- 2 Scottish Cups
- 4 Charity Cups
- 2 Glasgow Cups
- 8 Scotland caps
- Rangers Hall of Fame member
- An innovative manager

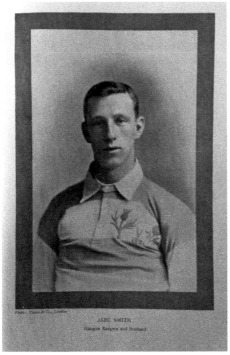

Alec Smith.
(Courtesy of The Founders Trail)

Alex Venters against Celtic.
(Courtesy of James Lepick)

Bill Struth, Tommy Muirhead and
Andy Cunningham in 1928.

Dougie Gray.
(Courtesy of James Lepick)

George Brown.
(Courtesy of James Lepick)

Jerry Dawson, Jimmy Simpson and
Sandy Archibald in 1932.

Jimmy Gordon. (Courtesy of James Lepick)

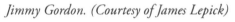

Jimmy Smith scores another Rangers goal.
(Courtesy of James Lepick)

J. M'PHERSON
(Inside Left, Rangers F.C.).

Photo: Agnew & Son, Glasgow
NEIL GIBSON

John McPherson.
(Courtesy of The Founders Trail)

Neilly Gibson of Rangers & Scotland.
(Courtesy of The Founders Trail)

Nicol Smith.
(Courtesy of The Founders Trail)

Jock Drummond.
(Courtesy of The Founders Trail)

NICOL SMITH, RANGERS F.C.

SCOTLAND'S CAPTAIN.

J. DRUMMOND, Rangers F.C.

R.C. Hamilton in Scotland colours.
(Courtesy of The Founders Trail)

Tully Craig.
(Courtesy of James Lepick)

Torry Gillick. (Courtesy of James Lepick)

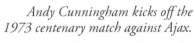

Andy Cunningham kicks off the
1973 centenary match against Ajax.

George Brown opens the Copland Road stand in 1979.

Nicol Smith benefit match ticket. (courtesy of The Founders Trail)

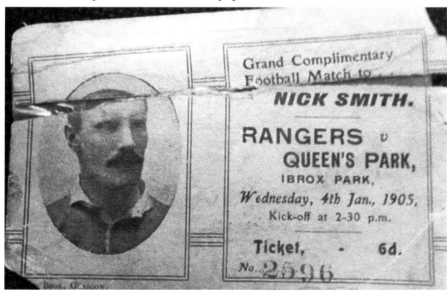

Torry Gillick tells the referee there are 12 Moscow Dynamo players in 1945.

The 1899 invincibles included Alec Smith, John McPherson, Neilly Gibson, Nicol Smith, Jock Drummond (wearing a bunnet) and captain R.C. Hamilton.

langers in 1907-08. Back row (left to right): J.Wilson (trainer), G.Wallace, G.Livingstone, A.Barrie, J.Macdonald, .T.Butler, R.C.Hamilton, J.J.Dunlop, A.Newbiggin, J.Spiers, G.Law, J.Gordon. Front row: A.Craig, Jo.Bell, J.Galt, J.Dickie, I.G.Campbell, J.Currie, A.Kyle, G.R.Watson, A.Smith. On ground: J.May. W.Henry.

The 1907/08 team including R.C. Hamilton, Jimmy Gordon and Alec Smith.

This 1925 team picture includes Sandy Archibald, Tommy Muirhead, Andy Cunningham and Tully Craig.

GLASGOW RANGERS F.C.

BACK ROW: Hamilton, Archibald, Gray, Osborne, Ireland, Purdon, McGregor, Hodge, Muirhead.
MIDDLE ROW: Henderson, Meiklejohn, A. Kirkwood, D. Kirkwood, Cunningham, Dick, Manderson, Marshall, Robb.
FRONT ROW: Craig, McCandless, McKay, Cairns, Dixon, Morton, Jamieson, G. Livingston (Trainer).

The 1930 clean sweep team, featuring Sandy Archibald, Tully Craig, George Brown, Dougie Gray and captain Tommy Muirhead.

A 1935 team picture featuring Jerry Dawson, Jimmy Simpson, Jimmy Smith, Alex Venters, George Brown, Torry Gillick and Dougie Gray.

The 1949 team with Torry Gillick, second in front row, and trainer Jimmy Smith, standing on the right.

Jimmy Gordon while in the army. (Courtesy of James Lepick)

PLAYERS 19 TO 72

19   ADAM LITTLE

The doctor who played for Rangers in three different decades

ADAM LITTLE was born on 1 September 1919 in Blantyre, the son of a miner. His family moved to Glasgow a few years later to accommodate a new job for his father in Cambuslang, and the young Little attended Rutherglen Academy. He excelled both academically and on the football field, representing his school and his county and winning a cap at international schoolboy level with Scotland. He always looked destined to be a professional player, and at the age of just 17 Little signed for Rangers after a visit by legendary manager Bill Struth to the family home. Not long before this, he had rejected the offer of a contract with Celtic.

Little was determined to also complete his studies; he had long wished to become a doctor, so as well as embarking on a football career he also completed his higher qualifications and was accepted to study medicine at Glasgow University. Struth was very encouraging for the young man to succeed with his studies, reminding Little that he had similarly encouraged previous Rangers stars Jimmy Paterson and James Marshall to also combine medical and football careers. Struth decided to allow Little to start learning his football trade in the juniors, and farmed him out to Blantyre Victoria where he would gain experience before returning to Ibrox a more hardened player.

Little returned to Ibrox the following year, and he made a first appearance for the first team in the famous Holditch Colliery Disaster Fund charity match at Stoke in September 1937 at the age of just 18. This was when Rangers were presented with the Loving Cup, which is one of the most famous exhibits in the Ibrox trophy room, and is seen every new year when the club toast the good health of the reigning monarch.

His introduction into the side was gradual, with a first competitive appearance not until a year later, when he played at inside-right in a goalless draw at Queen's Park in the Glasgow Cup first round. He also started in the replay, not an auspicious occasion as the Spiders won 3-2. Little started four times over the rest of 1938/39, all in the league, the first of which was in a draw at Arbroath on 24 September 1893, this time playing at wing-half. Of the six matches he started that season, he didn't enjoy a victory until the last one, a 3-2 win at Hamilton in the second last match of the season which was after the title had already been secured.

Season 1939/40 had hardly begun when the declaration of war changed life for everyone, and as medicine was a protected profession, Little remained at the university and was able to still play for the club during the wartime competitions. Apart from a solitary Glasgow Cup appearance, he wasn't used in the Western League campaign until after the turn of the year, but when called upon against Queen's Park on 6 January 1940 his excellent assured performance saw him force himself into Struth's plans, and after another short spell out the side he was brought back into the starting line-up for the title run-in, again against Queen's Park, on 20 April 1940. He scored his first goal for the club at Hampden in a 3-2 success when playing as a winger, and he kept his place for the remainder of the season. The Western League was won with Little eventually starting in nine of the matches, meaning a National Emergency War League Championship decider was needed against Eastern League winners Falkirk. On 1 June 1940, Rangers beat the Bairns 2-1 to be crowned wartime champions and Little scored one of the goals. He also collected a winners' medal in the War Emergency Cup, playing at Hampden before 90,000 spectators in a tight 1-0 win over Dundee United. And he topped off a medal winning burst with an appearance in the Charity Cup Final against Clyde, which Rangers won by virtue of forcing five more corners than their opponents after the match ended 1-1. Little was the creator of the Rangers goal after 20 minutes, sending Alex Venters clear on goal for him to open the scoring.

Although his medical studies were not due completion until 1944, Little missed all of 1940/41 to focus full-time on his practical learning with a year spent in a military hospital, but was then a mainstay of the wartime Rangers team who dominated the Scottish game from the following season, and he continued collecting winners' medals. He returned to the team on 30 August 1941 in a highly impressive 6-1 rout of Airdrie at Broomfield, now playing at right-half in what was to be the first-choice half-back line for the next few years alongside Willie Woodburn and Scot Symon. He started in 25 Southern League games as Rangers retained their title. He enjoyed a first winners' medal in the Glasgow Cup, beating Clyde 6-0 in the final after disposing of Celtic in the last four. Celtic were also dispatched in the semi-final of the Southern League Cup, and Little was in the team who lifted the trophy after a 1-0 final victory against Morton. He also picked up another Charity Cup medal after a comfortable 3-0 final win over Partick Thistle, a team-mate that day of the great Stanley Matthews. And he completed his massive medal haul for the season when Hibs were defeated in the final of the Summer Cup on the toss of a coin after a 0-0 draw at Hampden on 4 July. Despite all this success, he also played in a historic defeat in September 1941 when Hibs defeated Rangers 8-1 at Easter Road, still the heaviest competitive loss in the club's history.

The following season, Little was to play in a far more memorable 8-1 result, the famous new year thrashing of Celtic on 1 January 1943. This was another season of multiple trophy success; the Southern League was easily retained with Little playing in 28 of the games, scoring once. He again played in a Glasgow Cup win over Celtic then in the winning final, this time a handsome 5-2 win over Third Lanark. The Southern League Cup was also retained with Little in his usual right-half starting position, although there was no clean sweep this time as Celtic claimed the Charity Cup and St Mirren shocked Rangers in the Summer Cup Final.

In 1943/44 Little became an international player, albeit in a wartime match that didn't carry official status. He must have wished the selectors had chosen someone else, however, as a powerful England team (including his old team-mate Stanley Matthews) destroyed a weakened Scottish side by the embarrassing score of 8-0 at Maine Road in October 1943. He did continue to enjoy massive club success, however, with another almost ever-present Southern League season in which he scored twice. The Glasgow Cup and Charity Cup Finals were both won by beating Clyde, but Hibs prevailed in the Southern League Cup Final by winning one more corner in the goalless 90 minutes. The following year, 1944, was to be a momentous year for Little as he graduated as a doctor.

He continued to play for Rangers in 1944/45, but he also joined the Royal Medical Corps. He still managed to play enough games in the season to earn another Southern League medal, and was back in Glasgow to appear in the winning Southern League Cup Final against Motherwell and the Charity Cup Final win against Celtic in May 1945. He was stationed in Aldershot and turned out on occasion for Arsenal, meaning the three famous Rangers doctors – Paterson, Marshall and Little – had all played for the Gunners too.

The final season of wartime football in 1945/46 saw him mostly away on medical service, including a spell where he was stationed in Egypt. He did start nine games for Rangers between August and November 1945, the highlight being a fine 3-1 Glasgow Cup triumph over Celtic in the first round.

Adam wasn't the only Little family member who served with distinction during the war. His elder brother Gilbert was an aircraft designer and was instrumental in the design of the Wellington bomber. In post-war Britain, Gilbert became president of the British Water Board and was awarded a CBE for his service to the industry.

In all Dr Adam Little won an amazing 17 medals in his wartime appearances for Rangers, but once his military service was over and normality returned to the Scottish football calendar in 1946, he found his medical profession taking priority over his football career and appearances in Royal Blue were limited as other players took their chance to become first-team regulars. Although he remained a Rangers player until 1951, Little played only a handful of games for Rangers in the post-war period. He played at Motherwell in a 1-1 draw in the league in April 1948, a losing Glasgow Cup semi-final against Third Lanark in September 1949, and a last Rangers appearance in a league win at Ibrox over Morton on 9 December 1950. That final outing was his 204th start for the club, and it meant he had played in the Rangers first team in three different decades, a feat not achieved by a great many players in the club's history. In those 204 games, he scored eight times.

Although he loved life as a Rangers player, Little wanted to continue to combine his medical life with part-time football, and he joined Morton in 1951, which suited him perfectly as he was now a GP in Port Glasgow. He featured for the Greenock team for four years, starting over 100 games for them, before retiring from football in 1955 at the age of 35.

The good doctor then settled in Kilmacolm with his wife May. He enjoyed curling and especially golf, which he played at four handicap level.

On 12 June 2008, Dr Adam Little passed away at the age of 88.

- A Ranger from the age of 17
- Winner of 17 wartime medals
- 204 appearances across three different decades
- A doctor who served his country in World War Two

20 ALBERT GUDMUNDSSON

The former Rangers player who ran for the presidency of his country

ALBERT GUDMUNDSSON was born in the Icelandic capital of Reykjavik on 5 October 1923. A keen sportsman during his school years, he joined the sports club Valur when aged just 15. They had handball, basketball and football teams, and it was in football that Gudmundsson excelled. The Icelandic national league was very much in its formative years at this time, with just four Reykjavik clubs competing, and Valur came out on top in 1938 and 1940. Gudmundsson only played a minor part, however. But by 1942, the league had expanded and Gudmundsson was more of a regular, and he helped the club win successive titles in 1942, 1943 and 1944. It was in 1944 that life would change for him when he enrolled in a business course in Glasgow at Skerry's College in Bath Street.

While in Scotland he was keen to continue his football, and in 1945 when word reached Ibrox of the player's availability, Rangers offered him an amateur deal to allow him to play for them. Gudmundsson is not a name that features prominently in the club's history of the time. His time was brief and almost exclusively spent in the reserves, with his one and only appearance in the first team coming on Christmas Day 1945 when he played against Clyde at Ibrox in a Southern League match. He lined up at centre-forward alongside some great Ibrox names, including Willie Waddell who scored twice in a 3-1 victory. Despite not scoring, the Icelander made an impression on the legendary former captain Davie Meiklejohn, who reported on the match for the *Daily Record*. Meiklejohn singled out Gudmundsson for praise, commenting, 'This lad, I believe, has something, although he didn't shine here.' Rangers went on to win the wartime league again that season, so Gudmundsson played a very small part in the club's roll of honour.

After a further spell in the reserves, Gudmundsson left Rangers in 1946, moving to London where he again signed for a big club as an amateur. Arsenal manager George Allison was rebuilding the team at the time, their great pre-war side now long broken up. On 2 October 1946, he gave Gudmundsson a first-team opportunity when Sparta Prague visited Highbury for a friendly. Now almost 23 years old, Gudmundsson had an excellent game at inside-right in an entertaining 2-2 draw.

At the same time as he was making an impression with his new club, Gudmundsson joined up with a touring Iceland national team, delaying his next Arsenal appearance. This came on 19 October against Stoke City, and he enjoyed a fine competitive debut, playing well in a 1-0 win before a Highbury crowd of over 60,000. He also started the following weekend in a London derby against Chelsea, but tasted a 2-1 defeat. This was to be his last competitive appearance for the club, as although Arsenal were eager to sign the player, Gudmundsson failed in his application for a UK work permit and he therefore had no option but to leave Highbury. He did play in one last friendly, against Racing Club of Paris in mid-November. Arsenal lost 2-1 but Gudmundsson impressed his French hosts so much that they offered him a contract. The approach, however, was trumped by another French club, Nancy, who had representatives at the match. After some further negotiations, Gudmundsson agreed to sign for Nancy in early 1947.

Season 1947/48 was when Gudmundsson finally made his mark in professional club football. He ended the season as Nancy's top goalscorer despite them struggling at the wrong end of the table, and his all-action displays attracted attention from a much bigger club. So after just one season in France, he was on his travels again, joining Italian giants AC Milan. The San Siro club had high hopes for a potent strike partnership between Gudmundsson and Swedish international forward Gunnar Nordahl, and went into 1948/49 hopeful they could improve on the previous year's second-place finish in Serie A.

Gudmundsson played 14 times for Milan, scoring twice. Then in a fateful clash with Lazio he suffered a terrible knee injury that put his career in serious doubt. The club decided that the cost of surgery was too much to pay, so Gudmundsson looked to have played his last professional match. Milan were in a tight battle with city rivals Inter for second place at the time, and it caused some controversy when the Inter club doctor offered to carry out the knee surgery the player needed. Maybe unsurprisingly, Milan refused him permission to do this, so Gudmundsson in desperation bought out his playing contract to become a free agent again, and able to take up the medic's offer.

The Inter doctor's confidence was justified as the procedure was a complete success, and after a period of rehabilitation he finally did sign up with Racing Club, and moved back to Paris for 1949/50. He played three seasons in the French capital. His first saw him score nine times in 26 starts, helping Racing Club to the French Cup Final where he played in a 2-0 defeat to Reims. His second season was more prolific, 14 goals in 24 appearances. His form attracted another old club, Arsenal offering him a contract and taking him on a pre-season tour of Brazil. But the offer had to be withdrawn after he again was refused a UK work permit.

He instead stayed in Paris for a third season, with seven goals this time from 19 matches. Racing were happy with mid-table safety but Gudmundsson was more ambitious, and decided he wanted to move on. His eventual destination in the south of the country, Nice, couldn't provide him with any title challenge either, however. He played for them in 14 league games in 1952/53 but didn't enjoy the experience. At the end of the season he decided to return home, leaving full-time professional football behind and rejoining his first club, Valur.

His career lasted for five more seasons, all spent in Iceland. The final three years were at Hafnarfjorour, and when he retired in 1958 he had played six times for his national team, scoring twice. But football was becoming increasingly secondary to Gudmundsson as he was becoming a highly successful businessman. His imports business was growing rapidly, originally set up to bring women's fashion clothes into the country from France, and now it was dealing in all types of products, including French wine and cars. In the early 1960s he was an official agent for Renault, and as well as business he was starting to take a very active interest in both politics and football administration.

In 1962, he became his country's French Consul. In 1967, the Icelandic Football Association, the KSI, presented him with a Silver Award for services to the game, and within a year he had become the KSI's chairman. At this time he was a prominent member of Iceland's Independence Party, a Eurosceptic organisation of the centre-right, and in 1970 he successfully stood for election on to the Reykjavik City Council.

In 1973 he left his role as KSI chairman and was awarded an upgraded Gold Badge for his service to the game. That same year Gudmundsson travelled to Glasgow to participate in Rangers' centenary celebrations at Ibrox, and despite him only playing once for the club he proudly took part in a special presentation to the crowd of over 200 former players during a special celebration match against Arsenal.

He was now chairman of Reykjavik City Council, but his political ambitions went higher and in 1974 he was elected to the Icelandic parliament, the Althing. He successfully gained re-election four years later, and in 1980 he received the Independence Party nomination for the country's presidency. In the presidential election that year he received almost 20 per cent of the popular vote, which gave him third place behind the winner Vigdis Finnbogadottir, the first democratically elected female president anywhere in the world.

Gudmundsson remained in parliament until 1987, joining the government in 1983 and serving as both Minister for Finance and Minister for Industry, although he resigned following headlines over his tax affairs, both standing down from parliament and leaving the party. But rather than fade away he formed his own party, the Citizen's Party, winning 11 per cent of the vote in the 1987 election. He remained chairman of the party for two further years, before being appointed as the country's ambassador to France, a role he filled until 1993.

On 7 April 1994, Gudmundsson died at the age of 70. In 2010, the KSI commissioned a statue of him to stand outside the headquarters of the game in Iceland, and his statue is still there today.

- Only briefly a Ranger
- The first Icelandic professional player
- Played for three of the biggest clubs in Europe in Rangers, Arsenal and AC Milan
- A successful businessman, administrator and a top politician

21 ALEC BENNETT

The war hero with 152 appearances and 52 goals for Celtic, and 230 appearances and 68 goals for Rangers

BORN IN Rutherglen in 1881, Alec Bennett was an outstanding junior footballer at the turn of the 20th century. A tricky and intelligent forward with an eye for goal, he won the Scottish Junior Cup in 1902 with Rutherglen Glencairn and represented his country at that level before inevitably joining the senior professional ranks. In May 1903 he joined Celtic, where he quickly became an automatic starter in a team that was on the verge of dominating Scottish football.

Although Bennett had been mainly a centre-forward with Glencairn, Celtic had the prolific Jimmy Quinn as their main marksman, so he was utilised as a right-winger where his speed and creativity played a crucial role in a series of trophy wins. He scored a hat-trick in his first final, the 1903 Charity Cup, and over the next five years Bennett won four league titles and two Scottish Cups. On 25 April 1908 he scored the only goal at Ibrox to clinch Celtic's fourth successive championship. A thorn in Rangers' side, Bennett was a hero to the Celtic support, earning him the nickname of the 'Artful Dodger' for his ability on the ball and his consistent goals and assists.

On 2 May he starred in a Charity Cup win over Partick Thistle but was then mysteriously dropped for Celtic's next match in the competition, with the team line-up announced on 6 May including 'A.N. Other' on the right wing. The sensational news broke shortly afterwards that after five trophy laden years at Parkhead, 152 appearances and 53 goals, Bennett had crossed the Glasgow divide and signed for Rangers.

Celtic were however not prepared to let their man go easily. One press report told the story, 'On Friday May 29th 1908 at the first meeting of the new committee of the Scottish Football Association, a letter was read from Mr William Maley, secretary of the Celtic club in which he stated that he had been authorised by the board of directors to call the attention of the Association Committee to the signing on of Alexander Bennett by the Rangers club. The communication also stated "This player was asked to re-sign on April 15th but refused to do so and would give no reason but eventually stated that he had received a very big offer.

'"On 20th April he told Messrs Kelley, Colgan and Dunbar, all members of the board, that he had received such a big offer that it would be ridiculous to ask such terms of Celtic. On April 30th he again refused to sign for us and told our secretary he had decided to sign for another club but could not do so for a fortnight. He signed for Rangers on May 9th according to the evening papers. My club desires your committee to enquire into this case and to find from the player what club he had arranged with or had an offer from on April 15th which offer or arrangement was of course illegal and on learning the name of the club we would seek such club to be punished for infringing rule 55 of your association."

'Mr Mowar (Albion Rovers) moved that the commission be appointed.

'Mr Ward (Partick Thistle) seconded adding he knew Rangers desired an enquiry.

'Mr Williamson opposed the proposal saying that if they opened up all such questions they would have their hands full.

'Mr Robertson (Stenhousemuir) seconded.

'By the casting vote of the Chairman it was agreed to grant a special commission to be composed and given full powers under article 7.

'The commission sat in private eventually finding against the Celtic claim, stating 'the transfer not being one between two clubs but Bennett signing as a free agent.'

Rangers had paid the £50 release fee for the player, who in turn was now earning a far more lucrative salary. But to Bennett's close friends, including some Celtic team-mates, his move was no surprise. In private Bennett had been a vocal admirer of the Ibrox club, and he had long been uneasy at the Catholic ethos expected at Parkhead, even if players did not share that faith.

He made his Rangers debut in a 7-0 win over Port Glasgow in August 1908, when he also scored his first goal in Royal Blue. But already the press and public were looking forward to his first appearance against Celtic. It came on 26 September in the semi-final of the Glasgow Cup at Parkhead. Some 42,000 fans watched on as Bennett gave a man-of-the-match performance. He scored both Rangers goals in a hard-fought 2-2 draw. In his first season at Ibrox, Bennett didn't win the title, but he kept some of his best displays for the Celtic games. In addition to those two goals, he also scored against them in the first Scottish Cup Final draw (the trophy eventually withheld after a riot following a drawn replay) and a crucial strike in a 4-2 Rangers victory in the Charity Cup.

In the summer of 1909, Rangers brought in three players who alongside Bennett would finally bring back the glory days to Ibrox. Goalkeeper Herbert Lock, winger Billy Hogg, and striker Willie Reid just came up short in 1909/10, but over the next three seasons Rangers became Scotland's dominant team. The signing of Hogg allowed Bennett to move infield, and as an inside-forward the Artful Dodger was to create countless goals for the prolific Reid.

Bennett scored in a 3-1 Glasgow Cup Final win over Celtic, and scored six goals in 23 league appearances as the title was won with four points to spare. He was a regular again the following season as Rangers repeated the league and Glasgow Cup double, and then again in 1912/13, the same double achieved with Bennett scoring in the final success over Celtic. He scored again in the 1913/14 final, this time a 3-0 win over Third Lanark, as Rangers claimed the cup for the 4th year running. However, there was to be no fourth successive league win as Celtic's two league victories over Rangers proved to be the difference.

In August 1914, the world was plunged into war, and although Bennett was to feature for Rangers periodically, he enlisted in the Cameronian Regiment and saw active duty in the trenches. He did make one memorable appearance in November 1915, playing in goal against Falkirk after three Rangers players missed their train to the match due to fog, including regular keeper John Hempsey. His one and only appearance between the sticks ended in a 2-0 defeat. His brother James, a successful footballer with Queen's Park, also enlisted with the Highland Light Infantry. In 1916 Sergeant James Bennett was seriously injured by a gunshot to his back, which he survived, albeit his football career was ended as a result.

Alec Bennett also guested for Ayr United during the conflict, and was released by Rangers in 1918 after the end of the war. He then played for Dumbarton and Albion Rovers before retiring at the age of 40. He had represented Scotland 11 times, eight of these while a Rangers player, scoring against Wales in 1908 while at Parkhead and Ireland in 1913 while at Ibrox.

In all, Bennett played 230 times for Rangers, scoring 68 goals.

After retiring, he managed Third Lanark and Clydebank, before leaving football to become a sports writer for The Daily Record. He passed away on 9 January 1940 aged only 58. His sporting prowess passed on into his family, as his grandson Sandy Bennett Carmichael was a hugely successful rugby union international player for both Scotland and the British Lions.

- A multiple league winner for Celtic and Rangers
- A rare direct move between the two clubs
- A Scotland international
- A Great War veteran

22 ALEX STEVENSON

The future Republic of Ireland manager signed by Bill Struth

ALEXANDER EARNEST Stevenson was born in Dublin on 12 August 1912, into a family with a mixed religious upbringing. His parents Alexander and Rosalina were from families with Scottish, Irish and Italian bloodlines, and they decided to bring up their children in the Church of Ireland. Stevenson's football career started at the local team affiliated to his parents' church, the St Barnabus club, playing in the same team as his older brother Henry. At only 5ft 5in tall the 17-year-old Stevenson was mainly up against bigger and stronger rivals, but his natural ball skills and trickery saw him stand out.

He helped St Barnabus win the prestigious Leinster Cup in 1930, and the following year he was capped by Ireland at junior level, playing in a 3-2 defeat to Scotland at Falkirk. Several senior clubs were by now tracking his progress, and he signed for the Dolphin club of Dublin in 1931, who had former Rangers defender Arthur Dixon as their player-manager. Stevenson only played there for one season, making a huge impression as a goalscoring and creative inside-forward. He helped Dolphin to two cup finals, winning the Leinster Senior Cup but losing the all-Ireland FAI Cup Final to Shamrock Rovers. Towards the end of the 1931/32 season he was called up to the national team by the FAI for the first time, and made his debut for Ireland in a 2-0 victory away to Holland.

In the summer of 1932, Dixon left Dolphin to return to Rangers as the club's trainer. He was a hugely respected figure at Ibrox, a stalwart of six league title wins, and he recommended to manager Bill Struth that the club sign Stevenson. A fee of £250 was set, along with an agreement that Rangers would visit Dublin to play Dolphin in a challenge match, and Stevenson became a Rangers player.

The challenge match was played in April 1933 at Dalymount Park, Dublin. Rangers won a hard-fought encounter 3-1 thanks to a double from Northern Irish centre-forward Sam English. By the time that game was played, Stevenson had only played one first-team game for Rangers, with Struth preferring the experience and proven goals of Dr James Marshall at inside-right. Stevenson's debut had been on 17 September 1932 against Partick Thistle at Ibrox, a comfortable 3-0 win. It would be his only first-team appearance of his debut season, but 1933/34 would be different.

Stevenson started at inside-right on the opening day and gave an excellent display in a thumping 5-1 Ibrox win over Airdrie, with prolific centre-forward Jimmy Smith hitting four goals. Three days later, Smith and Stevenson were in even more sensational form as Smith hit the net six times and Stevenson grabbed a hat-trick in a 9-1 annihilation of Ayr United. By the end of September, Stevenson had started 11 times and scored seven goals. He had also made his first appearance in the Old Firm derby, a frantic 2-2 draw at Ibrox on 9 September.

Celtic were the opposition in the Glasgow Cup semi-final, and it was Stevenson who eventually decided the tie when he scored a late winner in an Ibrox replay after a Parkhead draw. He would only play once more for the club after that semi-final highlight, his 14th and final Rangers start coming in a 4-0 victory at Palmerston on 11 November. English giants Everton had been interested in the player prior to his move to Glasgow, and they were making determined efforts again to land him. He played in all three Home International games for the IFA's Irish side during the season, including a fine 2-1 win over Scotland (there were two different Irish football associations, each with a national team; the IFA were based in the north with the FAI based in the south). In February 1934, Rangers agreed a fee of £2,750 with Everton for the player and he moved to Goodison Park. Although no longer a Rangers player, he did receive a league winners' medal at the end of the season when the title was won.

Everton's chase for Stevenson proved to be time well spent as he went on to enjoy a fine career with the club. He formed several productive partnerships over his time on Merseyside, especially the legendary Dixie Dean during his early years, Tommy Lawton in the seasons after Dean retired, and with fellow Irish international Jackie Coulter, a left-winger with a talent for scoring spectacular goals. Stevenson scored 18 times in his first full season at Everton and although trophies eluded them, he continued to put in entertaining and match-winning performances. His best return was in 1936/37 when he scored 21 goals in 44 appearances, and by 1938/39 Everton were looking like a team capable of winning honours again.

Everton mounted a serious title challenge from the start of the season, with Lawton the most feared centre-forward in the division. He ended the season with 34 goals from 38 games, many of them created by the craft and intelligence of Stevenson. Years later, Lawton was quoted as giving Stevenson the highest of praise, 'He is one of the finest footballers who have ever kicked a football on an English ground.' Going into the hectic Easter fixtures, Everton were top of the table with Wolves their closest challengers. On Good Friday 1939 Stevenson starred in a hard-fought 2-1 win at Sunderland. The next day, Everton had travelled to London to play Chelsea, and despite the obvious tiredness, Stevenson scored a crucial opening goal in the 70th minute, and the points were secured when another former Rangers player, Torry Gillick, hit a second. On Easter Monday Sunderland visited Goodison in the reverse fixture, and Stevenson again scored in a handsome 6-2 win. Three wins in four days had all but secured the title and it was officially won the following Saturday with a point against Preston.

Stevenson was now a title winner in both Scotland and England. By the end of that season he had also played 14 times for the IFA's Irish team but strangely had never been called up again by the FAI; his only cap for the Dublin-based team had come before he moved to Ibrox.

Everton were unable to defend their title in 1939/40 as the season was suspended when war was declared. Stevenson could have returned home as the Irish Free State remained neutral during World War Two and their domestic league was unaffected. Several of his international colleagues opted to do this, but Stevenson chose instead to enlist with the RAF. A member of the ground crew, Stevenson was able to continue playing in wartime football as his service commitments allowed. He played over 200 times for Everton during the war years and he also made guest appearances for Blackpool and Tranmere. Included in his wartime career highlights was an amazing hat-trick against Manchester United in 1940 when he scored all three goals in the last five minutes of the match. Stevenson also played representative football during the war, including a memorable game between the IFA and a Combined Services XI which featured such household names as Stanley Mathews, Tommy Lawton and Matt Busby. The IFA team lost 8-4. He then missed much of the season in 1945 after being stationed in India.

Once football was able to resume in 1946/47, Stevenson was in the veteran stage of his career. He still managed eight goals in 30 appearances for Everton as they saw their much-delayed title defence end in a lowly tenth place, well behind new champions Liverpool. But the season was still a special one for Stevenson as after a 14-year wait, he was finally selected again to represent the FAI's national team. He travelled over to his home city of Dublin to play against England at Dalymount Park, and would go on to play six times for Ireland over the next two years. England won the match 1-0, but it could have been different if Stevenson's shot had been slightly lower rather than smashing off the crossbar. Stevenson was 36 years old when he won his last cap in December 1948.

By now he was very much in the twilight of his career, and had started to help coach the Everton reserve team as well as still occasionally play in the first team. He was Everton captain on 18 September 1948 when Goodison Park saw its all-time record attendance of 78,299 in a 1-1 draw with Liverpool. Stevenson left at the end of 1948/49, after 477 appearances and 181 goals when wartime matches are included.

He became player-manager at non-league club Bootle, where he enjoyed some success. Then in the summer of 1952 he moved back home after being appointed coach of the Irish national team. It's probably fair to say that not too many Rangers fans know that the club had a former player who became the Irish national manager. But back then the role was very different to now. The team itself was still picked by a committee, so the manager simply coached whatever players were picked for him, and between matches he travelled the country promoting the game. Stevenson didn't enjoy the job at all, and his spell was brief.

In February 1954, he left the FAI to take over as manager of St Patrick's Athletic. He decided to play as well as manage, and he guided the team to the FAI Cup Final where they lost to Drumcondra. His second season was even more successful, winning the league title while still turning out in the team occasionally despite being 43 years of age. He had added an Irish championship to those in Scotland and England. St. Patrick's retained the title the following season, before he moved to Waterford. He spent two seasons there, leading them to a League of Ireland Shield win and losing another FAI Cup Final.

This was Stevenson's last job in football, and after leaving Waterford he moved back across the Irish Sea to open a pub called The Shropshire Arms in Chester. Like many other footballers before and since, he found too much temptation when behind the bar. It ended his marriage, and after four years he left the pub trade, first working at a local Vauxhall factory then becoming a labourer in a construction site, before getting a job with the local council.

His later years were badly affected by heart problems, and Stevenson passed away on 2 September 1985 at the age of 73.

- Dublin-born and represented both Irish football associations
- A league winner in Scotland, England and Ireland
- Scorer of a cup-tie winner for Rangers against Celtic
- Served with the RAF in World War Two
- Briefly the Irish national team manager

23   ANDREW MCCREADIE

The diminutive centre-half who was part of many Rangers firsts

ANDREW MCCREADIE was born in Girvan on 19 November 1870. His football career started at Cowlairs in 1888 as a hard-tackling and aggressive centre-half. Despite being remarkably short for a central defender at just 5ft 5in, his displays at the heart of the Cowlairs defence quickly attracted other clubs, and the following year the 19-year-old joined Rangers.

He started his Rangers career in the months immediately before league football began in Scotland, and his competitive debut was memorable for him for many reasons. On 16 August 1890 he lined up in defence against Hearts in Rangers' first league match. It was further special as making his competitive debut also that day was his younger brother Hugh who played up front. Rangers won 5-2 on this momentous day, with Hugh scoring one of the goals.

Andrew started 15 of the 18 games in that first league season. His first goal came on 21 March 1891 and what a time to score it, a vital strike in a 2-2 draw away to Celtic. His only other goal that debut season came in another crucial match the following month when he opened the scoring against league leaders Dumbarton, who were beaten 4-2 in a match that would have seen them crowned champions with a victory. After 18 games, Rangers and Dumbarton finished level on points at the top, and the league was therefore to be decided by a play-off. Cathkin Park hosted the decider on 21 May 1891 and a 10,000 crowd saw Andrew McCreadie and Rangers roar into a two-goal lead through goals by David Hyslop and Hugh McCreadie. But Rangers couldn't hold on after a relentless Dumbarton onslaught, the match ending in a 2-2 draw. The league committee decided to jointly award the title to both clubs, so the McCreadie brothers became holders of Scotland's first league winners' medals.

Andrew's second season ended without further medals, although it was to be possibly his most consistent in Royal Blue. He started 30 times across the various competitions and even scored six times with five of these in the league. But Rangers' league challenge fizzled out from early on, leaving the cup competitions as the best chance of glory. He played in all three losing matches in the cups that season, a dismal loss to Queen's Park in the Glasgow Cup then two painful defeats to Celtic in the Scottish Cup semi-final and the Charity Cup Final.

Season 1892/93 saw McCreadie a virtual ever present again, with 24 starts. He added two goals to his Rangers total, against Third Lanark in the league and Northern in the Glasgow Cup. And it was in the Glasgow Cup where McCreadie next played his part in Rangers history. On 18 February 1893 he was at centre-half in the final against Celtic. Rangers had not yet defeated the Parkhead men in a competitive match, nor had they won the city's main cup competition. However, that all changed as goals by John Barker, Neil Kerr and the great John McPherson won the match 3-1. And just like the league decider almost two years earlier, Andrew had the extra pleasure of his brother Hugh being in the team line-up. Andrew also became an international player in 1893 when he made his Scotland debut in a thumping eight goal hammering of Wales in March.

McCreadie was part of history again in 1893/94. His 28 appearances this time yielded two goals, both in the unsuccessful league campaign. But this was the season Rangers would finally win the one competition they yearned for more than any other, the Scottish Cup. This was their 20th attempt and after a magnificent semi-final replay win over Queen's Park it was inevitably Celtic who were waiting in the final on 17 February 1894. Andrew wrote his name further into club history with an excellent performance in a convincing 3-1 triumph, with brother Hugh starting the scoring in a devastating three goal-burst in just ten second-half minutes. Captain and fellow Ayrshireman Davie Mitchell lifted the trophy to delirious celebrations from the Rangers support. Andrew also won a second and final Scotland cap in April, a 2-2 draw with England at Parkhead.

In the summer of 1894, McCreadie was tempted south by a big-money offer from Sunderland, who had just lost their championship crown and were determined to regain it. His debut was as easy as could be, an 8-0 thrashing of Derby County which featured goals from future Rangers players Jimmy Millar, Tom Hyslop and Johnny Campbell. His second start was even more familiar – a 1-1 draw at Ibrox in a friendly.

McCreadie made 27 starts that season in the league and another three in the FA Cup, immediately being a mainstay of the Sunderland defence. He also scored a very impressive ten goals, including a late penalty winner in the reverse fixture against Derby, and the opener on the final day against runners-up Everton. McCreadie added an English title medal to his collection, the Roker men ending the season five points clear.

He played a further 15 times in the First Division the following season but Sunderland struggled to maintain a challenge and he lost in place in the team just before Christmas 1895. In March 1896, after 45 appearances and 11 goals, Sunderland sold McCreadie back to Rangers. He played in only minor competitions until the season ended, not making his return to the league side until the opening day of 1896/97 From then on he was a regular again in the Ibrox rearguard. His 30 games featured two goals, against Hibs and Dundee. But there was no doubt his season highlights were in the cup competitions.

In November 1896 he played against Celtic in the Glasgow Cup Final. After a tense 1-1 draw, Rangers won the replay 2-1 thanks to a double by temperamental forward Peter Turnbull. Then in March 1897, McCreadie played in a thumping 5-1 win over Dumbarton in the Scottish Cup Final, the club's second victory in the tournament and his second winners' medal. This was now a Rangers team on the verge of becoming the dominant force in the country, with legendary players like Matt Dickie, Nicol Smith, Jock Drummond, Neilly Gibson, Alec Smith and John McPherson.

Season 1897/98 saw Rangers win two major cup competitions but it was also the final season of McCreadie's career. He started four of the first five league games, the last being a terrible 4-0 defeat by Celtic. And he never wore the Rangers shirt again. Still in his 20s, McCreadie disappeared from football, although his reasons why are not recorded. In 1901 the Glasgow census recorded McCreadie as living at 10 Slatefield Street in Denniston with wife Jemina and one-year-old son John. His occupation was listed as a 'shop man'.

Sadly, Jemina died in 1904 aged just 32. McCreadie's address changed to Annfield Street and he was listed as a weaver. But in 1916 he died aged only 45.

- One of great Rangers brothers, neither of whom are in the Hall of Fame
- Winner of the first Rangers league title
- Winner of the first Rangers Glasgow Cup

- Winner of the first Rangers Scottish Cup
- Also won another Scottish Cup, another Glasgow Cup, as well as an English league title
- 2 Scotland caps
- 140 Rangers appearances, 14 goals

24   ARCHIE KYLE

The Rangers star with the millionaire musical grandson

ARCHIBALD KYLE was born in Kinning Park, Glasgow on 13 July 1883 into a Roman Catholic family. A keen footballer from an early age, he joined Parkhead Juniors in 1903 where he immediately made a big impression as a speedy inside-forward with an eye for goal. After only one season in the junior ranks, he made the step up to the professional game when William Wilton signed him for Rangers in the summer of 1904.

Despite his relative inexperience and only just out of his teenage years, Kyle made his first Rangers appearance on 20 August in the opening league game of the season at Third Lanark. It wasn't the most memorable of debuts as Kyle was played out of position on the right wing, and the season started badly with a 2-1 loss. But his Ibrox bow a week later was more of a sign of things to come. Kyle was switched to his favoured inside-left position and scored in a convincing 4-0 defeat of Hibs.

Kyle made 34 starts in that first season, appearing in his first cup final in October 1904 in front of nearly 55,000 at Hampden when a goal by the legendary R.C. Hamilton wasn't enough to prevent a painful 2-1 defeat by Celtic in the Glasgow Cup. He scored his first goal against the men from Parkhead later in the season, but that was another defeat, this time 4-1 at home in the league. However, it looked like 1904/05 might end on a high note when Kyle helped defeat them in the infamous Scottish Cup semi-final when Celtic fans rioted to get the match abandoned after going 2-0 down and seeing their star centre-forward Jimmy Quinn ordered off. But Kyle endured heartache in the final when Third Lanark won the cup after a replay. A case of what might have been was made worse when, four days after the replay defeat, Kyle scored in a comfortable 4-1 win over the same opponents in the Glasgow League, and he then missed out on a place in the league championship play-off defeat against Celtic. In all Kyle scored 19 goals in 1904/05, including five separate doubles.

Season 1905/06 saw Kyle again a regular, although his form was somewhat inconsistent. After only hitting the net once in his first 11 starts he popped up with a vital strike in a hard-fought 3-2 league win over Celtic in late October. This started a brief purple patch in front of goal, with six goals in four games, including a first Rangers hat-trick when scoring all three in a draw at Motherwell. He then endured another barren spell before a memorable end of the season in May. He was among the scorers in a thumping 5-3 Charity Cup semi-final success at Parkhead before earning a first winners' medal in the final, where he also scored in the victory over Queen's Park.

In 1906/07, Kyle enjoyed a new strike partnership with future Ibrox director and converted full-back R.G. Campbell, with plenty goals scored between them. Kyle contributed 14 of them, although it was another season where the title stayed out of reach. Like the previous season, it ended in Charity Cup success with Kyle starting in the final. This triumph felt even more satisfying as Campbell scored the only goal at Hampden against bitter rivals Celtic.

Kyle's fourth and final season at Ibrox was probably his most frustrating of all. He scored against Celtic in the Glasgow Cup Final, in the new year game, and in the Scottish Cup. But all three games were lost 2-1. He played his 135th and final game for Rangers away to St Mirren on 13 April 1908, and scored his 58th and final goal in a 2-0 league win. His four seasons at Rangers had yielded just those two Charity Cup winners' medals.

During his Rangers career Kyle was selected twice to represent the Scottish League against their English counterparts. He scored in a heavy 6-2 defeat at Stamford Bridge in 1906, and also suffered defeat by 2-0 at Villa Park in 1908.

In the summer of 1908, English First Division side Blackburn Rovers signed Kyle, with high hopes that he would make a big impression. But after only a single season, where he scored eight times in 38 matches, he was sold to Bradford Park Avenue. Kyle never settled in England and never made a competitive appearance for Bradford. He was desperate to return north and accepted an offer from Bo'ness of the Central League. This proved to be an ill-fated switch, and he tried to resurrect his career in Belfast with Linfield. It looked like Kyle's career was heading in only one direction. Then in September 1910 he was given the chance to show he could still make an impression on Scottish football when signed by Clyde. Six goals in 27 league games later, he had helped Clyde to a solid eighth place in the First Division, prompting St Mirren to come calling for his services the following close-season. Kyle was enjoying something of a career Indian summer.

He became a key player in Paisley and was a virtual ever present. Now enjoying a slightly more withdrawn role, he still contributed 12 goals in almost 100 appearances. Although the Paisley side were far nearer the bottom of the league than the top, his near three seasons there were enough to persuade Hamilton Accies to sign the 30-year-old Kyle in January 1914. Mainly during the war, Kyle racked up 130 starts for the Lanarkshire side, scoring 32 times and creating many more.

As wartime ended, so did Kyle's senior career, and he settled his family to the East End of Glasgow. Little is known about his life after football, other than two scandalous headlines. First, in 1924 he was convicted along with former Celtic player John Browning of attempted bribery. They had met up with a Bo'ness player in a bar in Dundas Street and offered cash for the player to throw a match against Lochgelly. Kyle and Browning were sentenced to 60 days' hard labour. Then in 1931, there were further allegations he had been involved along with ex-Hamilton Accies team-mate Adam Miller in attempting to bribe a Hamilton player to lose a game against Leith. This time there was no criminal trial, although Accies did lose 3-2.

Kyle passed away in Bridgeton, Glasgow, in July 1957 aged 74. If his football career wasn't enough to remember him by then he has another claim to fame. He and his wife Letitia had a daughter christened Mary, but who was better known as Cathy. In the 1930s Cathy met and married local man Francis Miller. They had three children, daughters Letty and Anne, and a son named Frank after his father. The young Miller attended Sacred Heart RC school and was an altar boy at Sacred Heart RC church. He loved football, no doubt inherited from his grandfather, and he played for the local Harmony Row boys' club. He also passionately supported Celtic, something his grandfather may not have approved of.

But Frankie Miller would not find fame on the football field. His love of music, and a talent for songwriting meant he would become a household name with million-selling albums, hit songs such as 'Darlin' and 'Caledonia', and writing songs for world famous stars such as Roy Orbison, Ray Charles, Rod Stewart, Johnny Cash and The Eagles.

- A Catholic who was a Rangers regular
- Winner of two Charity Cup medals during his Rangers career, and runner-up in several finals
- Scorer of seven goals for Rangers against Celtic
- 13-year professional career in Scotland, England and Ireland
- Dubious character in later life
- Grandfather to a well-known Celtic-supporting musician

25   ARCHIE MACAULAY

The traffic warden who won titles with Rangers and Arsenal, and who outsmarted Matt Busby

ARCHIE MACAULAY was born in Falkirk during the grim days of the Great War, on 30 July 1915. A precocious talent at a young age, the red-haired inside-forward was a regular in junior football at just 16 years old, playing for Comely Park in 1931, Lauriston Villa in 1932 and Camelon Juniors in 1933 before signing for Rangers that year.

Despite joining a club enjoying domestic dominance, it was a sign of how highly Bill Struth regarded the young Macaulay that he was given a first-team debut on 16 September in a league match at Ayr United, replacing injured regular Alec Stevenson at inside-right in a 2-0 victory. Stevenson returned in the next game, but the teenager had shown enough to be considered ready when needed. Rangers went on an impressive run in league and cup, and by the time Macaulay made his next appearance they were well on course for the title. He opened the scoring in a midweek home win over Hamilton on 14 March 1934 and started four of the next five games, including on the right wing at Hampden in the Scottish Cup semi-final win over St Johnstone in front of 61,000 fans. Rangers won the double that season, with the young Macaulay starting six times and scoring that one goal.

Still only 19, 1934/35 was to be Macaulay's most memorable as a Rangers player. He started as the first-choice inside-right, the season opening with a 7-1 demolition of Dunfermline where Jimmy Smith hit six of them. Macaulay started ten of the first 12 league games, scoring in wins over Partick and Ayr, before making his first appearance against Celtic in the Glasgow Cup semi-final at Parkhead on 24 September. And what a start he made, scoring after only four minutes. A late Torry Gillick strike saw Rangers into the final thanks to a 2-1 win. Unfortunately, there was only a runners-up medal for him when he played in a surprise defeat by Partick Thistle. He lost his place just before the new year, but his four goals in 16 league starts played a part in the title being retained. Many articles on his career don't list him as receiving a winners' medal for the season, despite this appearance total being enough to have merited it.

Macaulay remained mainly a reserve in 1935/36 with Alex Venters preferred at inside-right. He started just seven games, six in the league, as Rangers finished runners-up. A player who often played on a short fuse, he was sent off in a bad-tempered win over Third Lanark at Cathkin Park in April 1936, but rounded off his season in a more positive way when scoring in a win at Kilmarnock.

Season 1936/37 was his last season in Royal Blue, and it ended with the title being regained. He started nine league games, scoring once in a rout of Kilmarnock. Strangely, despite this being far fewer appearances than in the title win two seasons earlier, he is listed as receiving a championship medal. He also won a Glasgow Cup medal, playing in the 6-1 final replay win over Partick in November. By the summer of 1937, Macaulay had played just 41 times for Rangers in four seasons, scoring eight times, and that close-season he was transferred to West Ham United of the English Second Division for £6000.

The volatile but skilful Macaulay was an instant hit at Upton Park, straight from his debut against Aston Villa on 28 August 1937. He struck a fine understanding with centre-forward Stan Foxall, and they ended the season as joint top scorers on ten apiece as the Hammers finished ninth. Season 1938/39 was even better, with 16 goals in 36 games making him their top scorer, and it included his first hat-trick in a big win over Tranmere.

Britain declared war on Germany on 3 September 1939, immediately ending national league football. West Ham were placed in a regional competition for London clubs along with Arsenal, Brentford, Charlton, Chelsea, Fulham, Millwall and Spurs. Macaulay did turn out in this competition, but he had also enlisted with the Essex Regiment of the Army, and became a PE Instructor at Aldershot barracks. At this time, the Football League decided to organise a national cup competition as Britain had not experienced any German bombing. This was the Football League War Cup.

The entire competition of 137 games including replays was condensed into nine weeks. West Ham reached the final by beating Chelsea, Leicester, Huddersfield, Birmingham and Fulham. However, by the time the final took place, the Luftwaffe had started their bombing offensive, but 42,300 fans ignored this threat and watched West Ham play Blackburn Rovers at Wembley in the final on 8 June 1940. Macaulay won his first medal in English football when Sam Small of West Ham scored the only goal.

During the conflict, Macaulay played 59 times for West Ham as his military service allowed, where he rose through the ranks to end the war as a sergeant major. He also represented Scotland in five wartime international matches, although none of these are officially recognised caps.

In the 1945/46 season he played for West Ham in the Football League South competition. However, he found it difficult to settle after hostilities had ceased and only played in eight games the following season before being transferred to the then more glamorous First Division Brentford in October 1946 for a fee of £7,500. Macaulay made his official Scotland debut against England at Wembley on 12 April 1947 alongside Rangers' Iron Curtain legends George Young, Tiger Shaw and Willie Woodburn, having now been converted to a wing-half. Such was his impressive form that he was also selected to play for Great Britain in a one-off match against a Rest of Europe team in May 1947. But despite his excellence, Brentford were relegated and in the summer of 1947 Macaulay was transferred to his third London club, Arsenal, for £10,000.

This was an Arsenal team full of international players, such as Joe Mercer, and the pair quickly gained the reputation as the best wing-half pairing in the country. He started 40 of Arsenal's 42 league games in his debut season as the Gunners captured the First Division title for the first time in a decade. He was now a champion in both Scotland and England. By May 1948 he had added further international caps, his seventh and final Scotland start being on 23 May in a 3-0 defeat to France.

By June 1950, Macaulay had played 108 times for Arsenal, adding the 1948 Charity Shield to his winners' medals after a thrilling 4-3 success over Manchester United. His Arsenal manager, Tom Whittaker, later recalled, 'Macaulay, a brilliant ball player and magnificently balanced, had the reputation of a temper in keeping with his red hair but while he was at Highbury, he was a loyal club servant and a fine footballer.' Whittaker, however, ended Macaulay's career at the club in disappointment, selecting fellow Scot Alex Forbes instead in the victorious 1950 FA Cup Final team.

Macaulay moved to Fulham in the summer of 1950 for £10,000, a hefty fee for a player almost 35 years old. He played at Craven Cottage for three seasons, the last of which was in the Second Division after relegation. After four goals in 53 Fulham appearances he moved into management, accepting an offer from Guildford City to become player-manager.

In his four years there, he developed a reputation as a fiery but innovative manager, resulting in him being appointed manager at Third Division Norwich City in the summer of 1957.

Norwich were at the lowest point in their history. They had finished bottom of the Football League, only just survived the re-election process, and had almost gone bust due to severe financial difficulties. In his first season in charge, Macaulay's priority was simply to stabilise a club in real danger of disappearing. He did a fine job in steering them to eighth place in the Third Division as well as earning some much-needed revenue by getting to the FA Cup third round. Nobody could have predicted the impression his team were to make in the tournament the following season.

Ever the innovator, Macaulay occasionally used a new 4-3-3 formation, which confused opponents. Norwich again reached the lucrative third round thanks to a win over non-league Ilford and a narrow replay victory over Swindon. The Norwich fans were celebrating as the draw paired them at home to Matt Busby's Manchester United. Carrow Road was covered in snow on 10 January 1959 as the mighty club from Old Trafford came to town. Robbed of a truly great team by the Munich tragedy the previous year, Busby still had a formidable line-up including the likes of Harry Gregg, Bill Foulkes, Dennis Violett and Bobby Charlton. However, it was the lesser-known Scottish manager who won the day before 38,000 fans, lowly Norwich outplaying United for a convincing 3-0 win with a double from Terry Bly. It was a result that put Norwich, Bly and Macaulay on the front pages.

The cup run continued with a fourth-round win over Cardiff City. Another full-house crowd of 38,000 saw Bly score an 88th-minute winner in a thrilling 3-2 victory. Surely the end of the road would be coming as the draw saw Norwich going to White Hart Lane to face a formidable Tottenham Hotspur team who included great players like Cliff Jones, Bobby Smith and Danny Blanchflower. Over 67,000 attended to see if the no-hopers could do it again, and they almost did as Spurs earned a replay thanks to a last-gasp Jones equaliser. The Carrow Road replay saw a third full house, and a third Bly fairytale goal, as Norwich won 1-0. Macaulay was briefly one of the most famous managers in England as his third-tier outfit were now in the last eight.

The quarter-final was away to Second Division Sheffield United. After a 1-1 draw, where Norwich keeper Nethercott played on despite a dislocated shoulder, the home replay had a very familiar outcome. Sold out, five goals, and Bly grabbing a double as Norwich won 3-2. A Third Division team just one win from Wembley; this was now historic, only the third time a team from the lowest league – the Fourth Division had not yet been introduced – had got this far.

First Division Luton Town stood between the Canaries and a place in the FA Cup Final. City fans once again returned to White Hart Lane in their thousands after Spurs' home was selected as the neutral venue for the semi-final showdown

The match ended 1-1 with Brennan netting a second-half equaliser for City. The result saw both sides do it all again four days later at Birmingham City's St Andrew's but sadly the semi-final replay proved a bridge too far for Norwich, whose remarkable run ended with a single strike from Luton's Billy Bingham being the difference between the two sides.

Despite missing out on a trip to the twin towers, the Canaries were given a heroic welcome back to Norwich by their proud supporters, with Macaulay the toast of the town.

Macaulay then extended success to the league when Norwich were promoted to the Second Division after finishing runners-up in 1960. He then took the team to a very respectable fourth-place finish in the second tier. Such success was always going to attract bigger clubs, and in the summer of 1961 Macaulay became manager at First Division West Bromwich Albion.

His two seasons at The Hawthorns were steady but unspectacular; mid-table both times, and he was sacked in 1963 after winning just 26 out of 67 matches. But he was out of football only briefly, quickly appointed manager of Fourth Division side Brighton & Hove Albion. He showed he remained a formidable manager at this level, guiding them to the title in 1965. But by 1968 he had enjoyed no further tangible success, and he left after almost five years in charge.

Macaulay briefly worked for Dundee and for Liverpool before leaving the game entirely in 1970. Just 55 years old, a man with a highly impressive CV as a player and a manager, he turned his back on football and returned to London. The last years of his working life were in the Chelsea area, where he patrolled the streets as a traffic warden. On retiring he moved to the Midlands, and on 10 June 1993 he passed away in the village of Knowle, near Solihull, aged 77.

- Rangers career: 1933–1937
- Teenage Rangers player
- League winner for Rangers and Arsenal
- Scotland international
- FA Cup sensation as a manager
- Innovator
- Wartime sergeant major
- Finally, a traffic warden

26 BILLY HOGG

The English international brought to Ibrox to help bring back the league title

IN RECENT history, many Rangers fans fondly remember the 'Souness revolution' in 1986, when the new manager raided the English First Division to bring top players from down south to Ibrox as the club brought to an end a period of misery on the pitch. There were many similarities in the long-forgotten summer of 1909, and this is the story of an England international brought to Rangers in similar circumstances.

Billy Hogg was born in Sunderland on 29 May 1879, in the aptly named Roker Avenue in the city. His family moved to Heaton, Newcastle-upon-Tyne when he was a youngster. His football career started at Wellington Athletic, and his pace, skill and shooting power soon attracted senior clubs. In October 1899 at the age of 20, he signed for Sunderland.

His league debut came in a home league match at Roker Park on 2 December against Notts County on the right wing, and he enjoyed a day to remember as Sunderland won

5-0 and he scored his first goal, the fourth of the afternoon. Sunderland had an excellent team at the time, and were challenging for the title, and Hogg wasn't yet a guaranteed starter. His next appearance came three weeks later and it was another memorable occasion for him, his first start in the Tyne-Wear derby against Newcastle United. Over 20,000 fans watched at St James' Park as Hogg helped Sunderland to a thrilling 4-2 win, coming from behind at half-time. Hogg's performances were already making him difficult to leave out and he was soon a regular in the team, making 22 appearances in his first professional season, and scoring an impressive 11 goals. These included winning goals in games against Bury, Notts Forest and Blackburn as Sunderland ended the season in third place behind champions Aston Villa.

They came even closer to title glory in his first full season of 1900/01, when Hogg started all 34 league games and scored nine times but saw the title thrown away when two defeats in the last four games saw Liverpool overtake them at the top on the last day. His goal at St James' Park in the final fixture to help win another derby was little consolation, but 1901/02 was to be different.

Hogg did miss a few games due to injury, but he appeared in 28 of Sunderland's 34 First Division fixtures and ended up joint top scorer with ten goals. Sunderland roared to the title and it was fitting that the final goal of the campaign was scored by Hogg in a home victory over Bolton Wanderers.

Hogg's excellent form by now had caught the eye of the England selectors and he was picked for all the matches in the 1902 Home Internationals. Tragically, his first match in Scotland was the Scotland v England Ibrox disaster, and he also played in the rescheduled fixture between the teams which ended in a 2-2 draw. The four caps he won in 1902 were his only appearances for his country, although he did play four times for the English League.

Hogg remained a mainstay of the Sunderland team for several more seasons, but 1902 remained his only English league title. He was top scorer again in 1903/04 when he occasionally started as a centre-forward, and in the following seasons he was seen there, on the wing and also as an inside-right. In 1903 he played in the Charity Shield, which Sunderland won. By season 1908/09 he was in his tenth season at Roker Park, and was adored by the Sunderland supporters. On 5 December 1908 he confirmed his place in their hearts by scoring a hat-trick in a historic 9-1 thrashing of Newcastle at the home of their biggest rivals, a result still celebrated in Sunderland folklore. This was Hogg's second hat-trick in a fortnight, having previously scored three in a victory away to Woolwich Arsenal. His 303rd and final Sunderland appearance came on 17 April 1909 at Ashton Gate, helping his side to a 4-2 win at Bristol City. Those 303 games contained 84 goals, with just two being penalties.

Sunderland ended the season in third place (incredibly, the title was won by the Newcastle team they had beaten 9-1), but Hogg was by now looking for a fresh challenge. Sunderland accepted an offer for their experienced and popular winger from Rangers in May 1909, and Hogg made the move to Ibrox for a fee of just £100.

This was a Rangers team desperate for success. The league title hadn't been won since 1902, the year when the club were rocked by the disaster during the Scotland v England international and had been forced to sell players to raise funds. The Scottish Cup hadn't been won since 1903 either, and to make things worse, Celtic were dominating the Scottish game. The previous season's Scottish Cup Final between the clubs had been declared void due to a riot by supporters, robbing Rangers of the chance to finally claim one of the major honours. Manager William Wilton had decided to look down south for the players to end this famine; as well as English international Hogg, he had also signed Willie Reid who had most recently been playing at Portsmouth, and English goalkeeper Herbert Lock was brought in from Southampton. This was an Edwardian version of the Souness revolution that excited Scottish football many decades later.

Wilton now had an array of attacking talent at his disposal, as along with Reid and Hogg there were wide men Alec Bennett and Alec Smith, and he decided Hogg would mainly play as inside-right with Bennett on the wing. But Hogg's first season at Ibrox didn't go to plan. League form was inconsistent and losing the first two away games meant the team were behind from early on. Hogg's first goal came in one of those defeats, at Airdrie, with his first Ibrox goals being a brace against Partick Thistle in the Glasgow Cup. His first experience of the Old Firm match came in the final, but it was a disappointing day as the match was lost 1-0. Rangers ended the season third in the title race, Hogg missed most of the end of the season due to injury, and the trophy cabinet remained bare. His personal highlight was scoring at Parkhead on New Year's Day to earn a creditable 1-1 draw. Overall, 1909/10 saw Hogg score eight goals in 30 appearances. But with no silverware, it was another season of disappointment, and one that Rangers in 1910/11 were determined to put right.

Alex Bennett was moved to inside-left by now, allowing Hogg to occupy his favourite position wide on the right, and it was a move that paid off. Rangers started the season well and were now genuine title challengers. But the first real sign of a possible change in the balance of power came in the Glasgow Cup Final on 8 October when again the opposition were the men from Parkhead. A crowd of 65,000 at Hampden saw an inspired Rangers performance, and although Hogg didn't put the ball in the net he played an important part in a devastating first 30 minutes when Rangers found the Celtic net three times through Smith, Bennett and Reid. The final score of 3-1 meant Hogg had his first medal in Scottish football, and it wouldn't be his last.

The next meeting with Celtic came just three weeks later in the league at Parkhead as Hogg settled a titanic struggle with the only goal. He then scored six goals in his next four starts as Rangers took top spot in the title race. Hogg appeared in all but four of the 34 league games played in 1910/11, and his 14 goals were a significant factor in the championship finally returning to Ibrox after nine long years. Sadly, his goal against holders Dundee in the Scottish Cup wasn't enough to prevent another early exit in the competition, but the season was rounded off in style on 10 May when Hogg enjoyed another cup final win over Celtic, this time a 2-1 victory in the Charity Cup thanks to two goals by the prolific Willie Reid.

Rangers lined up for season 1911/12 as holders of three trophies.

Hogg was to be a mainstay of the team again that season, and it was again one where he contributed to trophy success. He scored in each of the first three league games of the season, and in October a Hogg goal won the Glasgow Cup Final in a tight affair with Partick Thistle. By the new year he had scored in 12 different games, including his first Rangers hat-trick, on 30 December 1911 against Kilmarnock. The league title would be won with games to spare; Rangers able to afford three defeats in their last five matches and still finish a comfortable six points clear. The Scottish Cup, however, would still prove elusive with a second-round defeat to Clyde, a second defeat in three seasons to the team trained by Bill Struth. Hogg's contribution to the title was beyond question with a career-high 18 league goals in just 30 starts. His season ended prematurely, though, his last appearance being in late March against Raith Rovers where he picked up an injury meaning he had to sit out the Charity Cup competition, which was won by Celtic.

Hogg was now reaching the veteran stage of his career, and his final Ibrox season saw him miss several spells due to injuries, giving a new young future star in James Paterson his opportunity to stake a first-team claim. Hogg started the season still the first-choice right-winger and again scored on the opening day, against Airdrie. He also repeated his feat of the previous season by scoring in another Glasgow Cup Final win, a 3-1 victory over Celtic with the other goals scored by Alec Smith and Alec Bennett. He played in the new year defeat to Celtic, then lost his place to Paterson, and this coincided with a string of victories that saw Rangers ease clear at the top of the table. However, a disappointing Scottish Cup defeat at the hands of eventual winners Falkirk in late February saw the manager recall Hogg to the side. His last appearance in a Rangers shirt was on 24 March 1913 at Cathkin Park against Third Lanark, and it was fitting he scored the game's only goal, meaning in total he had scored a very good 52 goals in 126 starts. He had contributed five goals in 16 games in the league, and earned a third winners' medal in succession as Rangers retained the title by four points from Celtic.

Overall, Hogg had added three league titles, three Glasgow Cups and one Charity Cup to the English First Division and Charity Shield medals from his time at Sunderland.

Nearing his 34th birthday, Rangers allowed Hogg to leave the club in the close-season and he signed for Dundee in the summer of 1913. His one season there was relatively successful, scoring an excellent 17 goals in 34 games to help them to a much-improved seventh-place finish. In the summer of 1914 he was approached by Raith Rovers and offered the position of player-manager, which he accepted, but his stay there was extremely brief as on the declaration of war he decided to return home to the north-east of England and work as a fitter in an engineering works in Heaton, Newcastle-upon-Tyne, to aid the war effort. He made the occasional guest appearance with Dundee during the war years.

Once hostilities ended, Hogg was approached by St Mirren and offered a playing contract despite him being close to his 40th birthday. He declined this offer and instead took on a coaching position at lowly Montrose, still making the occasional appearance. His last appearances as a player came in 1921 when he started nine games for Dundee United, scoring twice. Hogg then moved permanently into coaching, firstly at Wolverhampton Wanderers, and he was part of the backroom team at Sunderland for several years before a final stint at Barnsley in the early 1930s. When he left football, he became a pub landlord in the Sunderland area.

Hogg was part of a reasonably successful footballing family. His brother Jack played for Sheffield United and Southampton, and his son William played for Bradford City.

Billy Hogg passed away on 30 January 1937 at the age of 57.

- A title winner once in England and three times for Rangers
- Winner of the Charity Shield, three Glasgow Cups and the Charity Cup
- Played for England four times, including being on the pitch the day of the terrible first Ibrox disaster
- An England international brought to Ibrox to bring back the glory years, and he succeeded
- Played until into his 40s, and was scoring goals in professional football for over 22 years
- Part of the first English revolution at Rangers

27   BILLY WILLIAMSON

The sailor with the unique Scottish Cup Final record for Rangers

BILLY WILLIAMSON was born on 12 February 1922 in Lenzie. A keen sportsman, he excelled at rugby and football, representing Lenzie Academy in both. For a while many friends and family thought he might have preferred to pursue a life playing the oval ball game, but football won the battle and he signed for junior team Kirkintilloch Rob Roy in 1939 aged 17. He was also a student teacher at Jordanhill College, which exempted him from a call-up when war broke out later that year. His football career had a brief spell at Petershill Juniors before signing for Bill Struth's Rangers in the late summer of 1941.

His first appearance for the club, in those dark wartime days, was a Glasgow Cup semi-final against old rivals Celtic. He played at inside-right in a stirring 3-2 win watched by 15,000 fans, the 19-year-old starting alongside legends like Tiger Shaw, Scot Symon, Dougie Gray and Jerry Dawson. He scored his first competitive goal for the club in a Southern League win over Airdrie later in the year, but his football career was put on the back burner when he decided to enlist in the Royal Navy, seeing active service while carrying out his main duty of being a ship PE Instructor.

During the conflict, he continued to turn out on the football pitch during periods of leave, playing 13 times for Rangers between 1942 and the war ending in the summer of 1945, and considerably more times for Manchester City where he played as a guest player. He enjoyed another Old Firm win during the hostilities, appearing in a 3-1 New Year's Day win at Parkhead. On leaving the Navy, he returned to Ibrox full time and became a regular starter in the last of the seasons of wartime competition in 1945/46.

Nicknamed 'Sailor' by his team-mates, Williamson made a scorching start to his reborn Rangers career. His versatility meant he was deployed in either inside-forward position or at centre-forward, but no matter where chosen by Struth he was making a significant impact. He scored seven goals in his first six starts, mainly at number nine, and these included two doubles against Celtic. The first was a 3-1 Glasgow Cup semi-final in front of 50,000 at Ibrox with the other goal coming from George Young, the second a 5-3 home win in the Southern League before 51,000 with Venters, Duncanson and Johnston sharing the other goals.

But despite his contribution, the number nine shirt had a natural owner, and the return of Willie Thornton to the club following his wartime service saw the manager more often selecting the legendary goalscorer, and Williamson rotating in and out the team. He still played 39 times overall that season across a variety of competitions, winning a Southern League medal, and scoring an impressive 22 goals. He also started in the iconic Ibrox friendly against Moscow Dynamo.

The rest of Williamson's Rangers career mostly followed this pattern – never really the undisputed choice, but a regular, dependable and effective deputy.

He only made ten starts in the first post-war season of 1946/47 but left his mark. In the league, Rangers were vying for the title with an excellent Hibs team. Williamson was recalled to the side in March 1947 for a Hampden League Cup semi-final game against Hibs after four months in the reserves, a match played just a few days after a Scottish Cup loss to the same opponents. Williamson didn't score, but played his part in a convincing 3-1 win in front of over 123,000 supporters. He kept his place and the following week scored four times as a 5-0 win over Clyde took Rangers to within an inch of the championship.

The following Saturday, 5 April 1947, saw Rangers face Aberdeen at Hampden in the first Scottish League Cup Final. Rangers cruised to a 4-0 win in front of 82,500 fans with Williamson carving a place in history by being among the scorers. He didn't play enough games for a league medal, but seven goals from just ten starts was an excellent return.

Season 1947/48 couldn't have started much better with an opening-day League Cup sectional tie at Ibrox against Celtic in front of 75,000 fans leading to a 2-0 Rangers win and Williamson scoring both goals. But despite six goals in his first six games, he lost his regular place, although he was picked for the first Old Firm league clash of the season in late September and opened the scoring in another 2-0 success. But after a shock defeat to St Mirren in late October, Struth didn't select him for months. Rangers reached the

Scottish Cup Final, and on Saturday, 17 April fought out a 1-1 draw with Morton before almost 132,000 people. For the midweek replay, Struth decided to replace inside-forward Willie Findlay and bring Williamson in from the cold. This would be his first Scottish Cup game for Rangers.

The replay attracted 133,750 spectators, and it was a tense affair with few chances. Extra time was needed and as the clock reached 115 minutes a second replay looked inevitable. Then a long, raking Torry Gillick pass found Eddie Rutherford on the wing. Rutherford, playing instead of the injured Willie Waddell, sent over an inviting cross, and the in-rushing Williamson leapt high to crash home an unstoppable header sending most of the huge crowd into delirium. The cup was won; what a first game in the competition for the most reliable of deputies.

The following season followed a familiar pattern with long spells out the team, but a telling contribution when selected. He only started 12 times, but one of these was on 16 October 1948 when an enormous 105,000 attended a League Cup game at Ibrox against Celtic and Williamson scored as Rangers won 2-1. Rangers went on to lift the League Cup but he was on the sidelines for the final victory over Raith Rovers. He hadn't started for five months when recalled for a vital league match at home to Albion Rovers as the league race with Dundee went to the wire. Sailor scored after just three minutes, setting up the win. The following week was Scottish Cup Final day, and after not playing in any of the other rounds, Williamson lined up at inside-left against Clyde. He had scored in the 1948 final in his first Scottish Cup match. He then scored in the 1949 final in his second match in the competition, the second Rangers goal in a 4-1 triumph. Two cup ties, two finals, two goals, two winners' medals.

Williamson played in the last two league games after the final; he didn't score, but was on the pitch when the title was won at Albion Rovers, the 4-1 last-day win securing the first treble in Scottish football.

Williamson had two Scottish Cup medals and a League Cup medal by now, and in 1949/50 he completed the set. He scored against Celtic in the semi-final of the Glasgow Cup and played in the final win over Clyde. He scored another against Celtic in a thumping 4-0 league win, and started 19 league games, enough for a medal when the title was won. In those 19 games he scored 11 times, and he added five more in the Scottish Cup, including one in the semi-final, but that wasn't enough to give him a place in the final victory over East Fife. He also showed his great sportsmanship in the League Cup semi-final, when with Rangers losing to East Fife at Hampden and time running out, he kicked the ball out of play to allow treatment for an injured opponent. The practice is common now, but had never been seen at that time.

Season 1950/51 was Williamson's last in Royal Blue and apart from a brief spell in November 1950 he was rarely selected. Williamson played his last Rangers game on 24 February 1951, a 3-1 defeat at Raith Rovers. After ten years, 130 games and 70 goals, he was transferred later that week to St Mirren. After just over a year in Paisley he moved on to Stirling Albion where he played for three seasons. Undoubtedly the biggest result of his career there was a shock 2-0 win over Rangers in the league in September 1953, the last season of Struth's Ibrox reign.

Williamson retired in 1956 aged 34, returning to his old school, Lenzie Academy, as a PE teacher. He was to become head of PE for boys, and an assistant rector, alongside his wife Mary, who was PE head for girls. His love of sport, and of Rangers, remained through his lifetime. He played rugby until in his 40s. He was a three-handicap golfer, an active member of the Scottish Schools Athletics Association, the Scottish Schools Cross-Country Championship organisation committee, and the Scottish Schools Rugby Association. He also enjoyed curling and orienteering in his spare time.

And all the while, he was a passionate supporter of Rangers, a regular at Ibrox and a shareholder.

Williamson passed away in February 2006, just short of his 84th birthday.

- Cup final goalscoring hero
- Treble winner
- Devoted Ranger
- War hero
- Sportsman
- Much more than just a deputy

28   BOB BLYTH

The man who shaped a famous English club and whose nephew was a legendary manager

BOB BLYTH was born in Glenbuck, Ayrshire in October 1869, and was a team member of the famous Glenbuck Cherrypickers, playing alongside members of his extended family, also appearing for Glenbuck Athletic in 1888. In 1889 he moved to England and joined Middlesbrough Ironopolis, before returning to Scotland with Cowlairs in 1890. He then signed for joint Scottish champions Rangers in 1891.

A wing-half, Blyth made his Rangers debut in a Glasgow Cup tie against Third Lanark in September of that year, impressing in a 2-0 victory. He kept his place in the team for the next couple of months, scoring his first goal in a 2-1 win over Cambuslang in the league, but then suffered an injury after scoring in a thumping 5-1 Scottish Cup success over St Bernard's in November. He didn't feature again in a competitive first-team match until almost two years later. He played six times in season 1893/94, his final appearance being a dismal 3-0 loss to old foes Third Lanark in the league on 23 December 1893. After 15 appearances and four goals, Rangers allowed him to leave in the 1894 close-season, with Blyth choosing to go back down south and join Preston North End.

After being the dominant force in English football at the beginning of the Football League, Preston had slumped to 14th place the previous season and were rebuilding in the search for former glories. Blyth made his Preston debut in September 1894 against Wolverhampton and went on to finally establish himself as a first team regular, being ever present in both 1895/96 and 1896/97. Although there were no trophies won, some respectability was restored with a fourth-place league finish and reaching the last eight in the FA Cup.

Blyth remained at Deepdale until 1901, except a very brief spell at Dundee, but relegation that year saw the end of his time there after 124 appearances and four goals. At the age of 32 he was then appointed player-manager of non-league Portsmouth, a move that started an association with the south coast club for the rest of his life. He also took on the added responsibility of being the team captain.

In his very first season, Blyth guided Pompey to the Southern League title, although this wasn't enough to gain election into the Football League itself. He also took the club to the quarter-final of the FA Cup, only losing to First Division side Derby County in a replay. Blyth remained manager for two more seasons and although they achieved two more top four finishes in the Southern League, their dream of joining the Football League remained out of reach. He retired as manager in the summer of 1904; to this day his win record is second-best of any manager in Portsmouth's history.

Blyth remained at the club as a director, and finally saw Portsmouth achieve league status in 1920, when he was vice-chairman. By 1929, Portsmouth had won the Third Division South, had been promoted out of the Second Division, and were a top-flight club, with Blyth now chairman. It was a proud day on 27 April 1929, when he watched his team compete in their first FA Cup Final, although it saw a a 2-0 loss to Bolton Wanderers.

Blyth remains the only man in Portsmouth history to hold every significant position at the club: player, captain, manager, director, vice-chairman and chairman. He stepped aside in the 1930s with Portsmouth an established top-ten club, allowing him to concentrate on a growing business empire of several hotels in the city. He passed away in the St James Hospital in his adopted city in February 1941 after a short illness aged 71. Sadly, he never got to see Portsmouth become champions of England towards the end of that decade, but his name was toasted by all at the club during the celebrations.

Blyth also had another famous football connection. Back in the village of Glenbuck, his sister Barbara had married a local man, John Shankly, and they had ten children: five boys and five girls. Among those nieces and nephews, Blyth must have been proud to watch on as all five boys made careers in football. Two of them became legends in the game.

Bob Shankly was a successful player and manager of Falkirk before going on to be the manager of the great Dundee team of the early 1960s who won the league title and reached the semi-finals of the European Cup. And the youngest nephew was a man still revered to this day as the architect of the modern Liverpool, the legendary Bill Shankly, an international player and an all-time great manager who won multiple trophies and started a dynasty.

Bob Blyth may be a minor and forgettable footnote in the history of our great club, but he left his mark on the wider game and was part of a football family famous the world over.

- A Ranger for three years but only made 15 appearances
- Player, captain, manager and chairman of Portsmouth
- The first member of an iconic footballing family

29   BOBBY NEILL

The scorer of the 'perfect' Rangers penalty

THE CALTON area of Glasgow isn't a place usually linked to Rangers, but in September 1875 a man was born there who would go on to score the most important goal of the greatest season in club history. His name was Robert Scott Gibson Neill.

Bobby Neill started his football career as a centre-half for junior club Glasgow Ashfield, and although short for a defender at only 5ft 4in he was attracting the attention of senior clubs with his pace, strength and decisive tackling. In 1894 he moved east to sign for Hibernian, where he played for two seasons. His last match for the Leith club was the 1896 Scottish Cup Final, but it was not a happy occasion as Hibs lost to rivals Hearts 3-1.

Neill was now an international, his first Scotland appearance coming in a 4-0 win over Wales in March 1896 when he scored twice. During his first season at Easter Road, Neill had played one match on loan at Liverpool when the English club were without several regulars, and in the summer of 1896 he moved permanently to Merseyside. In his only season down south, Neill played 26 times, scoring three goals, including a winner in a tense FA Cup tie away to West Bromwich Albion. Liverpool reached the semi-finals of the competition, but Neill's hopes of appearing in another national cup final were ended by Aston Villa, who beat them 3-0 at Bramall Lane. He played his last game for Liverpool a few weeks later on 10 April 1897 against Preston North End, after which a family bereavement caused him to ask Liverpool for a transfer, and he returned to his native city in late April 1897 to join Rangers.

This was a Rangers team who were just starting on their first sustained spell of dominance in Scottish football, with the 1896/97 season drawing to a close and both the Glasgow Cup and Scottish Cup already won, although they finished third in the league behind Hearts and Hibs.

Neill made his Rangers debut away to Clyde in the Glasgow League on 8 May, a very comfortable first appearance in blue as their opponents were demolished 7-0. But three days later came his first big test, a Charity Cup semi-final against Celtic at Hampden. Neill gave a solid performance in a highly impressive 4-1 victory before 20,000 fans, with legends John 'Kitey' McPherson and Alec Smith among the goals. A dream start to his Rangers career was complete a week later when Neill won his first medal, Third Lanark being hammered 6-1 in the competition final.

Neill added Glasgow Cup and Scottish Cup medals to his collection in 1897/98, and also took on the responsibility as the preferred penalty taker. His first success from the spot a vital one against Celtic in a 1-1 draw in the semi-final of the Glasgow Cup. Neill then converted another in the 4-0 win over Queen's Park in the final. He scored seven times that season, four of them penalties. One of these came in a 12-0 Scottish Cup win over lowly Cartvale, with Kilmarnock being the team who Rangers beat in the final by a more conventional scoreline of 2-0.

Rangers had finished second in the league behind Celtic in 1897/98, and were determined to go one better as 1898/99 got under way. This was to become a league campaign that would go down in not just the history of the club but in the world of football. Neill played every minute of all 18 matches and was one of five players to be ever present as Rangers racked up win after win. The first big test came on 24 September 1898 at Parkhead. Rangers stunned the 45,000 crowd with a quite devastating display, hammering the defending champions 4-0, including Neill scoring from the spot.

By mid-November, Rangers still had a 100 per cent record with ten straight wins. A trip to Easter Road on 19 November was seen as a tough test, and so it proved. The perfect record looked to be over as Hibs raced into a two-goal lead but William Wilton's men refused to concede defeat, and as the 89th minute began the scores were level at 3-3 and Rangers were pushing hard for a winner. A foul in the penalty box on centre-forward Robert Hamilton saw the referee award a spot-kick. This looked to be the last kick of the game. It was a penalty to either maintain the incredible perfect winning run or see a point finally dropped. Neill stepped up to take it as many on the pitch and among the 10,000 crowd held their breath. His strike was hard and true, and the Rangers players celebrated wildly as the goal won the points.

After such a scare, those who missed the return fixture against Hibs must have thought the newspapers had misprinted the scoreline. On Christmas Eve, Rangers wrapped up the title with a 10-0 win over the Easter Road team, and then had three more games to play. First, St Mirren were dispatched 3-2, then on 2 January 1899 Celtic visited Ibrox. A crowd of 30,000 attended, knowing this would be the day Rangers could make history look inevitable, and although their great rivals were determined to spoil the party the men in blue simply overpowered them. Nothing was to stand in the way of the quest for perfect season immortality as a hat-trick by Hamilton and a strike by Johnny Campbell gave Rangers a convincing 4-1 win.

On 7 January 1899, Neill and his team-mates lined up at Shawfield against Clyde, one win from completing the 100 per cent season. The result was never in serious doubt; a Neill penalty one of the goals in a 3-0 win. As the players, officials and fans celebrated a unique achievement, the name of Bobby Neill was toasted especially as the significance of that last minute Easter Road penalty was remembered.

In all, Neill played 180 games for Rangers, scoring 15 penalties among his 33 goals. He added further league medals in seasons 1899/1900, 1900/01 and 1901/02. His last

Rangers goal wasn't a penalty, and it came on New Year's Day 1903 in a thrilling 3-3 draw against Celtic. His appearances became infrequent in 1903/04, and he made his last start for the club on 30 January 1904 in a 2-1 defeat at Hearts.

Neill briefly moved to Airdrie but then decided to seek his fortune in Canada, giving up football and emigrating to Montreal in 1904. In 1909, the <u>Montreal Daily Witness</u> published an article on him as he occasionally turned out for local sides, and in his interview he stated, 'I played football for many years. The dear old Glasgow Rangers was my team.'

He returned to Scotland shortly afterwards, becoming a restaurant owner in Govan. Sadly, Neill took ill in early 1913, and passed away on 2 March aged only 37. The cause of his death was listed as chronic alcoholism.

- Rangers career: 1897–1904
- 180 appearances
- 33 goals
- 4 league titles
- 1 Scottish Cup
- 3 Glasgow Cups
- 2 Charity Cups
- 2 Scotland caps
- Scorer of the 'perfect' penalty

30   BOBBY PARKER

The Rangers deputy who became a hero on Merseyside and in the Great War

BOBBY PARKER was born in Possilpark in Glasgow in March 1891. Like many promising youngsters of that time, his playing career started in Junior football when at 16 years old the centre-forward signed for local side Ashfield. Already one of the Junior game's successful clubs, the arrival of the young scoring sensation propelled Ashfield to an even more impressive haul of trophies. The Glasgow Junior League was won in each of Parker's three seasons, and he ended his career with them by leading the line in the 1910 Junior Cup Final victory over Kilwinning Rangers at Firhill.

By now, Parker was one of the most sought-after players in the country, and in the summer of 1910 William Wilton added to his firepower by signing the forward for Rangers. Despite the powerful Parker being more than ready to take on the challenge of scoring the goals to bring the title back to Ibrox for the first time since 1902, manager Wilton already had a supreme goalscorer at his disposal in the great Willie Reid, who had scored eight goals in the final seven games of the previous season.

Reid started the 1910/11 season at centre-forward, but after scoring just twice in the first four matches the manager decided to try a Reid and Parker pairing against Aberdeen at Ibrox on 17 September, giving the youngster his debut in Royal Blue. It wasn't a dream start for Parker; his all-action physical presence made an impression but Rangers crashed to a 4-2 defeat despite Reid hitting a brace. Parker was back in the reserves the following week, and there he stayed for months as Reid and Rangers hit a rich vein of goalscoring. In his next 13 games Reid scored 20 times, including a crucial goal in a Glasgow Cup Final win over Celtic. As the Ibrox side built up an unstoppable title winning run, Parker only made one more appearance, replacing the injured Reid to score his first Rangers goal in a 4-0 home win over Queen's Park on 18 March 1911. Only two appearances, with one goal, was not enough for a medal as Rangers roared to the title. Reid ended the season with an amazing 38 league goals in his 33 starts.

Season 1911/12 followed the same pattern of Rangers consistently winning, Reid consistently scoring, and Parker watching on. Parker finally was given a start in January against Aberdeen when Reid was unfit, and he scored a vital goal in a 2-0 win. However, Reid was back the next week. Rangers again won the title and this time Parker managed three starts, scoring twice. Reid, meanwhile, hit 33 including three hat-tricks and two four-goal hauls.

The next season saw Parker feature more. Reid suffered several injuries while again regularly hitting the opposition net. Parker finally played in a match against Celtic, a painful single-goal defeat on New Year's Day 1913, but he took advantage of a longer first-team run later in the month when he hit successive hat-tricks against Hibs and Motherwell, and Wilton kept him in the starting XI when Reid returned for a Scottish Cup replay against Hamilton. Rangers won 2-0, Parker scoring a penalty. They both started again in the next round, a terrible 3-1 home loss to Falkirk. Despite it being Parker who scored the Rangers goal, he found himself dropped again with Reid back leading the line. Parker ended that season with 12 league goals from only nine starts, enough for a first championship medal.

Parker was growing increasingly frustrated at being an understudy, not helped by him scoring twice in only three irregular starts in the opening months of 1913/14. His last Rangers appearance saw him score in a 3-2 Ibrox win over Dumbarton before he was on the move in a £1,500 transfer to Everton. In his four seasons as a Rangers player, Parker had started only 22 games but scored a very impressive 20 times.

Everton had gone through a disappointing time, finishing out of the top ten in both of the previous English First Division seasons, and were desperate for a hero. Bobby Parker became that hero. He made his debut at Goodison Park on 6 December, making an instant impact with the only Everton goal in a draw with Sheffield Wednesday. Everton played to Parker's strengths, getting the ball into the penalty box quickly and allowing the Glaswegian to use his strength and aggression to create chances. He hit his first Everton hat-trick in a 5-0 Boxing Day thrashing of Manchester United. Parker ended the season with 17 goals, and although not helping Everton back into the top ten there were signs of better days ahead.

And those days were better than any Evertonian could have dreamed. After an inconsistent start, the Merseyside derby on 3 October 1914 sparked an incredible run. Liverpool hadn't won at Goodison in the 20th century and never looked like changing that statistic, with a Parker hat-trick the highlight of a 5-0 hammering. By Christmas, he had scored hat-tricks against Sunderland and Manchester City and all four in a win over Sheffield Wednesday. He also scored hat-tricks after New Year against Aston Villa and Bolton.

The title was now just a point away, and it was fitting that Parker scored one of the goals in a 2-2 draw at Chelsea that gave Everton their second championship. He ended as the division's top scorer with a magnificent 35 league goals, plus two more in the FA Cup.

Parker was the hottest goalscorer in England, but by now football had become secondary as war engulfed Europe. He enlisted as a private in the 4th Battalion Royal Scots Fusiliers. He made one guest appearance for Rangers against Partick Thistle in January 1916 before being transported to the front line. Later that year he suffered a severe injury, being hit in the back by a German bullet. Such was the extent of his injuries that he was transported back to Britain for extensive and painful treatment, and his war was over.

Parker bravely tried to resurrect his football career after the war. Having scored 55 goals in 65 games for Everton before the conflict, expectations were high that he would be the Goodison match winner again.

His first game back was in the derby at Anfield, and although he scored in a 3-1 defeat he lacked the mobility and aggression of years gone by. Given the scale of human loss the public had endured, the news of Parker's war injury was not widely known. This would explain some critical headlines in the local press, describing his play as 'unimpressive'. He still managed 16 goals in 27 games, but in 1921 he was released and joined Nottingham Forest. He contributed eight goals as Forest won the Second Division, but he only played intermittently before ending his playing days at Highland League Fraserburgh in 1925.

This wasn't the end of Parker's football career, however, as he accepted an offer from Bohemians of Dublin to become their manager. Parker was as much an instant hit in their dugout as he was in the Everton forward line. In 1927/28 he led his club to an unprecedented clean sweep of domestic honours – the League of Ireland, FAI Cup, FAI Shield and Leinster Senior Cup.

But Parker had never fully recovered from his wartime injury, and he drifted away from the game as his health deteriorated.

A *Football ECHO* report soon after the end of World War Two, 20 years after his managerial record season, recalled, 'Bobby Parker today lies at his Dublin home, a cripple through a hole in his back – the last-but-one-war caused this. Everton FC, to their everlasting glory, have never said a word about it, but I will tell you they have pensioned Bobby Parker all these years – a good deed done, without stealth or advertisement.'

The pain ended for Parker in 1950 when he died aged 59.

- Junior Cup winner
- Scottish league winner with Rangers, averaging almost a goal a game for the club
- English league top scorer
- English league winner with Everton, and still one of the best goal ratios in their history

- Suffered a life-changing injury in the Great War
- Irish clean sweep manager

31 CHARLES HEGGIE

Scorer of four goals in his only Scotland appearance

CHARLES HEGGIE was born in Glasgow on 26 September 1862, his school days coinciding with the beginnings of organised football in Scotland. Like many at the time, he was bitten by the football bug as a teenager he played as a defender for Govan based team Ailsa FC, then another local team, South Western FC. At the age of 19, in the summer of 1882, he became a Rangers player.

These were the days before league football, so much of the opposition and many of the competitions he played in no longer exist. His competitive Rangers debut was on 9 September 1882 in the first round of the Scottish Cup away to Jordanhill in a comfortable 4-0 win. However, his debut Scottish Cup season came to an end a few weeks later when a tough away tie at Queen's Park was lost 3-2. The Hampden team also knocked Rangers out of the Charity Cup, as the club endured some difficult times.

The following season Heggie was a mainstay of the team who reached the semi-final of the Scottish Cup, and played in the historic 14-2 win over Whitehill in the second round, which remains the joint biggest win in Rangers' history. Heggie was among the scorers in the quarter-final win against Cambuslang before a disappointing three-goal defeat to Vale of Leven in the last four. He played in the 1883 Charity Cup Final against Queen's Park as Rangers looked to win the trophy for the second time in their short history, but the day could hardly have gone worse for Heggie, who was not only on the end of a sound 4-1 beating but also had the misfortune to score an own goal just before half-time that allowed Queen's Park to equalise, and they then dominated the game.

Things changed for Heggie in 1884 when during an injury crisis he was pushed up front as an emergency centre-forward. The tall, rangy Heggie was a revelation, scoring 13 times in the various competitive and friendly games of the time. Even when the more regular forward players were fit again, Rangers kept Heggie in the front line.

By 1885/86 Heggie was a forward who opponents feared. He scored a highly impressive 29 goals and was now being talked about as a possible international player. In March 1886, he was selected in the reserve list for the upcoming match with Ireland in Belfast.

Before the game, Harrower of Queen's Park was forced to withdraw, and Heggie was promoted to the forward line to win his first cap. His international bow came on 20 March, and what a debut it was.

Heggie scored after 15 minutes. Ten minutes later he had a hat-trick, and on the hour he scored his fourth. Scotland cruised to a 7-2 victory and Heggie was the man of the match. Incredibly, he never played for Scotland again. You would think that scoring four goals in a sole Scotland appearance would surely be a record never equalled, but it actually happened again just two years later to William Dickson of Strathmore, who later starred for Sunderland, Aston Villa and Stoke City.

Heggie lined up that day alongside his Rangers team-mate, defender John Cameron, who was also winning his first Scotland cap. Like Heggie, this was to be his one and only appearance in his national team colours.

Later in 1886, Heggie scored the only goal as Rangers beat Everton in the FA Cup in a famous season where the club reached the semi-finals of England's foremost competition. This was a match that Everton later claimed to have scratched from taking part and instead only played as a friendly, but regardless of the match status it was Heggie who scored the only goal.

But Heggie rarely featured in the team after the arrival of 1887 due to a disagreement with the club which even made the pages of the press. One sports publication reported, 'It is an open secret that the Rangers and C. Heggie, their crack centre are at loggerheads. It would not reflect credit on either party if we rehearsed the cause of this unfortunate breach, but the sooner it is satisfactorily bridged over the better for all concerned. The Rangers, from present appearances and performances, can't get on very well without Heggie, although they may imagine so and Heggie shows to most advantage when he is in harness. Come down from your stools both of you and don't spoil by your stiffneckedness a season that has opened auspiciously, and which under prudent management should end gloriously.'

Whatever the cause of their disagreement, Heggie did not play in the losing FA Cup semi-final against Aston Villa, and it was no surprise when in the summer of 1887 it was announced he was no longer a Rangers player.

Heggie joined Edinburgh club St Bernard's, but it appeared his heart was no longer in playing and a career that promised so much drifted into oblivion. He wasn't completely lost to football, however, turning out as an occasional referee.

Heggie had married his childhood sweetheart Mary in 1886 and they welcomed son William into the world in 1889. But their marriage was to end in a bitter separation, with Mary taking young William to America in 1892, settling in Detroit. Charlie decided also to go seek a new life abroad, with Australia being his destination. He became a dock worker in Fremantle near Perth, remarrying in 1906, and was a proud member of the Fremantle Lumpers Union for dock workers until his death at the age of 62 in Perth on 15 July 1925.

He was buried in Presbyterian Cemetery, Karrakatta, ending the story of a unique life.

- Rangers defender and forward
- Played in the club's biggest ever win
- Scored for Rangers in the Scottish Cup and the FA Cup
- 4 goals for Scotland in just one appearance
- Left the club in mysterious circumstances

32 DAVID MCLEAN

Played for Rangers and Celtic, and the first man to be top goalscorer in both the English and Scottish top divisions

DAVID MCLEAN was born in Forfar on 13 December 1890. Aged just 14 years old he was a first-team player at local side Forfar West End, and when he then joined Forfar Celtic in 1905 he was given a trial by Scottish champions Celtic. He didn't impress enough to be offered a contract, but Celtic kept an eye on the young centre-forward who had a highly impressive goals return. McLean joined Forfar Athletic next, and his goalscoring exploits there made Celtic think again. He signed for them on 16 April 1907, when aged just 16.

Celtic were Scotland's dominant team at the time, and in centre-forward Jimmy Quinn they had a reliable and experienced goalscorer. McLean was seen as his long-term successor, and he was given a first-team debut on 26 October 1907 when still aged only 16 years and 317 days. Even now, he remains in the top ten youngest Celtic debutants. And what a first game to play in, a second replay of the Glasgow Cup Final against Rangers. A crowd of 56,000 at Hampden saw Celtic win 2-1 and the young unknown McLean score what proved to be the winning goal with a fierce shot.

He kept his place in the team for the next game, a league match at Parkhead against Port Glasgow Athletic. McLean scored a hat-trick. Overall, he started in ten league games that season, which saw Celtic champions again. He added eight more goals to his tally, including doubles against St Mirren, Clyde and Partick. He started a further 13 times the following season, hitting the net eight times as Celtic retained the title. But there were signs that McLean did not see eye to eye with the Celtic manager, Willie Maley. The pair had a dressing-room row in September after a 4-4 draw with Queen's Park when McLean felt the criticism he got from the imposing Maley was unfair as he had scored twice. Their relationship wasn't helped by the fact McLean was insistent that he should be the first-choice centre-forward despite his young age. Maley showed who was in charge by not selecting McLean for a single Scottish Cup tie that season, and when McLean was only selected in half of the first eight matches at the start of 1909/10, he made his feelings clear again. Maley decided that no player could dictate to him, and he sold McLean to Preston North End in November 1909 for a fee of £400.

As well as his unhappiness over team selection, McLean also voiced his disapproval on several occasions about another aspect of life at Celtic. He was a Protestant and found it difficult when regular money collections were sought by local Catholic church representatives in the dressing room. While respecting the club's support of these charity donations, McLean felt pressurised into donating when he would rather not have done so. It's not known if his public conversations on this matter were a factor in Maley's decision.

In the years to come, many Celtic fans thought the decision to sell McLean had been the wrong one. He had been their youngest goalscorer, their youngest hat-trick scorer, and their youngest player to score in an Old Firm match. Still only 19, he had played 29 competitive games for Celtic and scored 22 times. He continued this scoring form down south and in just a season and a half at Preston, McLean hit 25 league goals. Given his importance to the team, it came as a surprise that Preston accepted an offer for him in 1911 from The Wednesday – later to become Sheffield Wednesday – and the player was on the move again.

McLean was a sensation in Sheffield. In his first season there, he hit 25 league goals and was the division's joint top goalscorer with Harry Hampton of Aston Villa and George Holley of Sunderland. Wednesday ended the season in fifth place while his former club Preston got relegated. If that was impressive, the next season was even better. McLean hit 30 of Wednesday's 71 league goals, ending the season as the clear top scorer in the division. By the time football was suspended in 1915 due to the outbreak of the Great War, McLean had scored 100 goals for Wednesday in just 145 appearances. He was also a Scotland international, earning a cap in 1912 when he played against England at Hampden in front of over 127,000 fans.

With football in England suspended, McLean decided to return north to play as a guest in Scottish football, and he turned out for both Dykehead and Third Lanark. Then in the summer of 1918 he joined Rangers on loan for the season. Rangers had just won their first title since before the war after a dramatic final day. Most observers were predicting another close race with Celtic, and they proved to be correct.

McLean made his Rangers debut on 17 August 1918 at home to Falkirk. If there were any doubts about a former Celtic player leading the line they were immediately dispelled as he scored the game's only goal. He followed that up with a hat-trick in his next appearance, against Hearts, and by the end of September he had played in five league games, scored in them all, and was already on a total of nine. Some 11 years after that Glasgow Cup winning debut for Celtic, he then played in another Old Firm final in the competition, but this time wearing blue. He had a good game but wasn't a scorer as Rangers won 2-0. He ended 1918 by scoring four times against Kilmarnock, but his start to 1919 was a major reason why the title slipped away. A 1-1 draw with Celtic on 1 January was hard-fought and did no real damage, but he then played in two painful 1-0 defeats to Partick and Kilmarnock. Shortly afterwards, he picked up an injury that saw him miss two months of the campaign, during which Rangers dropped crucial points to Morton and Ayr United.

This put Celtic in pole position for the title, building a one-point lead with three games left. McLean started those last three and Rangers won them all by the same 4-0 scoreline. He scored one against Falkirk, two against Third Lanark, then a last day hat-trick against Clyde. But Celtic also won their final three games, a win at Ayr on the last day clinching the championship. Most Rangers fans were left to wonder what might have been if McLean had been fit for more games. He ended the season with 29 league goals from just 24 starts, which to this day remains the highest average strike rate for any Rangers player who played more than 20 games for the club. It also made him the league's top scorer for the season, meaning he became the first player to be top scorer in both the English and Scottish top divisions.

When the season ended, McLean returned to his parent club in Sheffield as English football was now resuming again. He only played three games for Wednesday before being sold to First Division rivals Bradford Park Avenue. Unsurprisingly, he ended 1919/20 as their top scorer with 18 goals. But the Bradford team were going through a difficult time and even McLean's goals couldn't prevent relegation in 1921, then again in 1922. Although now in his 30s, McLean had no desire to play in third-tier football, so after 49 league goals in 85 appearances in a poor team he returned north to sign for home team Forfar. His stay there was extremely short, moving on to Dundee where he again scored goals aplenty. McLean was their top scorer in 1922/23 with 22 goals, and he stayed at Dens Park until 1926.

The highlight of his time at Dens Park came in 1925, when he finally played in a Scottish Cup Final at the age of 34. The opposition were Celtic, and McLean shocked the majority of the 75,000 crowd by opening the scoring in the first half. Unfortunately they couldn't hold on, Celtic scoring twice in the second half to take the trophy.

In 1926, McLean left Dundee after adding another 43 goals to his career tally with them, and he returned to Forfar. He played there until 1931, his last match being on 5 September of that year against Arbroath. In his five years with his home club the veteran scored 76 goals in 153 games.

McLean's career had spanned 24 years, and he had played at the top level in Scotland and England. Including friendlies and wartime matches, he scored almost 500 goals. He scored 316 times in top-flight league football and is one of an elite band of players to have scored over 100 top flight goals north and south of the border.

Away from football, McLean was a keen cricketer, turning out regularly for the Strathmore club. His highlight in his other sporting love came in 1930 when the *Peter Pan* author J.M. Barrie opened the new pavilion, and McLean played against a team which included two of the touring Australian squad. He was also part of a football family, his brother George being an inside-forward with Huddersfield Town who finished runners-up to Arsenal in the First Division in 1934.

McLean spent the rest of his life in his beloved hometown of Forfar, and passed away on 23 December 1967 at the age of 77.

- Teenage sensation at Celtic
- The first man to be top scorer in the English and Scottish top divisions
- 29 league goals in just 24 Rangers games
- A winner in two Old Firm Glasgow Cup Finals, once for each team
- Scored almost 500 career goals

33   DAVID MITCHELL

The first Rangers captain to win the league and the Scottish Cup

THE RISE and successes of Rangers in the late 19th century featured many great players born in Ayrshire. Massively important men such as John 'Kitey' McPherson, Alec Smith, the McCreadie brothers and Nicol Smith are among them. And another man born in Ayrshire who left a historic legacy in Royal Blue was David Mitchell.

Mitchell was born in Kilmarnock on 29 April 1866. His passion for, and talent at, football was evident in his teens, and he joined Kilmarnock in 1886. After three years where he established himself in the left-half position, Mitchell made the move to Rangers for 1889/90, the final season in Scottish football before the start of league competition.

His competitive debut came in the Glasgow Cup first round on 21 September 1889 away to Pollokshaws, an easy start to his Rangers career as the hosts were defeated 5-1. His first goal for the club wasn't long in coming, scoring one of 13 goals in a Scottish Cup tie against the hapless Kelvinside Athletic the following week. Overall, he played in seven cup matches that first season, as well as several friendlies. And by the time the new Scottish league kicked off the following summer, the tough-tackling and inspirational Mitchell was now the team captain.

He lined up in his customary left-half position on 16 August 1890 when Rangers defeated Hearts 5-2 in the club's first league match. And he was an ever present that season, starting in all 18 matches, as a 4-1 win over Third Lanark in the final fixture meant Rangers and Dumbarton ended level on points at the top. As the rules dictated, a play-off was required, Mitchell leading out his team on 21 May 1891 at Cathkin Park before 10,000 fans to determine the first national champions. Despite taking a two-goal lead, the match ended in a thrilling 2-2 draw, the authorities then declaring the clubs joint champions. Mitchell's place in both Rangers' and Scottish football's history was secured as the first title-winning captain.

He stayed as captain and a mainstay of the team for many years. Season 1891/92 was one of disappointment even though he racked up 27 competitive starts. His only goal came in a thumping win over Queen's Park in the Charity Cup. Unfortunately he missed the final due to injury, and was helpless to prevent a 2-0 defeat by Celtic.

The following season saw him create another piece of club history. It wasn't in the league, where despite his 16 appearances Rangers slumped to two costly defeats in the closing stages, finishing runners-up behind Celtic by a single point. Nor was it in the Scottish Cup, a quarter-final loss to St Bernard's in January meaning the 19-year wait for the trophy went on. This time it was in the Glasgow Cup. Northern, Linthouse, Queen's Park and Partick Thistle were all defeated, setting up a final date with Celtic on 18 February 1893. This was a trophy Rangers had yet to win, and standing in their way was the rival who they had not yet beaten in any competitive match.

But everything changed in the Hampden Park rain. Mitchell's team-mates were men possessed, and goals by John Barker, Neil Kerr and John McPherson gave Rangers a convincing 3-1 win. Mitchell was able to claim the honour of being the first man to lift this old trophy for the club.

The following season saw Mitchell being captain in more momentous days. Celtic were thrashed 5-0 in September, a first league win over them and Cowlairs were defeated 1-0 in the Glasgow Cup Final in December, the first trophy Rangers retained. But although he had now lifted three major honours, like all at the club it was the Scottish Cup that Mitchell most wanted. In 1893/94, Rangers went on an impressive run in the competition. League form was inconsistent but Cowlairs, Leith Athletic and Clyde were swept aside to set up a semi-final with Queen's Park, still a major force in Scotland. A tense but deserved replay victory meant the first Scottish Cup Final for Rangers since 1879, and inevitably the opposition was to be Celtic. On 2 February 1894, Mitchell was skipper at Hampden as Rangers looked to finally triumph in the cup at the 20th time of asking. After a nervous and hard-fought first half, Rangers hit their rivals with a devastating three-goal burst in just 13 minutes with Hugh McCreadie, John Barker and John McPherson all scoring. A late consolation was soon forgotten as Mitchell collected the Scottish Cup in front of the wildly celebrating Rangers support in the 17,000 crowd.

Mitchell remained the first-choice left-half in the next two seasons, with almost 40 appearances over the period despite a significant spell injured. Rangers didn't add to their trophy haul during this time but did change captain. The team was now led by John McPherson, even though Mitchell was still a regular. And Mitchell played a big part in bringing more silverware to the club. He played 35 competitive games in 1896/97, more than any other season in his Ibrox career. His one goal came against St Mirren in the league, but that certainly wasn't the highlight. In November 1896 he starred in a thrilling Glasgow Cup Final replay win over Celtic when two Peter Turnbull goals clinched victory. Then in March 1897 he started his second Scottish Cup Final, gaining his second winners' medal in a magnificent 5-1 hammering of Dumbarton, before rounding off a hat-trick of cup successes in May when he won Rangers' first Charity Cup in 18 years when Celtic were hammered 4-1 in the semi-final then Third Lanark thrashed 6-1 in the final. Mitchell and new captain McPherson became the first Rangers players to win all four of the main competitions the club competed in.

Season 1897/98 saw Mitchell still starting most games, but now in his early 30s he did miss occasional fixtures. He scored twice in 28 starts, with only 11 of these in the league, and he added to his impressive medal haul. The Glasgow Cup was retained with a comfortable win over Queen's Park, and the Scottish Cup retained for the first time with a straightforward 2-0 victory over Kilmarnock. And Mitchell had one more historic Rangers achievement still to come.

Rangers' 1898/99 season is legendary in world football, with 18 league games played and all 18 won to complete a unique 100 per cent league campaign. Now a veteran, Mitchell started in the first 13 of those 18 matches to win his second league medal. He regained his place for the latter stages of the Scottish Cup but tasted defeat in the final.

He stayed at Ibrox for one more season, although only making three appearances, with his 241st game for Rangers being in the Glasgow League against Queen's Park in March 1900. Those 241 appearances brought six goals, two league titles, three Scottish Cups, four Glasgow Cups and a Charity Cup.

In the summer of 1900, he travelled to Denmark to coach KB Copenhagen players who were due to face Queen's Park in a tour of the country after a similar tour two years earlier had resulted in heavy defeats. *The Scottish Referee* reported, 'David Mitchell … has proved an able coach to the Danes, and the close result is proof that they have been very apt pupils.'

He was a born and bred Ayrshireman, living there all his life. He married Mary Wilson of Dreghorn in 1896 and they had two children, Jeanie and David. Mitchell lived to the age of 82 before passing away on 6 December 1948 in Irvine. He is not a member of the Rangers Hall of Fame but there is a good argument that he deserves to be.

- 11 years at the club, 241 appearances
- The first Rangers captain to win the league
- The first Rangers captain to beat Celtic
- The first Rangers captain to win the Glasgow Cup
- The first Rangers captain to win the Scottish Cup
- A member of the Invincibles
- Winner of ten major honours

34   DAVID MURRAY

The life-saving Rangers trialist who perished in the great war

DAVID BRUCE Murray was born on 4 December 1882 in Cathcart, Glasgow, but spent his early years mainly in Busby where he developed an interest in several sports. A very keen swimmer, Murray began his football career as a full-back for local youth team Busby Rosemount, then progressing into the Juniors with Leven Victoria at the beginning of the 20th century.

While a Junior player he continued to pursue other sports, taking up hammer throwing and also participating in swimming competitions. This ability in the water turned out to be life-saving, when one day out walking near the Busby Dam he noticed a young boy in the water in great difficulty. Murray immediately jumped in to rescue the youth, saving his life and being recognised by The Royal Humane Society for his bravery.

Rangers had the magnificent full-back partnership of Nicol Smith and Jock Drummond at this time, but were casting their eye around for backup players. They offered Murray a temporary contract and a trial match to give him the chance to impress, which he accepted eagerly. Murray wore the Royal Blue at left-back at Port Glasgow in early 1903, but a good display in a winning team didn't convince the watching Rangers management they were looking at a future first-team player. His temporary contract was allowed to expire but Murray was to succeed in wearing blue in senior football as he was then snapped up by English First Division giants Everton.

The left-back position at Goodison was firmly in the possession of Jack Crelley, so Murray started 1903/04 in the reserves. Although he showed up well, he never was seen as the first choice, his only two First Division starts coming in November 1903 when Crelley was injured. Murray was on the losing side both times, a 1-0 loss away to Sheffield Wednesday then another single-goal defeat the following Saturday at home to Sunderland. Murray played out the rest of the season back in the second XI, and won a medal as Everton's reserves took the Lancashire Combination championship.

After just one season as a top-flight footballer, Everton sold Murray to their local rivals Liverpool, who were preparing for a season in the Second Division after suffering relegation. He made his Liverpool debut at Anfield on 1 September 1904 in a 2-0 victory over Burton United. Murray kept his place for the next few months, playing 12 times before dropping out. Those 12 starts were enough to earn him a championship medal as Liverpool won the title and promotion back to the top division at the first attempt.

Murray started only three games in 1905/06 in the top tier, and suffered defeat in all of them. A 4-2 loss to old club Everton in the Merseyside derby on 30 September 1905 was to be his last game for the club, and he switched back to the Second Division with Leeds City – renamed Leeds United in 1919 – in early December of that year for a fee of £150. This was where Murray enjoyed his most consistent spell as a professional. Liverpool, meanwhile, went on to win the First Division title in their first season back in the top flight.

He was pitched straight into first-team action in Yorkshire, featuring in ten games on the bounce during which he was asked to fill both full-back positions. He was also nominated as City's penalty taker and opened his account for the Peacocks from the spot in a 4-1 defeat of Leicester Fosse on 20 January. Murray missed three games in February, but ended his first season for City with three goals from 23 appearances, establishing himself as a mainstay of the side.

Murray took over as City captain after John George lost his place early in the 1906/07 campaign, and he continued to give consistent displays, though he missed large chunks of the season between December and April through injury. He remained a regular choice throughout 1907/08, and missed just four games. However he was unavailable for the start of the following season with a cartilage injury and had a barren time, not appearing in the first team at all until 23 January. He was only selected twice more by Leeds before leaving in the summer of 1909. Overall, he had played 89 times for Leeds, all the while in the Second Division, and scored his only nine senior professional goals for them.

Murray's football career ended in non-league football, playing for Mexborough United and Burslem Port Vale in the Midland League and Frickley Colliery in the Sheffield Association League. But like so many others, his life was changed completely when war was declared in 1914.

In early 1915 he enlisted in the Great War effort, joining the 11th Service Battalion of the Argyll and Sutherland Highlanders. Private Murray was sent to the Western Front in France in September 1915 and took part in the Battle of Loos, the first engagement of the conflict where the British Army used poison gas. Tragically, like so many other brave men, Murray was killed in action while serving his country. He was declared dead on 10 December 1915, aged just 33.

Private David Bruce Murray is remembered on panel 125 on the Loos Memorial.

In our recent history, the name of David Murray is well known, and it is a name that is associated with good times and with bad. But over 100 years ago, there was another David Murray who briefly was associated with the club. And all Rangers supporters will agree that this one really was a hero.

- Saved a young life by risking his own
- Briefly on trial with Rangers
- Played for both halves of Merseyside
- Won a league title with Liverpool
- Captain of Leeds
- Made the ultimate sacrifice for his country

35   DAVID TAYLOR

The former Ranger who won the English title after a near-fatal heart attack

DAVID TAYLOR was born in St Ninians, near Stirling on 5 August 1884. Mainly a left-back, he started his football career at Bannockburn Juniors in 1904, then had a short spell with Glasgow Ashfield where he was spotted by scouts from Rangers. He signed for the club in the summer of 1906.

It wasn't left-back where Taylor made his debut, however, manager William Wilton seeing him more naturally suited to centre-back. His first Rangers appearance was on 24 September 1906 in the middle of the defence in a 1-1 home draw with Hearts. This was to be the start of a five-year Rangers career, one that never saw Taylor as anything other than a reliable deputy. He made nine starts that first season, including a baptism into the Old Firm game in late October when Rangers lost 2-1 at Parkhead.

Season 1907/08 saw the most appearances of any Ibrox campaign for Taylor, with 12 league starts and three more in the Charity Cup. Unfortunately, one of these was Celtic's title-clinching victory at Ibrox in late April when future Rangers team-mate Alec Bennett scored the only goal. He made just six starts the following season, one cup appearance in 1909/10 (when he went on loan to Motherwell for a spell), and a single league appearance in 1910/11, his 32nd and last Rangers start being on 26 September 1910 in a comfortable 4-0 win against Hibs which included a hat-trick from Willie Reid. Within days he was transferred to English First Division side Bradford City.

His Bradford career was relatively short but memorable. Taylor's debut was in a 1-1 draw at Sunderland on 1 October, and he immediately made the left-back position his own. Bradford finished a very acceptable fifth in the First Division that season, but it was the FA Cup that made it special. New Brompton, Norwich City, Grimsby Town, Burnley and

Blackburn Rovers were all beaten to set up a final in London against Newcastle United. After a tense goalless draw at the Crystal Palace, Taylor played in Bradford's only FA Cup Final victory in the Old Trafford replay when former Rangers team-mate and future fallen war hero Jimmy Speirs scored the only goal.

Taylor played 51 times for Bradford, and it came as something of a surprise in December 1911 when they accepted an offer from Second Division Burnley for his services. Burnley narrowly missed out on promotion in his first season, but a second-place finish in 1912/13 saw them return to the top league. Now history was to repeat itself for Taylor as Burnley comfortably finished mid-table but embarked on his next unforgettable FA Cup run. Derby, Bolton and Sunderland were all difficult opponents but all beaten, then a tense semi-final replay win over Sheffield United meant a final date with Liverpool. On 25 April 1914, almost 73,000 fans packed into the Crystal Palace to see Taylor win his second FA Cup winners' medal when prolific ex-Everton centre-forward Bert Freeman scored the winning goal.

Season 1914/15 would be severely disrupted due to the declaration of war, and in 1915 English football was put on hold. Taylor enlisted in the Artillery Regiment and turned out as a guest player for Ayr United, Falkirk, Chelsea, and made one last appearance for Rangers in a 0-0 draw against Aberdeen on 29 April 1916. All the while, he was still a registered Burnley player, and after the war ended he joined one last club as a guest in December 1918. That club was Celtic.

Season 1918/19 was a neck-and-neck title race between the two Glasgow giants. Taylor's Celtic debut was to be against his old club on New Year's Day at Ibrox, and he received numerous accolades as the best player on the pitch when Celtic played a determined defensive game to steal a point in a 1-1 draw. The *Glasgow Herald* report stated, 'Success attended the inclusion of Taylor (Burnley) on the visiting side,' and added, 'The visitors were helped by the magnificent rearguard tactics of Taylor.' He only played four more league games for Celtic, who won the title by that single point gained on 1 January. Such was manager Maley's gratitude he arranged for a special medal to be struck for Taylor as he had not played enough for an official one.

Taylor returned to Burnley in May 1919, now almost 35 years old. He was made club captain for the coming season, but before it had even begun, Taylor was to face his greatest battle yet after suffering a serious heart attack in July 1919. His life stayed in the balance for many months, and to most observers this was the end of a fine career. But incredibly, he not only won the fight for his life but he recovered to such an extent that he made a comeback for Burnley in 1920/21, playing 11 times as Burnley roared to their first English championship. Rarely can a league medal have been won against such odds.

Taylor played on at Turf Moor until 1924 as an occasional stand-in before retiring at almost 40 years old, having played over 250 games over 13 war- and health-interrupted years, scoring five times. That summer, he was appointed manager of newly promoted St Johnstone where he stayed for seven seasons. His team beat both Rangers and Celtic in 1926/27 but were relegated in 1930, before he left the job the following year when failing to steer the club back to the top flight. He joined Blackburn as a trainer, before his next managerial post in 1936 at Dunfermline. Money troubles and poor signings saw him suffer another relegation, and he resigned in April 1938 with his team a lowly tenth in the Second Division. He had one last brief job as manager of Carlisle which was brought to an end in 1940 by the Second World War, prompting Taylor to retire.

On 6 August 1949, just over 30 years after his near-fatal heart attack, Taylor passed away at his daughter's home in Bridge of Allan at the age of 65.

- Played for Rangers and Celtic
- Won the FA Cup with two different clubs
- Won the English league after a near-fatal heart attack

36   GEORDIE HENDERSON

The forgotten first great goalscorer of the Bill Struth era

BORN IN Forfar in April 1897, George 'Geordie' Henderson started his professional football career with his hometown club, arriving at Ibrox via a short spell with Dundee in November 1919.

A powerful forward, he had to bide his time to make his debut as William Wilton's side were enjoying a consistent winning run. It wasn't until 20 March 1920 that he made his first league appearance for the club in a 2-0 victory at Aberdeen.

Henderson kept his place for most of the remainder of the season, although not making the most impressive of starts to his Rangers career, with just two goals in eight appearances. His first goal in Royal Blue was scored against Airdrie at Ibrox in a 3-2 win in April. The season ended with the championship returning to Ibrox by three points over holders Celtic, but Henderson played in the massive shock defeat in the Scottish Cup semi-final to already relegated Albion Rovers. That cup jinx remained throughout his brief but spectacular Rangers career.

The close-season in 1920 was dominated by the untimely and tragic death of Wilton, so 1920/21 was to be the first season under Bill Struth. The new boss saw great potential in Henderson, but decided not to start him when the season got under way as he concentrated on developing his raw talent into a more productive striker.

Rangers began brilliantly, dropping only one point in their first 15 games, the forward line from the previous season now even more deadly with the addition of legendary left-winger Alan Morton from Queen's Park. Goals were flowing, with Andy Cunningham playing centre-forward and leading the scoring charts. Henderson made only one appearance in the first three months of the campaign, scoring in a 2-1 Glasgow Cup win against Queen's Park at Hampden in September.

However, in November injury allowed Henderson a chance to stake a claim in the team, and rarely has any player taken his chance so spectacularly. On 6 November 1920 Struth selected Henderson for the first time in a league game, with Dundee the opponents at Ibrox.

Henderson hammered home four goals in a 5-0 rout. The following week he repeated the feat with another four-goal haul, this time in a 4-2 victory at Clydebank. He rounded off an incredible November by helping himself to two more when Hamilton were defeated 4-0. Three games, ten goals. Struth had unleashed the first of the many goalscoring machines, which would be a feature of his 34 years in charge. Henderson ended that season with 21 league goals, all scored from November onwards, as he won his first league championship medal. These included a third four-goal haul, this time against Ayr. He couldn't add the Scottish Cup to his medal collection, however, playing in the surprise Hampden final defeat to Partick Thistle. And he suffered a second cup final heartbreak when starting the end-of-season Charity Cup Final which was lost 2-0 to Celtic.

Season 1921/22 saw the title lost by a single point to Celtic, but it was the first of four successive seasons where Henderson finished as Rangers' top scorer as he banged in 21 league goals in 28 starts, including three hat-tricks. And although suffering yet another Scottish Cup Final calamity when Morton shocked Rangers 1-0 in the final, he did add winners' medals in both the Glasgow and Charity Cups. The former was won with a tight single-goal victory over Celtic thanks to a goal by Davie Meiklejohn, the latter a 3-1 comeback win over Queen's Park that featured a treble by Sandy Archibald.

Henderson continued his sensational scoring form the following season and carried on collecting medals. He won his first league championship badge, with his 23 league goals in 28 appearances a crucial factor in an eventual five-point winning margin over Airdrie. His only hat-trick of the campaign came on 2 December 1922 against the men from Broomfield, a massive result in the title race. Earlier, he had scored his first Old Firm league goal when Celtic were vanquished at Parkhead and he also scored his first cup final goals at the end of the season when he hit a double in the 4-0 Charity Cup win over Queen's Park. With another Glasgow Cup also won, this time against Clyde, it was only the failure to lift the Scottish Cup that prevented Henderson from enjoying a clean sweep. Ayr United this time provided the shock result in the second round, Henderson ending his Rangers career some years later as one of many great club servants who never enjoyed success in the national cup competition.

Henderson scored 19 league goals in 1923/24 as another championship was secured. He missed three weeks of the season in February and March 1924 due to injury, and while on the sidelines he had to watch on helplessly as Hibs knocked Rangers out of the Scottish Cup. His first-round hat-trick against Lochgelly and second-round winner at St Mirren therefore counted for little. He also had contrasting fortunes in the two minor tournaments, scoring the semi-final winner against Celtic in the Glasgow Cup and another goal in the final win over Third Lanark but unable to find the target in the Charity Cup Final loss to the men from Parkhead.

A first and only representative honour was given to Henderson during the season, and he scored the only goal of the game on 31 October 1923 to help the Scottish League team defeat their Irish counterparts. Despite his consistent goalscoring for the best team in the country, Henderson was never picked for the full Scotland international side.

If his goalscoring feats so far hadn't been enough, Henderson was even more prolific in 1924/25. He started the season by scoring all three goals in a 3-0 win at Ibrox over Raith Rovers, and went on to hammer in 27 league goals as Rangers wrapped up a third successive championship. These included a double on New Year's Day at Ibrox in a commanding 4-1 thrashing of Celtic, and he also hit a double against them in another 4-1 Glasgow Cup Final triumph. Amazingly, Celtic turned the tables in the Scottish Cup, Henderson unusually blunt in a dismal 5-0 semi-final reverse. A Charity Cup win at the end of the season did little to ease the pain of that particular result.

Season 1925/26 saw a combination of injury to Henderson and the emergence of Jimmy Fleming as another magnificent goalscorer, meaning Geordie was limited to only 15 appearances. He still scored eight goals but the season overall was a huge disappointment and ended trophyless. Fleming was now the undisputed first choice to lead the attack. Henderson scored his last Rangers goal on 2 October 1926 in a seven-goal blitz over St Mirren, and played his last game on 8 January 1927 at Ibrox against St Johnstone. He left that month to join English side Darlington for a sizeable fee of £2,250.

His goalscoring record in his time at Rangers stands up in comparison with almost any of our great centre-forwards. Henderson can lay claim to the title of being Bill Struth's first goalscoring sensation. He scored over 150 times for Rangers, with only one of these a penalty.

Henderson had a nomadic career after his great years at Ibrox. His time at Darlington was brief, they were relegated despite him scoring a goal almost every two games for them, so he was on the move again in the summer of 1927, crossing the Atlantic to play in the American Soccer League with New York Nationals. His one and only season there saw him add to his medal collection as the Nationals made it to the National Challenge Cup Final, where they beat the Bricklayers and Masons Football Club of Chicago 3-0 in a replay at Soldier Field, Chicago. Typically, Henderson scored two of the goals.

Once the season was over, Henderson returned to Scotland to sign for Dundee United, then of the Second Division. Manager Jimmy Brownlie wanted an experienced goal-getter to help in their promotion push, and who better than a player who had guaranteed goals wherever he played. This caused some upset at his former club Darlington, who believed they had retained his registration when he left for America, but their protests were found to be unwarranted. Henderson was declared free to sign for the Tannadice club.

Henderson delivered exactly what his new manager had hoped. Despite now being utilised as more of an inside-forward than leading the attack, he notched 12 league goals as United won promotion back to the First Division. He also scored the only goal against neighbours Dundee to win a highly charged local derby in the Scottish Cup. On 2 March 1929, Henderson had an emotional reunion with many former colleagues as United travelled to Ibrox to play in a Scottish Cup quarter-final. However, there was no fairytale ending for him as Rangers eased to a 3-1 win thanks to goals by Marshall, McPhail, and the man who had taken his centre-forward place a few years earlier, Jimmy Fleming.

He was now a First Division player again, and he showed he was more than capable of holding his own at that level by scoring 13 times for United in 1929/30. These included a consolation at Ibrox on 28 September 1929 in a 3-1 defeat, and a double against Celtic at Tannadice the following month in a 2-2 draw. But despite Henderson's goals, United struggled badly, and their stay in the top league ended with an immediate relegation.

Rather than spend another year in the Second Division, Henderson accepted an offer from Welsh outfit Rhyl to become their player-coach. This was his last club, Henderson then retiring from the game. He became a publican for a time in Dundee, before his untimely death on 14 June 1953 at the age of just 56.

Henderson was the first of Bill Struth's great centre-forwards. Unlike Fleming, Smith, English, Thornton and Simpson, he is not inducted in the Rangers Hall of Fame. He could be the greatest forgotten goalscorer in club history and deserves to be remembered.

- Rangers career: 1919–1927
- Over 150 goals for the club at a strike rate of around three goals every four games
- 4 league titles
- 4 Glasgow Cups
- 2 Charity Cups
- Also a winner in New York and on Tayside

37   GEORGE GILLESPIE

The international goalkeeper who played at left-back for Rangers in the cup final

BORN ON 22 June 1859, George Gillespie had a short but unique Rangers career. He joined the club in 1875 as a teenager, and made his Scottish Cup debut as a full-back in a first round tie against Queen's Park Juniors on 30 September 1876, alongside iconic names from the club's foundation in Moses McNeil, Peter Campbell and Tom Vallance. A 4-1 victory set Rangers on the path to their first Scottish Cup Final. Gillespie featured at left-back in all three final matches, the legendary tussles with Vale of Leven, who prevailed 3-2 in the second replay on 14 April 1877. He also lined up in the Charity Cup Final the following month against Queen's Park, but again tasted defeat as our 'bigger' rivals won 4-0.

The iconic 'gallant pioneers' photograph taken to commemorate that first Scottish Cup Final is probably the most famous team picture of any in the club's long history. Gillespie stands at the back left. He was just 17 years old when he played in that final.

Season 1877/78 saw Gillespie remain as the first-choice left full-back and he once again played in a losing cup final, lining up alongside the McNeil and Vallance brothers in a 2-1 defeat by Third Lanark in the Charity Cup on 1 April 1878.

A talented athlete who won several track competitions as well as being a fine footballer, Gillespie then showed just how versatile he was when in the summer of 1878 he took over as first-choice goalkeeper from James Watt. Some unfair comments were directed at him for being too 'soft' to play outfield, but this stands little scrutiny when you think of the physical challenges made on goalkeepers in those early days, a far cry from the protection offered in the modern game. Gillespie made the position his own, impressing onlookers with his agility. With Gillespie in goal, Rangers embarked on another Scottish Cup run in 1879 and reached their second final, with Vale of Leven again the opposition just as two years earlier. Gillespie therefore played for Rangers in two different finals, one outfield and one in goal. On 19 April, recent history repeated itself with the match ending 1-1. There would be no replay this time, however, as Rangers protested strongly that a disallowed Willie Struthers goal should have stood and they had in fact won. Despite presenting a strong case, fronted by Tom Vallance and the former goalkeeper and now honorary treasurer James Watt, Rangers were ordered to replay the final by the SFA. So strong was the feeling of injustice at the club that Rangers decided not to turn up for the replay, meaning their opponents were awarded the cup.

Just a few weeks later, Rangers were to play Vale of Leven in the Charity Cup Final, the events surrounding the Scottish Cup still fresh in the memory. Fuelled by the anger of being denied the country's biggest trophy, Rangers, with Gillespie in goal, defeated Vale 2-1 to win their first trophy. Perhaps fittingly, Willie Struthers scored.

Gillespie remained Rangers' goalkeeper for a further four seasons but failed to add to his winners' medals. He did, however, become a Scotland international, making his debut in March 1880 in a 5-1 home win against Wales. He then played in successive huge wins over England, 6-1 away in 1881 and 5-1 at home in 1882. The 1881 victory at the Kennington Oval was a historic occasion as Scotland's Andrew Watson became the world's first black international footballer. Overall, Gillespie represented his country seven times and remained unbeaten during his international career.

In January 1884, Gillespie left Rangers for Queen's Park and played in the FA Cup Final that year against Blackburn Rovers at the Kennington Oval. Rovers won 2-1 with the winning goal scored by a familiar name to Rangers fans, Jim Forrest. Incredibly, Queen's Park then reached the final again the following season but history repeated itself as Gillespie once conceded twice to Blackburn, with Forrest on the scoresheet for the second successive year.

Gillespie remained at Queen's Park until 1892, and by then he had finally won a national final. He was the last line of defence in the 1886 win over Renton, a 3-1 victory at Cathkin Park. Then four years later, he won a second Scottish Cup Final, gaining some belated revenge over Vale of Leven when they were defeated 2-1 in a replay at Ibrox in front of 13,000 fans.

After hanging up his gloves, Gillespie became a successful businessman, owning a popular bar in the Finnieston area of the city. A resident of Radnor Street, facing Kelvingrove Park, he took ill at the very beginning of the 20th century, and passed away at his home on 3 February 1900 aged just 40.

Just two days after his death, the minutes of the Queen's Park committee meeting contained this tribute to him, '

Mr. James Lawrence made reference to the sudden death of Mr. George Gillespie, which had taken place on Saturday morning. Mr. Gillespie, who came from Rangers to Queen's Park, was known as "the prince of goalkeepers". He had been a member of the club for a long period, was highly esteemed by all who knew him, and had in his time done excellent service for the club. He had been cut off in the prime of life, leaving a widow and family to mourn his loss. Mr. Gillespie was a marvellous goalkeeper. He had previously played in other positions, until he found his true vocation was the part of custodian.'

The title of 'Prince of Goalkeepers' is one familiar to those with an interest in the history of Rangers, it being the well-known nickname of the legendary Hall of Fame goalkeeper of the 1930s and 1940s, Jerry Dawson. George Gillespie remains very much part of the Rangers history.

- Friend and team-mate of 'The Gallant Pioneers'
- Played outfield and in goal for Rangers in cup finals
- Played in the first ever final won by the club
- A Scotland international

38   GEORGE LIVINGSTONE

The only man to play for Rangers, Celtic, Manchester City and Manchester United

GEORGE LIVINGSTONE was born on 5 May 1876 in Dumbarton. His nomadic football career started at Junior level, representing Sinclair Swifts in 1892, Artizan Thistle in 1893 and Parkhead Juniors in 1894, before becoming a senior professional player at local club Dumbarton in 1895. But he never broke into their league team, and moved east to Edinburgh to join Hearts the following year in search of regular football.

He made an instant impact at Tynecastle, scoring both goals at inside-forward in a debut 2-2 draw with Dundee in September 1896. Despite this, he remained mainly a reliable deputy during his four seasons with Hearts. He only made three starts in the league that season as Hearts won the title, not enough for a medal. He did have an excellent scoring record when called upon, including four in a 6-2 win over Leith. His longest run in the side was in 1898/99 when Hearts were runners-up behind the immortal Rangers team who went through the entire season without dropping a point. In all, Livingstone played 59 times for Hearts across various competitions, scoring 30 times.

In 1900 Livingstone moved south. He played a trial match in March for Everton, and must have impressed as the Merseyside club's board minutes of May 1900 disclosed they were to make a £250 offer for the player. But it was by then too late as Hearts had accepted a £175 bid from Sunderland, with Livingstone already on his way to the north-east. He teamed up with another recently arrived Scot, Jimmy Millar from Rangers. Livingstone described himself as 'Rangers daft', and the team-mates struck up a formidable partnership on the field as well as being good friends off it. Sunderland had been champions three times in the previous decade with their 'Team of All the Talents', and they were confident this new-look side would bring back title glory. However, inconsistent away form and a mini collapse in the run-in saw them finish second to Liverpool, with Livingstone their top scorer in the league with 11 goals.

This was to be Livingstone's only season at Roker Park as in the spring of 1901 he surprised his friends by agreeing a move back to Scotland to join Celtic. Rangers daft he may have been, but that didn't prevent Livingstone from making a big impact at Parkhead. He made his debut against Rangers in a Charity Cup match in May 1901, which Celtic won 1-0. He was to play against Rangers three times in 1901/02. A league draw at Ibrox and a Rangers 4-2 win at New Year at Parkhead saw the Ibrox club narrowly take the title for a fourth successive year, with the other meeting in the Glasgow League at the end of the season. He scored four times against his boyhood heroes in a 5-1 Celtic victory. It would be a season without a winners' medal though, as Celtic lost 1-0 in the Scottish Cup Final to Hibs, Livingstone coming closest to salvaging a draw when his shot struck the post. His record for Celtic in the main competitions was 23 games played and seven goals scored (the Glasgow League was not counted as a main competition). Meanwhile, in England, the Sunderland team he left had won the First Division championship.

Livingstone was back on his travels in May 1902, joining Liverpool for £200. He was by now a Scottish international, although his debut was later annulled from the records as it was the tragic Ibrox disaster match against England in April of that year. His Anfield debut was a memorable one, scoring in a handsome 5-2 win over Blackburn Rovers on the opening day of 1902/03. He started 31 of the 34 league fixtures for Liverpool, scoring his fourth and final goal for the club in a 9-2 demolition of Grimsby. Liverpool finished fifth, only four points behind champions The Wednesday. Again, this was to be his only season with the club, as he joined Second Division champions and newly promoted Manchester City in 1903.

Arguably, this was to be the best footballing period of Livingstone's career. He forged an instant and highly effective right-sided attacking partnership with the great Welsh winger Billy Meredith, scoring on his City debut on 5 September in a 2-1 win at Stoke. He would score six times that season as City took the top division by storm, finishing runners-up to The Wednesday. They also reached the FA Cup Final for the first time and Livingstone finally got his hands on a winners' medal. His brilliant through ball sent Meredith clear on goal for the only goal against Bolton Wanderers at the Crystal Palace in London on 23 April 1904, before 61,000 fans.

Livingstone spent three full seasons with Manchester City. Although he got no more medals, they were firmly established as a major force in England, finishing second, third and fifth during his time there. He made 88 appearances, with his 30th and last goal coming in his final start in a 3-1 win at Bolton in March 1906. He also finally won a recognised full Scotland cap when he played in the April 1906 win over England. He missed the start of season 1906/07 due to injury and couldn't regain his place, so in January 1907 he left Manchester to return north and finally signed for the club he most wanted to play for, Rangers.

Manager William Wilton was rebuilding his team, as it had been five years since Rangers' last league title and rivals Celtic were the dominant team in the country. Livingstone was pitched straight into the side, his debut coming in a 2-1 away Scottish Cup first round win at Falkirk. His first two Rangers goals came in the second round in a comfortable 4-0 win at Galston, but the cup run ended abruptly in round three with a dismal 3-0 home loss to Celtic. In all, Livingston started 16 games in this first partial campaign at Ibrox, scoring seven goals. Undoubtedly the highlight came in the last game of the season when he played a prominent role in a hard-fought but deserved 1-0 Charity Cup Final win over Celtic at Hampden.

Livingstone was a first-team regular again in 1907/08 with 32 starts. He started the season on fire, with six goals in his first six appearances, but his total of 13 goals couldn't prevent the heartache of seeing Celtic again lift the title and also inflict painful defeats in both the Glasgow and Scottish Cups. Now at the veteran stage of his career, Livingstone remained a regular choice in the first half of the following season but was no longer an automatic pick. His last goals for Rangers came on 2 January 1909 when he helped himself to four in a 6-0 rout of Partick Thistle, with his 62nd and last appearance the following week against Dundee. Those 62 games featured a total of 26 goals.

At almost 33 years of age, and with manager Wilton preferring younger legs at inside-forward, Livingstone left Rangers that January, returning to Manchester but to the red half of the city by joining Manchester United. Ironically, his debut on 23 January was to be against their city rivals and his former club. He completed the full set of Glasgow and Manchester derby appearances in style, scoring twice as United easily defeated City 3-1.

United were a team on the up, with the experience of Livingstone providing calmness to their play when selected. He was mostly now a wing-half rather than a forward and made regular but intermittent starts. United won the league title in 1910/11, with Livingstone appearing in ten games, which these days would have qualified for a medal but it wasn't enough back then. Manchester United was to be his last club and he remained there until retiring in April 1914, just short of his 38th birthday. In five years he made a total of 46 starts, only adding two more goals to his memorable debut derby double. He had a dual role towards the end of his career there, making the occasional first-team appearance while also being player-coach of the reserves.

After retiring, he started a plumbing business in Glasgow in 1915, but kept in touch with the numerous contacts he had made in the game. He also joined the King's Own African Rifles and served in East Africa.

After the Great War ended, he accepted the job of Dumbarton manager in 1919, but this was unsuccessful and he resigned after just one season. He did put on the boots one last time during an injury crisis, making his last senior appearance at the age of 43. Then in

1920, he was contacted by new Rangers manager Bill Struth with the offer of a job as the first-team trainer. For seven seasons he was a key part of the backroom team who started a period of dominance in Scotland. A player who had so few medals to show for a long career at top clubs then enjoyed seeing the players he trained win title after title.

In early 1927, Livingstone took ill with a complex and serious appendicitis. Hospitalised for a significant period, he resigned from his role to focus on his recovery. As his strength returned, he missed his involvement in the game, and quickly accepted an offer from Bradford City of the Third Division North to become their trainer. This reunited Livingstone with legendary former Rangers player Tommy Cairns who was now Bradford's captain. City had almost gone under due to severe financial problems after a recent relegation and desperately needed to regain their second-tier status. Livingstone showed how shrewd a signing he was as he helped guide Bradford to a memorable title success in 1928/29 in his first season, with big crowds flocking back to help ease their money problems.

Livingstone remained at Bradford until retiring in 1935. He died on 15 January 1950 in Helensburgh aged 73.

- The only man to play for Rangers, Celtic, Manchester United and Manchester City, and score for them all too
- If you include his Everton trial, he also represented both halves of Merseyside
- Played in the Edinburgh derby
- Played in the first Ibrox disaster match
- Won an FA Cup Final
- Worked under Bill Struth

39 HARRY RENNIE

The pioneering goalkeeper whose mistake led to the Hampden riot

HARRY RENNIE was born on 1 June 1873 in Greenock, the son of a local wine merchant. An intelligent young man, he combined training as a law clerk with a junior football career in his teenage years. He was a quick and cultured half-back for local sides Greenock Volunteers, Belgrove Ramblers and Greenock West End and made such an impression that he earned a Junior international cap for Scotland. In 1894 he moved into senior football when he signed for Morton, then of the Scottish Second Division.

Rennie had suffered a severe facial injury playing cricket when younger, a disfiguring abscess being the result, and his appearance made him the target of some cruel taunts from spectators. This may have been a reason why he developed an uncompromising attitude throughout his long football career, refusing to budge from what he thought was right regardless of what others would say. In training, he enjoyed going in goal and he showed such ability between the sticks that Morton first announced him as their official backup goalkeeper, and by 1897 he became the club's regular custodian.

He was known for an almost fanatical attitude to his job, throwing himself repeatedly to the concrete floor in the dressing room to 'toughen myself up' in the days when goalkeepers were subject to overly physical attention in games. Rennie's agility and reading of the play attracted bigger clubs, and after 39 league appearances for Morton (more than half in goal), he joined First Division Hearts for £50 in 1898.

From his league debut against Rangers in September 1898, Rennie was an automatic choice for the Edinburgh club. He brought a scientific approach that had never been seen anywhere before. He studied angles and made marks on the pitch to help him understand exactly where attackers were in relation to the posts. He believed in looking at player body language as a way of predicting what attackers were going to do. And he even kept dossiers on the opposing attackers he thought most dangerous to him keeping the ball out the goal. In his two years with the club, he made 43 competitive appearances and helped them to finishes of second and fourth. In March 1900 he made the first of his 13 Scotland international appearances in a 3-0 victory over Ireland.

That summer, Rennie attracted the attention of Celtic, who wanted Scotland's new goalkeeper in their team to try to reclaim the title from the dominant Rangers team of the time. Hearts agreed to a transfer but Rennie was unhappy with the contract on offer and he never signed it. During the stand-off, Hibs approached Rennie and he persuaded them to pay him the wages lost during the contract dispute as well as pay him more than the Parkhead offer, so he subsequently signed for Hearts' rivals.

Rennie's consistency, bravery and his seeming ability to intimidate opposing forwards was a huge part of some memorable successes for the green side of Edinburgh. He also would rush from his goal to break up attacks as well as having the ability to find team-mates with the ball, unheard of at the time. A 'sweeper keeper' before the expression was ever invented. He was outstanding in the 1902 Scottish Cup Final when Hibs beat Celtic 1-0, making several breathtaking saves to deny the team who wanted him two years before. He won a Charity Cup Final the same year when the competition expanded to allow more matches and raise extra funds following the Ibrox disaster when a stand collapse caused tragic loss of life. This time Hibs beat Celtic 6-2. Then in 1902/03 he was ever present as Hibs won the First Division title, becoming Scottish champions for the first time.

Rennie made 195 league starts, and many more cup appearances, in eight seasons at Hibs. Then in April 1908, at the age of almost 35, he made a surprise move when William Wilton brought him to Rangers. The Ibrox club were going through a difficult period, Wilton concerned that the title would not return until the defence conceded fewer goals. He saw the experienced and hugely influential Rennie as a good bet to deal with that problem. Rennie's debut came in the end-of-season Charity Cup in a draw with Third Lanark, and in 1908/09 he became the Rangers regular.

He made an excellent start to the season, only conceding one goal in the first five league games, all of them won. But defeat in a replay to Celtic in the Glasgow Cup semi-final seemed to knock Rangers' confidence. Rennie started 31 times in the league as his team finished fourth, although just six points behind winners Celtic. He also was in goal for most of a Scottish Cup run that saw Rangers meet Celtic in the final. On 10 April 1909 Rennie was in the team who took to the Hampden pitch, and he would unfortunately make the mistake that his Rangers career would be remembered for. With time running out, Rangers had come back to lead 2-1 and their supporters in the 70,000 crowd were starting to celebrate. Then in the 84th minute, Rennie saved a Munro shot but then twisted to evade an on-rushing challenge from centre-forward Quinn. The referee adjudged Rennie had carried the ball over his goal line and awarded the equaliser, crediting the custodian with an own goal.

A replay was needed, Rennie showing his strength of character by not only starting but having a fine match in a 1-1 draw. However, his display was quickly forgotten when the game did not go to extra time and the fans rioted in protest. The cup was withheld as all of Scottish football condemned the terrible scenes. It would never have happened but for that unfortunate own goal in the first game.

Rennie did end the season on a happier note as on 15 May he was in goal for the Charity Cup Final, again against Celtic, and he won his second winners' medal in the tournament as Rangers powered to a 4-2 victory.

That summer, Rangers signed Englishman Herbert Lock who became the first-choice goalkeeper. Rennie remained at the club for one more season, playing his 48th and last game in a win over Airdrie in March 1910. He left Ibrox that summer, and after brief spells with Kilmarnock then his first club Morton, he retired in 1911.

After his playing career ended, Rennie listed his occupation as an engineer, but retained a keen interest in the game and became a coach and mentor to young goalkeepers. There was no doubting the identity of his star pupil, the great Jimmy Cowan of Morton and Scotland who was the hero in a memorable Wembley victory in the 1949 Home International championship. Rennie, undoubtedly a pioneering goalkeeper, died in 1954 at the age of 81.

- Represented Scotland both outfield and in goal
- Regarded as the 'father of modern goalkeeping'
- League and cup winner
- Scorer of the own goal that led indirectly to the Hampden riot
- Signed for Rangers but wouldn't sign for Celtic

40 HERBERT LOCK

The first English goalkeeper brought to Ibrox to bring back title glory

IN THE summer of 1909, after a disappointing season when Rangers finished fourth behind a Celtic team winning their fifth successive championship, manager William Wilton made three significant signings. Forward Willie Reid would go on to be the club's goalscoring machine in the coming years. The other two surprised Scottish football by both being top-division English players from down south. First, goalkeeper Herbert Lock was signed from FA Cup semi-finalists Southampton, then three weeks later forward Billy Hogg, a full England international, moved from Sunderland.

Although not the first non-Scottish goalkeeper for the club, Herbert Lock became the first to make the jersey his own, and enjoyed a long and successful spell at Rangers. He was also the first English player the club had signed from an English club.

Born on 22 January 1887, the 22-year-old Lock was known as something of a penalty stopper, his final season at Southampton seeing him save eight from 12 he faced. But he was better known as a goalkeeper whose bravery and determination to prevent the opposition from scoring resulted in some serious injuries. He actually missed his club's FA Cup semi-final after sustaining several broken bones in a league match at Watford in March 1909.

Rangers opened their league season on 16 August 1909 with Lock between the posts in a comfortable 3-0 Ibrox victory over Kilmarnock. His agility and bravery quickly found favour with the support and Wilton, and he played all but two matches as first choice that season, when a poor start to the campaign meant Rangers were unable to finish better than third. The trophy cabinet stayed bare, Lock suffering Glasgow Cup Final heartache by a single goal to Celtic, and going out the Scottish and Charity Cups to a very good Clyde team.

However, 1910/11 was to see the club finally end Celtic's league dominance, with Lock an ever present in a triumphant title-winning season. Lock enjoyed 14 shut-outs, the most significant being a crucial 1-0 win at Parkhead in October, when fellow Englishman Hogg scored the only goal. Rangers won the league by four points from Aberdeen, and Lock added both the Glasgow and Charity Cups to his trophy haul for the season with hugely satisfying wins against Celtic in both finals.

With Reid scoring more than a goal a game, the title was retained the following season, and Lock was again a key player. He only missed one game, a meaningless defeat at Rugby Park after the title was won. The Glasgow Cup was also retained, Lock keeping the Partick attack at bay in the final, allowing Hogg to score the decisive goal. Season 1912/13, however, was a third title in a row for Rangers but a painful one for the English stopper. After a solid start Rangers were drawn against Partick Thistle in the semi-finals of the Glasgow Cup. A goalless draw at Firhill meant a replay at Ibrox on 7 October. With the score at 1-1 and with just a few minutes remaining, Thistle right-winger Callaghan burst unchallenged into the penalty box. As he prepared to shoot, the Ibrox crowd saw certain defeat staring at them. Not Lock. As Callaghan started to shoot, he flung himself at the flying boot of the winger. The goal was saved, but the sickening contact between boot and goalkeeper saw Lock sidelined for months.

Lock then lost his place to a fine deputy goalkeeper, John Hempsey, and over the next few years they shared the number one jersey. Lock didn't appear again in the first team until January 1914 when he kept a clean sheet in a draw at home to Motherwell. That season of 1913/14, the last before the Great War, saw Rangers lose their crown to Celtic, despite a winning run of seven successive games after Lock was reinstated.

During the conflict, Lock worked towards the war effort in the local shipyards, his football career taking second place. As this work allowed, he did still turn out for the club, playing 26 times in 1914/15, 16 times in both 1915/16 and 1916/17, and seven times in 1917/18. Season 1917/18 was the only of these to see a Rangers title win. During that time, his finest display was undoubtedly on 30 October 1915 when 45,000 at Ibrox watched his heroics keep out a potent Celtic forward line in a resounding 3-0 victory.

After the war was over, 32-year-old Lock enjoyed one last memorable season at Ibrox. In 1919/20 manager Wilton had assembled a magnificent team, with names like Cunningham, Archibald, Gordon, Cairns and Meiklejohn. Behind them as last line of defence was Lock. Rangers lost only twice in 42 league games that season, conceding a miserly 25 goals while scoring 106. That was a defensive record any goalkeeper in the history of the club would be proud of.

Also that season, Lock kept goal in front of the record domestic attendance up to that time, when at least 85,000 crammed into Ibrox to see a him keep a clean sheet and Tommy Muirhead score the winner in the Scottish Cup quarter-final against Celtic.

This was to be Lock's swansong as a Ranger, injury in April 1920 seeing him lose his place to another great in Willie Robb, who played the remainder of the season and kept his place for 1920/21 under the new manager Bill Struth. Lock's 267th and last game for the club was fittingly a clean sheet, a vital point won in a tense 0-0 draw at Tynecastle in the run-in to the title.

Lock left Rangers in August 1921 for QPR, and had spells at Southampton and Bournemouth before retiring at the age of 37.

He settled in Southampton, working as a carpenter for Southern Railway, and died on 16 March 1957 at the age of 70. In 2010, four of his hard-earned medals were made available at auction, including two Scottish league medals. The sale prices achieved were undisclosed, but the starting bid for each medal was set at £500. A small price to pay for honours won by such a brave and popular Ranger.

- Rangers career: 1909–1920
- 267 appearances
- 3 league titles
- 2 Glasgow Cups
- 1 Charity Cup
- Like Chris Woods many decades later, an English goalkeeper who helped win back the title but never won the Scottish Cup

41   IAN MCPHERSON

The decorated RAF pilot who won titles with Rangers and Arsenal

IAN MCPHERSON was born in Glasgow on 26 March 1920 and signed for Rangers in 1939. A goalscoring winger in his age group, he made a positive early impression on Rangers manager Bill Struth and made his senior debut in a 3-1 victory against Arbroath at Ibrox. He shared the pitch with several legendary Rangers names, with the goals coming from Hall of Fame members Willie Thornton, Willie Waddell and Alex Venters. This match turned out to be the penultimate fixture in the Scottish Football League before the competition was suspended with the outbreak of World War Two. Little would the 19-year-old footballer realise just what this would mean for his future career.

That Arbroath match would be the only 'official' appearance for McPherson at Ibrox. But he was to play a big part as Rangers competed for and won the newly created Scottish Regional League Western Division. The young, dynamic and direct winger played 11 times in 1939/40, scoring 11 goals including a hat-trick against Clyde and doubles against Ayr, Dumbarton and Partick. Rangers won the Western League, setting up a national championship decider against Falkirk. McPherson started at inside-right, helping the team to a hard-fought 2-1 win thanks to strikes by Venters and Dr Adam Little. As well as the regional title, he helped Rangers to the Charity Cup in May 1940, playing in the final win against Clyde.

The next season saw him play his last four matches for the club in August and September 1940. McPherson kept up his excellent scoring record, hitting doubles against Hibs in the league and Third Lanark in the Glasgow Cup. His final start in a Rangers shirt came on 4 September in the semi-final of the Glasgow Cup when he played his part in a tense 1-0 win over Partick. This was McPherson's last game for the club as he had enlisted with the RAF. His record in his short Ibrox career was highly impressive with 15 goals in only 17 starts.

He moved from Glasgow to be stationed at Marham with the 105 squadron. After his training, McPherson became a pilot officer and flew De Havilland Mosquito aircraft, fighter-bomber planes with a two-man crew. He and his navigator became veterans in quick time, and had several lucky escapes as they encountered the enemy. There were three occasions where the plane was damaged after being struck by German guns, and each time McPherson was able to guide it home with only one usable engine. Even more frightening was the occasion where the aircraft lost electrics, and after being forced to dump fuel and turning back to Britain the crew discovered there was no way to identify themselves as friendly while crossing the Channel, meaning the British gunners assumed them as the enemy. Luckily, their shooting wasn't as deadly as McPherson had been on the football pitch, and they got home without further damage. One other sortie ended in a crash landing due to the plane's landing gear being made unusable by shrapnel damage.

In June 1944, McPherson was awarded the Distinguished Flying Cross after 57 sorties into German air space. The DFC states that it is awarded for 'an act or acts of valour, courage, or devotion to duty whilst flying in active operations against the enemy'. By June 1945, as the conflict was reaching its successful conclusion, he was further awarded a Bar for his DFC. By then, McPherson had flown over 100 missions across enemy lines and held the position of flying officer.

In all of World War Two, there were only 563 DFCs awarded by the RAF. McPherson was in a small and extremely elite band of men. When awarded the Bar in 1945, his recommendation for it from his superior officers stated, 'Since the award of his Distinguished Flying Cross, Flying Officer McPherson has completed numerous sorties. Throughout all his operations he has consistently displayed exemplary courage and tenacity of purpose which, together with outstanding skill and fine leadership, are worthy of high praise.' Despite this all sounding like a 24/7 job, McPherson did turn out on a very occasional basis for Arsenal during wartime. Then once peace was confirmed and his RAF service was completed, McPherson joined Notts County and played in the regional league in 1945/6, the last season before normal league football could resume. He then signed in August 1946 for Arsenal, a return to Highbury after his brief introduction to the club during the hostilities.

His official debut for the Gunners was something of a disaster, a humbling 6-1 defeat on the opening day of the season at Wolves. Manager George Allison rung the changes after that humiliating start, but McPherson kept his place at outside-right for virtually the entire season. He made 32 league appearances overall in his first campaign at Highbury, scoring six times. He also scored once in the FA Cup. It wasn't the season Arsenal fans had hoped for, and manager Allison resigned, replaced by Tom Whittaker.

Whittaker's first season in charge could hardly have gone better. McPherson was switched to outside-left and became an integral part of the team as they mounted a genuine title challenge. His speed and powerful shot were a feature of his play, as was his frustrating inconsistency. Something of a fans' favourite, but not good for Whittaker's blood pressure. McPherson played in 29 league matches in 1948/49, scoring five goals as Arsenal roared to the title by an impressive seven-point margin, helped by the deadly finishing of centre-forward Ronnie Rooke who hit the net 33 times.

This was to be the high point of McPherson's Arsenal career. He missed the Charity Shield win at Wembley over Manchester United the following season, although he did still make 33 starts in the league, which saw Arsenal finish fifth. Then in 1949/50, despite another 27 league appearances, he wasn't selected for the FA Cup Final, which Arsenal won by beating Liverpool.

He was now more of a deputy than a first choice, and left Arsenal in the summer of 1951 at the age of 31. He rejoined former club Notts County and could look back on a satisfying career at Highbury which yielded a league medal and 21 goals from 163 appearances.

He stayed at County for two years, playing 50 times, before a brief stint at Brentford brought his league career to an end in late 1953. McPherson then scored six goals in 17 appearances for non-league Bedford Town before rejoining the RAF as a physical training instructor in the summer of 1954, turning out occasionally for Cambridge United as his service commitments allowed.

Little is known of his life in the following three decades. However, he appeared in public in early March 1983, attending a testimonial lunch at Lord's for the great Leslie Compton, an Arsenal team-mate who also had a career as a top cricket international. Just two weeks later, McPherson passed away in St Albans at the age 62. He was one of the gallant few.

- Teenage scoring sensation at Rangers
- Winner of wartime honours with Rangers
- Highly decorated World War Two pilot
- Title winner at Arsenal

42   JACK SMITH

The Rangers failure who became the first player to score in both the Scottish Cup and English FA Cup Finals

'J. SMITH' is famous at Ibrox for the great Jimmy Smith who scored more goals for the club than any other player. But there was another J. Smith who was also expected to be a Rangers goalscoring sensation, only finding glory only before and after his brief spell as an Ibrox striker.

John Reid Smith was born on 2 April 1895 in Pollokshaws in Glasgow. He was known as Jack by friends and family, and began his football career with Battlefield Juniors in 1913 before turning professional at the age of 19 the following year when signing for Albion Rovers of the Second Division. His time there was almost immediately interrupted by war, and with the Second Division put on hold, he returned to the Junior game with Wishaw Thistle and then Battlefield Swifts while helping the war effort at home.

In 1919, Kilmarnock had appointed a new club secretary, Hugh Spence, who previously had assisted William Wilton at Rangers and had good contacts within the Glasgow senior and Junior clubs. Killie had a poor start in their league campaign in 1919/20, suffering some heavy defeats that included conceding seven to Rangers at home. Despite signs by December that their form was improving, the team desperately needed extra firepower in attack, and Spence identified Smith as an ideal signing. Now also known as 'J.R.', the arrival of Smith helped not just improve their league position, but his goals also were a big part of a great Scottish Cup run. He scored twice against Queen's Park in a 4-1 victory in the third round, and followed this with another goal in the quarter-final win against Armadale. He got two more in the semi-final 3-2 comeback victory over Morton at Hampden on 27 March 1920, and to the surprise of all in Ayrshire, Kilmarnock found themselves in a final against lowly Albion Rovers, who shocked hot favourites Rangers in the other semi-final.

On 17 April, a massive crowd of over 95,000 saw Kilmarnock lose an early goal but recover to take the trophy for the first time in their history by another 3-2 scoreline. The third, and ultimately winning goal, was scored by Smith. Kilmarnock ended the season in a respectable ninth place in the league, a great comeback from where they were before Smith had signed. Smith played in an end-of-season benefit match at Ibrox against Rangers, the league champions and cup winners competing for the Scottish War Memorial Trophy. In a possible sign of things to come for his Ibrox career, Smith was sent off and his team lost 5-0.

In his relatively short Kilmarnock career, Smith scored 40 goals in just 60 starts, but he became disillusioned with life at Rugby Park after a contract disagreement and he was sold to Cowdenbeath of the Second Division in 1921. In just one year in Fife he was a goalscoring sensation. He hit four hat-tricks in a total of 32 league goals for the club, all in just 32 games. He hit a club record seven goals in a single match, a 9-1 Scottish Cup hammering of lowly Vale of Atholl. In all he scored 45 times for Cowdenbeath. Such goalscoring was bound to attract bigger clubs, and in the close-season of 1922 Bill Struth brought Smith to Rangers for a fee of £3,000. This further strengthened the goalscoring options for the manager, as the previous season George 'Geordie' Henderson had scored 27 times from just 36 appearances.

Smith started at centre-forward on the opening day of the league season at home to Alloa on 15 August 1922 with Henderson unavailable. He scored a debut goal in a 2-0 victory. Struth was unsure who to make his first choice centre-forward, as Danish player Carl Hansen was given the nod in the next league game against Third Lanark. Smith was back in the team for the following game, and he again scored, this time in a fine 4-0 win at Motherwell. He kept his place for the next two fixtures, a Glasgow Cup win against Partick and then a dismal 2-0 league defeat to Falkirk on 9 September. Henderson was now available again, and Smith was dropped to allow him to return to the forward line.

Those four starts and two goals would be the total of Smith's Rangers career. Henderson rediscovered his scoring form and Smith could do nothing but watch from the sidelines, growing increasingly frustrated. In November 1922, just three months after his debut, Smith was sold to Bolton Wanderers of the English First Division, who needed a replacement for their centre-forward Frank Roberts after his move to Manchester City.

He made his Bolton debut on 25 November 1922 and made an immediate impact, grabbing a last-minute winner in a 2-1 win over Roberts's new club. Smith would go on to have an excellent career in Bolton, playing there until 1928 and scoring 87 goals in 174 appearances. This was despite an unfair reputation as being injury prone due to an ungainly running style which made it appear he was limping. But it was to be in the FA Cup that Smith would make a lasting impact in football history.

Bolton reached the FA Cup Final in Smith's first season, beating the likes of Norwich, Huddersfield and Sheffield United to get there. This was to be the first final at the new Wembley Stadium, and the opposition in front of King George V were West Ham United. The new venue was a great attraction to the football public and an enormous crowd flocked to see the match. Although the vast new stadium was said to be able to hold 125,000 fans, it was soon evident that far more than that were squeezing through the turnstiles for a game that was not all-ticket. In famous scenes, the huge crowd of an estimated 250,000 spilled on to the pitch, delaying the kick-off for over an hour, and the game could only start at all thanks to the efforts of mounted police (including the famous white horse named Billie, ridden by PC George Scorey), who managed to cram spectators right round the touchlines, leaving virtually no room visible other than the dimensions of the playing surface.

Many players were uneasy at playing the game at all, but it eventually began and Bolton struck first through David Jack. In the second half came Smith's moment of football immortality. He fiercely struck home a cross from inside-forward Ted Vizard, despite West Ham protests that the ball had actually struck the post. The referee judged that the ball had indeed gone in but had rebounded back into play off spectators crammed behind the goal nets. Bolton won the match 2-0, and Jack Smith became the first man to score in both the Scottish Cup and FA Cup Finals, as well as the first man to score at both Hampden and Wembley.

Smith continued the lead the Bolton line, with his best season in front of goal coming in 1924/25 with 21 league goals as they finished in third place. In 1925/26, Bolton embarked on another winning FA Cup run and Smith again found himself playing at centre-forward in a Wembley final. Incredibly, they had avoided First Division opposition at every stage prior to the final, Smith scoring in the fifth round win over South Shields. This time the Wembley opposition were Manchester City on 24 April 1926. City were struggling near the bottom of the First Division and Bolton started as hot favourites. After the chaos of 1923, the FA now made the final an all-ticket match, but tickets were sold too early in the season and before the finalists were known, resulting in Bolton bitterly complaining that many of their supporters were unable to attend.

Smith had been out injured for several weeks prior to the match, but was passed fit to play. As in 1923, the King was present to watch the match, and as in 1923 the opening goal was scored for Bolton by David Jack. This time, however, there would be no further scoring, and Bolton captain Joe Smith lifted the trophy with Jack earning his second winners' medal in the tournament.

Jack remained a Bolton player until 1928, but by then he had lost his place in the forward line to Harold Blackmore, so he joined Bury for £1,500 in March of that year. He made an immediate impact, hitting a hat-trick on his debut against Sheffield Wednesday, and he remained at the club for five years, during which time he hit an excellent 112 goals in 169 appearances.

Now in his late 30s, Smith played for Rochdale in the 1933/34 season, scoring eight times, and he retired in 1935 after spells at a couple of non-league clubs. Just before the start of the Second World War he returned to football as assistant trainer at Cardiff City, where he worked under manager Bill Jennings, who had been a team-mate at Bolton.

Smith died in the Cardiff suburb of Whitchurch on 1 September 1946, aged 51. His son Jack and his grandson Barry both became Bolton Wanderers players.

- Winner of the Scottish Cup and the FA Cup
- The first man to score in the final of both competitions
- A regular goalscorer in Scotland and England
- But unable to claim a place in the great Rangers forward line of Bill Struth

43 JACKY ROBERTSON

The Rangers star who became the first player and manager of Chelsea

JOHN TAIT Robertson was born in Dumbarton on 25 February 1877. Known to his friends as Jacky, he was a cultured and intelligent left-sided footballer, and started out in Junior football in 1892 with Poinfield, moving on after a year to Sinclair Swifts. He then joined senior club Morton in 1894 at the tender age of 17. He was a highly ambitious player as well as a skilful one, and he had played in fewer than 40 competitive matches for the Greenock club before deciding to try his luck in England when offered the chance to join Everton the following year.

His Everton debut came in October 1895 in a home match against Wolves, and the young Scot made an instant impression. He wasn't a first-team regular, however, until 1897/98 when he started 31 times in the left-half role, scoring once. His form attracted the attention of the Scotland selectors and he made his international debut on 2 April 1898 against England at Parkhead in a match lost by 3-1. He shared a dressing room that day with several Rangers players who would become club team-mates before long, namely Jock Drummond, Neilly Gibson, Jimmy Millar and Alec Smith.

It was something of a surprise when the following month Everton accepted an offer for him from Southern League club Southampton, Robertson incredibly becoming the 12th Scottish player on their books. He was a virtual ever present and a key man as Saints won the Southern League in 1898/99. He also added a second international cap while playing on the south coast, again against England, which ended in another defeat.

That international appearance would be the last time a Southampton outfield player played for the Scotland national side for over a century, the next being ex-Ranger Neil McCann in 2003. With his international status, Robertson was keen to renegotiate his contract with the club, who offered him the licence of local pub The Stewart Arms as an inducement. They thought this was a deal-clincher but Robertson declined the offer, and Southampton had little option but to sell their prized asset. A huge fee of £300 was agreed with Scottish champions Rangers, and Robertson moved to Glasgow.

This was a Rangers team already setting unsurpassed standards in the game after going through the previous season's entire league campaign without dropping a point. Opponents must have watched on in horror as one of the country's most highly rated players was added to an already invincible team. Robertson made his debut on the second weekend of the new season at Shawfield on 26 August 1899, scoring in a 6-2 thrashing of Clyde. It wasn't to be another invincible season, but it was still one that Rangers dominated. He played in his first Old Firm match on 7 October in the league, which ended all square, before the two sides met for the season's first trophy in November in the Glasgow Cup Final. A replay was needed before Rangers took the trophy thanks to a Bobby Neill penalty. Robertson had won the first of many medals as a Rangers player.

He started in 15 of the 18 league matches as the title was retained, adding two more goals to the one scored on his debut. The season ended with two wildly contrasting cup ties against their bitter rivals. First, Robertson endured a sickening 4-0 Scottish Cup semi-final defeat to the Parkhead team, and then enjoyed a sensational 5-1 Charity Cup Final hammering over them in May 1900. Three trophies won out of four in his debut season at Ibrox was a dream start, and he further enjoyed 1900 when given the honour of leading out Scotland against England in April, a match that saw the English humbled 4-1 with a hat-trick from future Rangers player R.S. McColl and a sensational display from Robertson's team-mate Neilly Gibson.

Over the course of his Rangers career, Robertson would add 14 caps to the two he won before joining the club, scoring three times (all of them against Wales). He could have added a couple more, but twice refused to travel to play against Ireland as his fear of sailing made the boat journey one that he was unwilling to make. He also represented the Scottish League six times while at Rangers, and was on the Ibrox pitch playing for Scotland in the tragic 1902 disaster match against England, his cap for this game being made unofficial.

His second season with Rangers, 1900/01, saw the title won for the third successive year and a 100 per cent home record. Robertson started every league match, scoring three times. He also scored in the Glasgow Cup Final, a 3-1 win over Partick. Unfortunately he also played in two 1-0 defeats to Celtic that ended the Scottish and Charity Cup campaigns.

Injury significantly interrupted his next campaign, only starting eight league games in 1901/02. But he played in the crucial new year victory at Parkhead, a thrilling 4-2 win in which he scored his first Old Firm league goal. He also won another Glasgow Cup Final, although in strange circumstances when Celtic refused to play in an Ibrox replay after a 2-2 draw in the first match, also at Ibrox. His medal collection was only missing a Scottish Cup, and that remained the case when Robertson was unable to prevent a deserved 2-0 win for Hibs in the semi-final.

After winning the title in each season at Rangers, things changed in 1902/03. The club was severely impacted, both on and off the pitch, by the awful loss of life at the Scotland v England match, and priority was on raising funds both for the families involved and for stadium renovation. Some players were sold, and combined with a squad that had some key men past their peak, it meant there would be no further league medals for Robertson in his remaining Ibrox career. He made 20 starts in the league in 1902/03, scoring twice, and also suffered defeats in the Glasgow and Charity Cups. But his focus, and that of the whole club, was on trying to win back the Scottish Cup as a tribute to those impacted in the disaster. Robertson was outstanding as Celtic were brushed aside 3-0 at Parkhead in the third round, and he scored twice in the 4-1 semi-final win over Stenhousemuir. Hearts were the final opposition and it took three extremely tight and tense matches before Rangers prevailed. The third match saw Robertson have to put in even greater effort as the team lost Jock Drummond to injury, but the men in blue would not be denied and won 2-0 thanks to goals by Alec Mackie and R.C. Hamilton.

Robertson would have two more seasons at Ibrox, but by now Celtic had overtaken them as the top team in the country and he would only win one more medal. Season 1903/04 saw a third-place finish in the league in a season he played 28 times in all competitions. The defence of the Scottish Cup ended in heartbreak, the final against Celtic seemingly won after two early goals only for the Parkhead men to come back to win 3-2. Robertson suffered along with all at the club that day, but helped to ease the pain a few weeks later when he scored twice against them in a resounding 5-2 Charity Cup Final victory.

His last season at Ibrox saw him score a decisive goal in the Scottish Cup semi-final win over Celtic, a match abandoned after Celtic fans invaded the pitch and tried to attack the referee. The final, however, ended in disappointment as Robertson and his team-mates simply failed to perform and lost easily to Third Lanark. The campaign also saw the first league play-off since the opening season of league football in 1891. After finishing tied on points, Robertson started the winner-takes-all match against Celtic on 6 May 1905. Despite Robertson scoring his sixth career goal against them, Celtic won 2-1 to take the title and this was his 178th and last appearance for Rangers. After numerous medals, multiple international caps and 30 goals he moved on in the summer of 1905.

Robertson's destination this time was a historic one. The newly formed Chelsea FC in London had been granted entry to the Second Division but they had a stadium without a team or a manager. The club wanted Robertson as their first boss, and when he signed on as player-manager he became both the first manager and the first registered player in the club's history. At 28, this was exactly the kind of exciting new challenge that the ambitious Robertson was looking for.

Robertson used his contacts in the game to quickly build an impressive squad. Among those he brought in were William 'Fatty' Foulke, the massive England international goalkeeper who weighed over 22st, and Joe Kirwan, the star winger of the Ireland national side. He took the team to third place in their first season with their performances attracting some huge crowds. For his second season in charge, he had spotted and signed Fulham's George Hildson, who became a scoring sensation and earned the nickname 'Gatling Gun' as he rattled in over 100 goals in his Chelsea career.

But there were tensions behind the scenes, and after an argument with the board Robertson resigned in November 1906 when he had been informed that team selection would become the responsibility of the directors. Robertson had laid successful foundations as Chelsea won promotion at the end of the season.

He reappeared as player-manager of Second Division Glossop North End in January 1907, where he stayed for two years. Unable to progress the small club above their status, Robertson then left in 1909 when appointed reserve team manager at Manchester United. But this was short-lived, and the ever-ambitious Scot then made the move abroad in 1912 when becoming a coach in the Hungarian capital of Budapest for local side MTK.

Back then, the standard of Hungarian football was far inferior to that in Britain, but Robertson's coaching methods must have paid off as the team climbed to second place in their championship. He had gone back home to the UK by the time MTK became champions in 1914, and they retained the title every year until 1925. After Robertson's death many years later, one Hungarian football official said, 'It was Jacky Robertson who laid the foundations of the cultured style of football played here.' He remained a popular figure among those still in the game until his passing aged 57 on 24 January 1935 after a long illness. Robertson's funeral at Rutherglen cemetery was attended by many of his former team-mates.

- A Scotland captain, and one of the best players of his generation
- Multiple league winner with Rangers
- Scorer of cup final goals against Celtic
- The first player and first manager for Chelsea
- A football visionary in Hungary

44   JAMES FIDDES

The cup final scorer against Celtic who was awarded the British Empire Medal

JAMES FIDDES was born in Grangemouth in the middle of the Great War, on 3 October 1916. Like many young Scottish footballers of the time, as a teenager he joined his local Junior team, Grange Rovers. A thoughtful and tricky right-winger and occasional inside-forward, his displays caught the eye of local Ibrox scouts who knew there was a space to fill in the Rangers squad since the career of the great Sandy Archibald had ended. In June 1934, Bill Struth offered the 17-year-old Fiddes a contract and he became a Rangers player.

Bobby Main was the established first choice in the right-wing position, young Fiddes starting his Ibrox career in the reserves and learning from those around him. He didn't have long to wait for his first appearance in the top team, however, Struth selecting a relatively inexperienced 11 on 27 August to play Celtic in a testimonial match for their long-serving and legendary goalscorer Jimmy McGrory. It wasn't the usual Celtic line-up either, but 10,000 fans attended and expected the customary competitive match. It was a night to remember for Fiddes, as playing at inside-right he scored the third goal and Rangers cruised to an emphatic 4-0 win.

Fiddes had to wait until the following April for his competitive debut. Rangers had a Scottish Cup Final the following Saturday, so rested both Bobby Main and George Brown for the trip to Aberdeen on 13 April. The two replacements were at opposite ends of their Rangers careers. Brown was replaced by the great Tully Craig, making his last Rangers start, while Main was replaced on the right wing by Fiddes. Rangers won 3-1 and the newspaper reports of the game all agreed that Fiddes showed great promise. He also started the last two league games of 1934/35, defeats to Hamilton and Queen's Park, but the title had already been secured.

Season 1935/36 started inconsistently for Rangers, both in results and team selection. Several players were tried at inside-right in the opening weeks, with Archie Macaulay, George Brown and a single appearance by Egyptian Mohamed Latif. However it was

Fiddes who got the nod for a Glasgow Cup semi-final against Clyde, and his clever and incisive play saw him retain the jersey. On 12 October 1935, Fiddes started in the Glasgow Cup Final at Hampden against Celtic in front of 50,000 fans. Following a tense first half Rangers exerted their superiority after the interval. And it was Fiddes who got the breakthrough on 65 minutes with his first competitive goal, a fierce shot crashing back into play off the woodwork, but the officials were well placed to see it had clearly crossed the line first. Rangers won 2-0, the second goal scored by Torry Gillick direct from a corner, and 19-year-old Fiddes had his first winners' medal.

Fiddes went on to play 17 league games that season, many in his initial position on the right wing. He was a winger when scoring a hat-trick in a 6-2 away demolition of Dunfermline in February 1936, but despite his six league goals Rangers relinquished their title to Celtic. They did, however, reach a third successive Scottish Cup Final, and on 18 April 1936 Fiddes won his first and only winners' medal in the tournament when a Bob McPhail goal defeated Third Lanark at Hampden.

Season 1936/37 was a good one for Rangers, claiming back their title, but it wasn't memorable for Fiddes who lost his place in early October through injury after playing in two Old Firm games in a matter of weeks. On his return to fitness, Struth preferred to stick with a winning team, and Fiddes only made a total of five starts. He again wasn't an automatic choice the following season, but did play more often. He played both wide and inside in his 14 league starts in an unsuccessful campaign, but his season's highlight was winning a second Glasgow Cup Final in a 2-1 defeat of Third Lanark in October 1937.

Season 1938/39 was to be his last full campaign at Ibrox, and it was the one he saw most first-team appearances. Nineteen of these were in the league, with his best display at Ibrox on 17 December 1938 when he scored four goals against a good Aberdeen team in a 5-2 victory. Rangers were champions again, and Fiddes had his second league medal. Fiddes also added a first Charity Cup winners' medal to his haul, starting in a tepid goalless final against Third Lanark in May 1939 that was won virtue of winning more corners.

He started the first three games of the following season, scoring in an Ibrox win over St Mirren on the opening day, before the outbreak of World War Two. Fiddes played his last game for Rangers in a defeat to Morton in the Western League on 30 December 1939. He left at the start of 1940, moving back closer to home to join Falkirk, managed by the same Tully Craig who played his last Rangers league game the day Fiddes had played his first. In all, he had started 73 games and scored 16 goals.

Although now a Falkirk player, he enlisted in the RAF, and made a couple guest appearances for Dunfermline as well as turning out for his parent club as his training allowed. On 5 March 1941, Fiddes completed his RAF training and became an acting pilot officer for the remainder of the conflict. His football career was now on hold but when granted leave he returned home to Falkirk where he now played as mainly a right-half.

After the conflict, Fiddes became a mainstay of a good Falkirk team. In the League Cup of 1947, Fiddes and the Prince of Goalkeepers Jerry Dawson were in the side that beat

Rangers 1-0 in the semi-final. Still managed by Craig, they lost the final in a replay to East Fife, who themselves were managed by a future Rangers great, Scot Symon.

In all, including wartime, Fiddes played 239 times for Falkirk, scoring 29 goals, and he turned out for them in every outfield position. In 1951 he went part-time and took on a job as a tanker driver at the BP refinery in Grangemouth. His part-time football career was brief with short spells at Ross County then Stenhousemuir before retiring. But Fiddes now enjoyed a second type of career. A keen trade unionist, he became a shop steward at the refinery, becoming both a branch chairman for the TGWU union and also an active member of their national Commercial Services Group. By 1969 he was also chairman of this group, and his long union activism saw him receive the British Empire Medal in 1970 in recognition of his services to the petroleum industry and the TGWU.

Sadly, Fiddes was not able to boast of his honour for long as in 1970, he passed away suddenly at the age of just 53.

- First competitive Rangers goal was in a cup final against Celtic
- 2 league medals
- 1 Scottish Cup
- 2 Glasgow Cups
- 1 Charity Cup
- Scored four in a game against Aberdeen
- Hampden cup finalist with Falkirk
- RAF war hero
- Holder of the British Empire Medal

45 JAMES MARSHALL

The London doctor who scored more than 100 league goals for Rangers

JAMES MARSHALL was born in January 1908 in the small Stirlingshire village of Avonbridge (only three miles away from another tiny village called Slamannan, the birthplace of his famous future Rangers team-mate Jimmy Smith). A talented and pacy inside-forward with an eye for goal, the young Marshall played Junior football for Shettleston, where he caught the eye of Bill Struth and his Rangers scouts. The long-serving Andy Cunningham was still the regular inside-right but he couldn't go on forever and Struth was searching for a potential successor. Convinced that Marshall could be that player, Struth signed him for Rangers in 1925 at the age of just 17.

Season 1925/26 was horrendous for the club, a combination of injuries and loss of form seeing Rangers stumble to their worst ever league placing of sixth. March 1926 saw Rangers suffer four successive defeats, including a Scottish Cup semi-final to St Mirren. The season was over and with four games remaining, Struth decided to give young Marshall his opportunity. How he grabbed it. Marshall's debut was on 3 April 1926 away to Morton. The 18-year-old scored twice in a 3-1 victory, helping halt that losing run. In the three remaining matches, Rangers won two and drew the other. Marshall scored two more doubles and a single, meaning seven goals recorded while scoring in all four of his starts.

A highly educated young man, he combined his football career with studying medicine, his medical career being his ambition and football his passion. Season 1926/27 started with a home game against Dundee United. Rangers won 2-0 with Marshall scoring both. He started 18 out of the first 20 matches in that league season, with highlights being a five-goal haul against Morton, a hat-trick against Clyde and a goal in the new year game versus Celtic, his first appearance against them in an Ibrox 2-1 win. Marshall won his first league winners' medal that season, eventually playing 25 games and scoring 20 goals. Marshall was used as an inside-right, a right-winger and even a centre-forward, his versatility a huge asset to the manager.

Cunningham was preferred for the majority of 1927/28, meaning Marshall's appearances were restricted to just six starts in another title-winning season. This was the year the Scottish Cup finally returned to Ibrox after a quarter of a century of heartache, Marshall not involved in any of the cup matches at all. He did hit six goals in those six appearances, however, reminding the manager he had plenty to offer when called upon.

Over the following seasons, he gradually established himself as the number one inside-right at the club. A second league medal was won in 1928/29, with 18 appearances in the campaign. His eight goals in all competitions included another against Celtic, but sadly it wasn't enough to win the Glasgow Cup tie which ended in a 2-1 loss. He also scored his first Scottish Cup goal in a 3-1 win against Dundee United, but wasn't selected for the tournament's later stages which saw Kilmarnock beat Rangers in the final.

Rangers, with Marshall ever more influential, then had a season to remember in 1929/30. He started the most league games yet in his Ibrox career, 26 appearances, as the title was won convincingly. In those 26 games he hit the opposition net 14 times, with doubles against Ayr, St Johnstone and Clyde. But Marshall won far more than just a third league medal. He scored in the Glasgow Cup semi-final win over Partick to help set up an Old Firm final, and then enjoyed a thumping 4-0 win in the final replay, a match that saw the great Jimmy Fleming score a hat-trick. Then in April he started his first Scottish Cup Final, a tense 0-0 draw with Glasgow rivals Partick Thistle. Marshall then opened the scoring in the replay, which was won 2-1 thanks to a late winner by veteran Tully Craig. Only the Charity Cup remained to be won, and this would give the club their first clean sweep of the four available trophies. Marshall opened the scoring in the final against Celtic on 10 May 1930. Fleming was also again on target in a match that saw Celtic snatch a 2-2 draw in injury time, then Rangers won the trophy by captain Davie Meiklejohn winning a nerve-shredding toss of a coin.

Marshall added plenty more medals in the next few seasons. His fourth league championship was secured in 1930/31 as he hit 20 league goals for the sole time in his

Rangers career. But the only cup that was won was to be the end-of-season Charity Cup, Marshall scoring the extra-time winner in a 2-1 victory over a plucky Queen's Park team at Hampden.

Season 1931/32 would see the league title lost for the first time in six years, the best Motherwell team in their club's history claiming the championship for the only time. Marshall had another fine season, however, claiming another 15 league goals in 34 starts. These included what proved to be the winner in the new year derby at Parkhead in a 2-1 success, and he also scored twice against Celtic in a Glasgow Cup semi-final trilogy, netting in both the drawn matches before a Jimmy Smith goal settled the second replay. Marshall played in the final as the trophy was regained with an easy win over Queen's Park, and he also scored twice in the Scottish Cup semi-final win against Hamilton to set up a Hampden date with Kilmarnock in April. He won his second Scottish Cup when the Ayrshire team were defeated 3-0 in a replay, and Marshall completed a hat-trick of cup successes in the season when Third Lanark were brushed aside in the Charity Cup Final.

April 1932 also saw him become a Scotland player when he lined up alongside Ibrox team-mates George Brown, Sandy Archibald and Alan Morton at Wembley against England. The match was lost 3-0, but Marshall was to get some revenge the following year when he played a starring role in a 2-1 home win over the same opposition. His third and final Scotland cap came in 1934, again at Wembley in another 3-0 loss. These three 'Auld Enemy' clashes were the only matches he played for his country.

Season 1932/33 saw Marshall help Rangers to three more trophy successes. He scored 16 league goals from 34 matches as Motherwell were beaten into second place by just three points, both clubs displaying tremendous consistency. Marshall scored in every round of the Glasgow Cup, including the only goal of the final to beat Partick. He also scored the only goal of the Charity Cup Final to beat Queen's Park. The sole failure of the season was in the Scottish Cup, Kilmarnock knocking Rangers out at Rugby Park in the third round.

By the summer of 1933, Marshall had completed his medical studies and graduated. It was therefore Dr James Marshall who lined up for 1933/34 and the season was just what the doctor ordered, another clean sweep of all four competitions. Marshall started in 21 league games, scoring seven times in a campaign that saw Rangers only lose twice. He scored an equaliser in the Glasgow Cup semi-final against Celtic, which Rangers won 2-1 thanks to a late Alex Stevenson winner, then he started in the final against Clyde and added to his medal collection thanks to a 2-0 victory. He also scored a crucial Scottish Cup semi-final goal to settle a close-fought match with a very good St Johnstone team, then collected his third national trophy in a one-sided final where St Mirren were hammered 5-0. Marshall started his last match for Rangers in May 1934 in the Charity Cup Final, and enjoyed a fitting finale to his Ibrox career by beating the Parkhead men 1-0.

In the summer of 1934, Marshall accepted an offer to take up a medical position in London, meaning the end of his Rangers career. The club, and Bill Struth, were fully understanding of his position, although this didn't stop the press from speculating on the player's future. Arsenal manager George Alison had been a long-term admirer of Marshall and in a blaze of publicity he signed for the Highbury club in July 1934. The fee was said to be 'one of the highest on record'.

He would score for Arsenal in a Charity Shield victory over Manchester City, but he struggled initially to combine his work with his job, and rarely featured at Highbury. Marshall only stayed at Arsenal for one season and made just five competitive starts for them. He then moved to West Ham, where he played far more often, scoring 14 goals in 57 appearances. He retired in 1937 at the young age of 29 to concentrate full time on medicine.

Overall Dr James Marshall scored over 140 goals for Rangers in his nine seasons, a fantastic strike rate for a player who was primarily an inside-forward. He only ever took one penalty in that tally, and is a member of an elite club to have scored more than 100 league goals for Rangers.

After a successful medical career, mainly in the Bermondsey area of London, Dr Marshall passed away in December 1977 at the age of 69.

- Over 100 league goals for Rangers
- 6 league titles
- 3 Scottish Cups
- Multiple Glasgow and Charity Cups
- Twice winner of the clean sweep
- 3 Scotland caps
- Not a Hall of Fame member but surely a candidate

46   JIMMY DUNCANSON

The first scorer of a Rangers league hat-trick against Celtic in the 20th century

THE TWO Rangers players to have scored the most goals for the club in matches against Celtic are both in the Hall of Fame, the legendary R.C. Hamilton leading the way with 35 strikes in all matches between the clubs, followed by the more recent Ally McCoist who hit the Celtic net 27 times. But the man who sits in third place in the list goals doesn't have his name on the Hall of Fame board at the top of the marble staircase. His name is Jimmy Duncanson.

Duncanson was born in Denniston in Glasgow on 13 October 1919, and on leaving John Street Secondary School in Bridgeton in 1934 he played football for Dunoon Milton Rovers. It took some time for his ability to be noticed by senior clubs, as it wasn't until 1939 that he joined Rangers.

The move came just as the world was again plunged into the horrors of war, and the first part of his Rangers career was spent playing in the various competitions that took place during the conflict. His debut came on 6 January 1940 against Queen's Park at Ibrox in the Western League. Playing at inside-right in a forward line containing future

Hall of Fame legends Willie Waddell, Willie Thornton and Alex Venters, the 20-year-old Duncanson instantly took to the Royal Blue shirt by scoring twice. He played ten times in that successful campaign, adding three more goals in the process.

His first three seasons saw Bill Struth ease him slowly into the team, with Duncanson seeing frequent action but never being an automatic choice. He made eight more league appearances in 1940/41, now in the Southern League. Duncanson also scored his first cup-tie goal for the club in the Summer Cup first round win over Falkirk. In 1941/42 he was restricted to just six starts up until the last few weeks of the campaign, but from then on he became a reliable and deadly part of a highly successful team both during and after the war. A sign of things to come came in the semi-final of the Charity Cup at Ibrox against Celtic in mid-May 1942 when a 2-1 win was achieved thanks to a double by Duncanson. These were his first goals against Celtic and he would go on to score 20 more in the next eight years. The final a few days later saw him score the clinching third goal in a 3-1 win over Clyde, his first of many cup final successes.

Duncanson hardly missed a game in 1942/43 after sitting out the first couple of weeks of the season. Rangers cruised to the Southern League title again, with the unforgettable 8-1 new year win over Celtic the undoubted highlight. Duncanson scored that day as well as in the return match at Parkhead, and he also scored against Celtic in wins over them in the Glasgow Cup, the Southern League Cup and the Summer Cup. His 22 goals in total over the campaign made him undroppable now, and he scored even more the next season.

His 25 goals in 1943/44 included his first Rangers hat-trick in a 4-1 win over Morton, as well as yet more strikes into the Celtic net, the highlight of these being a crucial double in a hard-fought 4-2 Southern League Cup semi-final at Hampden in front of a massive 90,000 crowd.

Duncanson completed a hat-trick of Glasgow Cup Final wins the following season, the big surprise being he didn't score when Rangers beat Celtic 3-2 in the final. He did hit a purple patch of scoring form in the title run-in, however, finding the net ten times in just five games between late February and early April 1945 to ensure another Southern League was won shortly before the conflict in Europe was over. And he finished the season in customary fashion, hitting the opener as Rangers took the Charity Cup back from Celtic by defeating them 2-1 in the final.

Season 1945/46 was the last of wartime competition before the return to football normality. Duncanson started in his usual fashion, scoring in another Southern League Old Firm win. He missed a spell due to injury but was back to help the team wrap up the league again, Rangers being wartime title winners in every season of the temporary competition. The season ended with the Victory Cup, a tournament celebrating the end of war and marking the end of wartime football. Rangers beat Celtic in the semi-final, without Duncanson scoring for once, and set up a final at Hampden against Hibs. The trophy was won on 15 June 1946 before a 100,000 crowd, and they saw Duncanson score twice to ensure a victory.

In August 1946 the Scottish league restarted. The first match of 1946/47 for Rangers was at home to Motherwell on 10 August. Duncanson played in his first 'official' league match for the club and scored twice in a 4-2 win. By the end of September, he had started in all of Rangers' first ten league matches, scoring 12 times with three doubles plus a hat-trick against St Mirren. One of those doubles came at Parkhead where he hit both goals in the first half an hour of a 3-2 win. He started in 27 of the 30 league matches over the season, ending with a total of 18 league goals as Rangers won the first national title after World War Two, meaning they had now been champions in each of the last nine seasons of league competition. Duncanson also played in the first Scottish League Cup Final, on 5 April 1947 against Aberdeen at Hampden, and he scored the third and fourth goals in a comprehensive 4-0 triumph.

Duncanson had played in a couple of wartime unofficial matches for Scotland, but in November 1946 he won his first, and only, recognised cap for his country. The match was against the Irish, and Duncanson had three of his club colleagues in Bobby Brown, George Young and Willie Thornton to help him feel at home. But the Scots played poorly, lucky to escape with a 0-0 draw, and Duncanson was never selected again.

The title was lost in 1947/48 to Hibs, and the League Cup defence ended in a 1-0 semi-final defeat to a Falkirk team managed by Rangers great Tully Craig and who had Duncanson's old team-mate Jerry Dawson in goal. But Duncanson still collected more winners' medals. He scored in the Glasgow Cup Final win over Third Lanark, and scored one and created the other in a Charity Cup Final win over Celtic at Hampden at the end of the season, watched by a record crowd for the competition of almost 70,000. And he won his first Scottish Cup Final when starting both matches against Morton in the final, the replay decided by a classic Billy Williamson goal. Both these matches had crowds of over 130,000 as fans flocked to see post-war football. Duncanson had already scored his customary Old Firm goal that season when hitting the last goal in a 4-0 Parkhead thumping on 2 January.

Season 1948/49 was a historic one for Rangers as they won the first treble of league title, Scottish Cup and Scottish League Cup. The league went to the last day with Dundee holding a one-point advantage, but they lost at Falkirk, allowing Rangers to snatch the championship by winning 4-1 at Albion Rovers. The great Willie Thornton scored three times that day, with the other coming from Duncanson. But it was on New Year's Day 1949 that Duncanson made his own bit of club history. In front of a 95,000 Ibrox crowd, he became the first Rangers player of the 20th century to score a league hat-trick in the Old Firm fixture with goals in the 26th, 43rd and 88th minutes. The last league hat-trick scored by a man in Royal Blue had been way back in 1899 when R.C. Hamilton also scored three in a new year win, and it remains a rare occurrence to this day with nobody achieving the feat since Johnny Hubbard in 1955.

Duncanson played in both the major cup finals that were won, scoring in the Scottish Cup win at Hampden over Clyde before 120,000 spectators. This was to be the last season he could be described as an automatic choice as injuries and competition for places restricted his appearances in 1949/50. Duncanson started in 12 league games as the title was retained by a single point from Hibs. His only goal in the league turned out to be a vital one, the sole goal of the game at Dens Park in April to turn one point into two. He did play in the Scottish Cup Final, however, collecting a third successive winners' medal as East Fife were beaten 3-0. He also played in the match that made the title a virtual certainty, a 0-0 draw against Hibs in late April that saw over 100,000 cram into Ibrox stadium.

That goal at Dundee would prove to be his last for Rangers. Duncanson just started once in 1950/51, a 0-0 draw at home to Dundee, before leaving Ibrox to join St Mirren. He played at Love Street for three seasons, followed by a brief spell at Stranraer in 1953 before he hung up his boots at the age of 34.

Duncanson continued to attend matches at Ibrox for as long as he was able, he and his wife Nancy remaining devoted supporters of the club that he had served with such distinction. He passed away on 1 September 1996 at the age of 76.

- Rangers career: 1939–1950
- Won multiple wartime honours
- Scored in the 8-1 win over Celtic
- 3 league titles, including the first treble
- 2 Scottish Cups
- 2 League Cups
- Over 150 Rangers goals, with 22 against Celtic
- First league hat-trick against Celtic in the 20th century
- Not yet in the Hall of Fame

47   JIMMY GALT

The war hero and businessman who won titles with Rangers and Everton

JIMMY GALT was born in Saltcoats on 11 August 1885. A left-sided defender and occasional inside-left, he began his illustrious career in the Juniors with Stevenston in 1903, Ardrossan Winton Rovers in 1904 and Ardeer Thistle in 1905. His displays impressed watching senior scouts and it was no surprise in the summer of 1906 when he left the Junior game. His destination was Rangers.

His competitive debut was on 25 August 1906 at left-half in a 2-0 league win at Port Glasgow Athletic. Among his team-mates that day was forward Jimmy Speirs, who made his bow the previous week. Both players went on to serve their country in the battlefields of the Great War.

Galt quickly established himself as an effective and influential defender, sharp in the tackle and accurate in his passing. He started 25 times in his first season at Ibrox, with

21 in the league as Rangers were unable to prevent Celtic from retaining their title and finished third. He did, however, gain his first winners' medal, helping keep out the star Celtic forward line in the Charity Cup Final in May 1907 as an R.G. Campbell goal won the trophy.

Season 1907/08 saw no trophies won (the biggest disappointment was a Glasgow Cup Final loss to Celtic after two replays), but Galt remained a pivotal player in the team. He scored his first Rangers goal on 31 August 1907 in a crazy 4-4 draw at Falkirk, and added goals against Morton in the league and Third Lanark in the Charity Cup for his most prolific season, three goals in 37 appearances. He also became a Scotland international, making a winning debut in March 1908 against Wales and then scoring in a 5-0 win over Ireland.

Galt didn't hit the net at all the following season, but he remained a fixture in the team, the left-half position now his own. Inconsistent league form meant that Rangers' challenge fizzled out, but Galt helped the team to a Scottish Cup Final date with champions Celtic. This was to be a final infamous in Scottish football history when a riot after a drawn replay saw the cup withheld. Galt played in both drawn matches, then lined up again against the same bitter rivals the following month in the Charity Cup Final. The crowd of 25,000 witnessed a fine Rangers victory, Galt earning his second winners' medal in the competition as two goals by his good friend and fellow Saltcoats man Jimmy Gordon saw Celtic defeated 4-2.

Season 1909/10 saw great optimism among the support that this could be the team to finally bring back the title. Prolific goalscorer Willie Reid and established English stars Billy Hogg and Herbert Lock were now Ibrox regulars, but the league campaign ended with a sixth successive title going to Parkhead and Rangers in third. Galt was still the club's undisputed first-choice left-half, racking up a further 31 starts. The closest he got to a winners' medal was in the Glasgow Cup when he played in an unfortunate 1-0 defeat to Celtic.

It was to be Galt's fifth season as a Ranger before the balance of power swung back to Ibrox. He made 25 starts in 1910/11, missing several games through injury. He managed one goal, in a league win over Hearts, but he won three winners' medals. The league title was won by four points from second-placed Aberdeen, with Willie Reid scoring an amazing 38 times. In the October, Galt played behind a forward line who blew Celtic away with three goals in the first hour of the Glasgow Cup Final, then in May he enjoyed another final success over them, a 2-1 victory in the Charity Cup.

Rangers were at last the best team in the land again, and they retained both the league title and the Glasgow Cup the following season, Galt playing his part with another 31 starts. He started the campaign with an opening-day goal in a big win over Raith Rovers, and added one more to his modest tally in a new year win over Partick Thistle, who were also beaten in the Glasgow Cup Final. Like every season of his Rangers career, however, Galt failed to add a Scottish Cup medal to his collection, Clyde being the latest team to end that particular dream.

Galt started another 34 games in 1912/13, now an occasional captain as well as an ever-dependable defender. Unfortunately, injury robbed him of a third Glasgow Cup winners' medal when he sat out the final victory over Celtic, but he won a third successive league championship as William Wilton's men finished four points clear of the chasing pack.

His final season in Royal Blue was injury interrupted but he still added 21 appearances to his Rangers total. After three years as champions, the title was lost narrowly to Celtic but Galt did add a third Glasgow Cup medal to his collection, playing in a comfortable victory over Third Lanark. By the summer of 1914, Galt had amassed 240 Rangers appearances, with three winners' medals in the league and both the Glasgow and Charity Cups. Now 29, he was subject of a substantial transfer offer from English giants Everton and made the move to Merseyside, joining up with former Ibrox team-mate Bobby Parker.

Galt only played for one season at Everton, with war ending English competition in 1915. But what a season it was. Right from day one, his debut in an opening-day victory away to Spurs, he was captain of the team. Parker's goals at one end, combined with Galt's experience and organisational skills at the other, made a winning combination. After a slightly shaky spell in September, a thumping 5-0 derby win at Liverpool set them on an impressive run of wins. By 7 December they were up to fourth place and genuine title contenders when Galt returned to Glasgow as a director of the new Lorne Cinema in Cornwall Street in Ibrox, a business venture along with good friend and Rangers star Jimmy Gordon. The appearance of the two Royal Blue favourites, along with Parker, guaranteed a sell-out opening night of 700 paying patrons.

When back down in Merseyside, Galt's Everton were the team in form. In March they surprisingly lost to Chelsea in the semi-final of the FA Cup, but a few weeks later a win away at Bradford saw them hit the top of the First Division table, where they stayed. Galt was the captain in 25 of their games, and was the last skipper to lift the championship trophy for some time as football was suspended due to the war.

Galt returned to Scotland and enlisted in the Army Services Corps. He played a handful of games as a guest for Partick Thistle, Third Lanark and Fulham and even made a last unofficial international appearance against England in 1916, when he scored. But his time was mostly now on active duty. He rose to the rank of second lieutenant in the Argyll and Southern Highlanders, until in 1917 he suffered severe shellshock on the front line and was returned home to recuperate. His injuries were such that a return to football was unlikely, but he did attempt a brief playing career with Partick and then Alloa before inevitably accepting his days on the pitch were over.

Galt then concentrated on his business interests, and in 1919 he founded the firm of James H. Galt (Ltd.), motor agents, 52 Woodlands Road, Glasgow, which had Jimmy Gordon as a partner. He had the oldest Alvis agency in Britain, having taken it when the car was first manufactured 1919.

Galt was a vice-president of the Motor Agents' Association, and had spells as chairman of the local division and had also been vice-chairman of the Scottish Centre of the Motor and Cycle Trades Benevolent Fund. He and Gordon also opened several successful billiard halls.

Away from business, he was a member of the Scottish Flying Club and was an excellent golfer. In his younger years he had almost won the Scottish amateur golf championship.

On 17 November 1935, Galt passed away at his home at Burnside Road, Whitecraigs, Giffnock. He was just 50 and had served his club and country with great distinction.

- 240 appearances, six goals
- 3 league titles
- 3 Glasgow Cups
- 3 Charity Cups
- Title-winning captain at Everton
- Hero of the Great War
- Highly successful businessman

48 JIMMY MILLAR

The Rangers player with a familiar name who was an invincible and a world champion

JIMMY MILLAR was born in Annbank on 2 March 1870. He stood out in local football as a nimble and skilful goalscorer, and at the age of just 19 he joined Rangers in 1889.

That was just before league football started in Scotland, so his appearances were mainly in friendlies and minor long-forgotten competitions. His first start in a match which would nowadays be regarded as competitive was on 7 September 1889, a 6-2 Scottish Cup win over the quaintly named United Abstainers Athletic. No record exists of who scored that day so we don't know if Millar was among the goals, but he did score in a fine Glasgow Cup win over Third Lanark two months later.

When league football started in the summer of 1890, Millar had been tempted south by a lucrative contract offer from Sunderland, who had just been voted into the English Football League. They were a team who had been given the nickname 'The Team of All the Talents' the previous season when despite their non-league status had thrashed some of England's top sides in friendly matches, including a 7-2 demolition of Aston Villa. This prompted Villa chairman and Football League founder William McGregor to remark that Sunderland had talent in every position. Their team was crammed full of Scottish players. Johnny Campbell signed from Renton and was the star man, alongside other former Renton players Davy Hannah and John Harvie, Tom Porteous from Kilmarnock and captain John Auld from Third Lanark.

Millar's first game for Sunderland was in a 5-1 friendly win over Renton, and he played in the club's first league fixture, a 3-2 defeat to Burnley in September 1890. His first league goal came two weeks later in a crushing win over West Brom, and he ended that first season with ten goals in 17 games as Sunderland finished seventh. But it was Sunderland's second league season in 1891/92 that Millar started his incredible medal-winning run.

The season opened with a Millar hat-trick in a 5-2 win over Wolves. They then lost their next three games despite more Millar goals before winning all but two of their remaining 22 fixtures to roar up the table from 14th to first. Millar only missed four games all season as Sunderland claimed their first English title and also reached the FA Cup semi-final. His 18 goals played a huge part in the Roker men's triumph. Their home ground was a fortress, winning all 13 games. Millar also paid a visit to his former club, playing in a 1-0 friendly win at the old Ibrox in April 1892.

Sunderland maintained their position as England's top club in 1892/93, with Millar again a vital player. His 18 league goals included hat-tricks against West Brom and Everton, and he added a third in an FA Cup tie against Royal Arsenal as the championship was retained by a massive 11-point margin. The following season saw Millar end top scorer for the first time, but it wasn't enough to stop the title slipping away and a second-place finish behind Aston Villa. He scored home and away against Villa that season among his 21 league goals, and he also scored in another Ibrox friendly, a 2-2 draw over the new year period.

Season 1894/95 would end in a historic triumph for Millar and Sunderland, not only regaining their English title for a third championship in four seasons but winning the unofficial 'World Championship' too. An 8-0 season opener against Derby County set things off, featuring a Millar double. A further Scottish forward had been signed that season, Tom Hyslop, who would later be a Rangers player. He scored seven league goals and Millar hit 13 as the title never looked in doubt from the turn of the year onwards. Miller also scored five times in an 11-1 FA Cup win over Lancashire League team Fairfield; to this day he is one of only four Sunderland players to score five in a competitive fixture.

After winning the title, Sunderland agreed to take on Scottish champions Hearts for what was billed as 'The World Championship Match', an occasional one-off game that had taken place over the previous two decades, but this was the first time it had been between both league champions. The fixture in Edinburgh attracted 10,000 spectators and they witnessed a classic game of attacking football. After an uncertain start, the visitors roared into a two-goal lead at half-time. But the home crowd were in a frenzy within 20 minutes of the restart as three Hearts goals seemed to put the Scots on the road to victory. Then the tide turned again when Millar weaved his way through the home defence with a surging run, and he equalised with a firm shot. Hearts were now deflated and two late Sunderland goals gave them a 5-3 win, and allowed themselves the title of the football world champions.

Despite their claim, the following season was a disappointing one. Dogged by inconsistency, the title was gone by the new year and despite three goals by Millar in two ties, there was an early FA Cup exit. Millar played his last game in Sunderland colours on 11 April 1896, scoring the only goal in a 1-0 win against Small Heath. By now, the Scottish league was well established and the top clubs could finally compete with those down south in terms of wages. And in the close-season of 1896, Rangers were able to attract Millar back to Ibrox.

There was a familiar face alongside Millar in the forward line when he made his second Rangers debut on 15 August against St Mirren with ex-team-mate Tom Hyslop starting his first full season with the club. Both men scored in a 5-1 win. Millar was a fixture in the team from then on, enjoying a glittering first season, and he played in the Glasgow Cup Final win over Celtic. Although not prolific, he scored important goals, including one in the league win over Celtic in December. He scored four Scottish Cup goals, including the first and last strikes in the final, a 5-1 hammering of Dumbarton. And he ended the season by winning a third cup medal in the Charity Cup win over Third Lanark. A third place in the league apart, Millar was keeping up his impressive record of winning medals. His first season back had seen him hit 16 goals in 29 starts.

His excellent form earned Millar a long overdue Scotland cap in April 1897, and he scored the winner in a 2-1 win over England at the Crystal Palace in front of 37,00 fans. Millar played twice more for Scotland the following year, enjoying a win over Wales then suffering a defeat against England where he scored Scotland's consolation goal.

His second season saw him twice score four times in a match, against Partick Thistle in the Glasgow Cup and Dundee in the league. He won a second Glasgow Cup Final, an easy victory over Queen's Park with new scoring sensation R.C. Hamilton on target. Despite Hamilton's regular goals, and Millar weighing in with ten in just 15 games, Rangers only finished runners-up in the league. But Millar was one of the 11 who retained the Scottish Cup, meaning two of the three main cup competitions were won again.

Millar had collected an impressive collection of medals by now, but he can't have expected his next year at Rangers to have gone any better. Season 1898/99 is iconic to all Rangers fans as the year the league title was won without dropping a single point, and Millar more than played his part. He played in 16 of the 18 games and scored 11 times, including one at Parkhead in an early title warning to the holders when Rangers romped to a 4-0 success. In November he scored an important goal in a nervous and pivotal 4-3 win at Hibs, then a hat-trick in a big win over Clyde. Then on 7 January 1899, after 17 wins from 17, Millar was among the scorers as Rangers beat Clyde 3-0 to clinch the perfect season.

Incredibly, for the last five matches of that season, there was a second Jimmy Millar in the team. This one was a half-back born in Elgin, who would go on to have an excellent career with Bradford City.

Despite the invincible league season, Millar's campaign ended with double disappointment in Cup competitions as he played in the losing Scottish Cup Final to Celtic before also losing to them in the Charity Cup. But Millar's place in Ibrox history was secured forever, a key man in the unique perfect campaign.

His last season in Royal Blue saw him pick up a second league title in a row, but his form was inconsistent and he didn't feature as often as before. His only league goal from seven starts was in an opening-day win over Third Lanark but he ended the season in style, scoring in a 5-1 humbling of Celtic in the Charity Cup Final. In all Millar had played 114 times for Rangers and scored a very respectable 59 goals.

Down south, his old club Sunderland had suffered relegation then won promotion again during his absence, and were building another strong team. In the summer of 1900, Rangers accepted an offer for Millar to return to Roker Park.

His second Sunderland debut was also the first appearance for the club of fellow Scot and future Celtic and Rangers forward George Livingstone, with Millar opening the scoring in a 2-2 draw at Notts County. Millar played in 30 league games, scoring nine times as Sunderland finished a close second behind Liverpool, leading the table right up to the last day.

Millar and his team-mates were determined to go one better in 1901/02, although the previous season's top scorer Livingstone had left for Parkhead. And they were to be successful, only losing twice as Millar earned his fourth English championship medal. Now in his 30s, he was employed in a slightly less advanced position but still chipped in with nine goals in 32 starts. These included a crucial hat-trick in a 3-0 defeat of Bury in the run-in as glory beckoned.

During the following season he notched eight times but Sunderland could only finish third. His highlight came on 28 February 1903 when he scored twice in a 3-0 win over Corinthians in the final of the Sheriff of London Shield, a forerunner of the Charity Shield. This was to be the last season of regular football for Millar and his final competitive Sunderland start was in a dismal 3-0 home defeat to Derby County on 26 March 1904, although he took part in an end-of-season tour of Ireland and scored his last two Sunderland goals in a thumping win over Cliftonville.

In all, Millar made 260 Sunderland appearances in his two spells, hitting 128 goals and even to this day the fan website A Love Supreme lists him as the sixth greatest player in their history. Sadly, there is no happy ending to Millar's story. After retiring from playing in 1904, he returned to the game a couple years later when appointed as trainer at Chelsea, managed by former Rangers star Jacky Robertson. But in the summer of 1907 he died suddenly at the age of 37 after a short illness.

For many years, Millar's contribution to Rangers and Sunderland was unrecognised, mainly as both clubs for some reason often used the spelling Miller in their team line ups that included him, leading many publications since to talk of a 'James Miller' in the Rangers team of the time. But he most certainly was one and the same man, and with the same spelling as his famous 1950s and 1960s goalscoring namesake.

- 2 separate spells at both Rangers and at Sunderland
- 187 goals in 374 career appearances
- 4 English titles
- 2 Scottish titles
- 2 Scottish Cups
- 2 Glasgow Cups

- 2 Charity Cups
- 1 Charity Shield
- 3 Scotland caps and two goals against England
- An Invincible
- A world champion

49 JIMMY PATERSON

The star winger who won the Military Cross for gallantry

JAMES ALEXANDER Paterson was born on 9 May 1891 in London, where his Scottish parents were living at the time. His father was a Presbyterian church minister, and they returned north when James was still a young child. He was brought up in Maxwell Street and attended Bellahouston Academy, where he became the school sports champion. As well as being a talented athlete and highly intelligent studious pupil, Paterson was also a fine football player and helped the school team to the Glasgow Secondary Schools League title. A quick and skilful winger, he was signed by Queen's Park where he played in their reserve team, known as The Strollers.

It was there that Paterson was spotted by Rangers scouts, and manager William Wilton signed him for the Ibrox club in September 1910. He combined his football with studying for a medical degree, making his Rangers debut at Ibrox on 26 September 1910 on the left wing in a 4-0 win over Hibs. That position was the property of the great Alec Smith, who was out injured, and as soon as he was fit again Paterson was back in the reserves. He did play one more time that season, however, deputising for Smith again in a vital 1-0 win over Celtic at Parkhead in a season that saw the title finally returning to the club after a long nine-year absence.

Paterson took part in a close-season tour of Denmark, but he remained mainly a part-time reserve and part-time medical student the following season, starting just seven first-team matches. These included a Scottish Cup first round tie against Stenhousemuir where he scored his first Rangers goals, grabbing a double in a 3-1 win. These games were mostly on the right wing, deputising for first-choice Billy Hogg, and in 1912/13 Paterson finally made his breakthrough, almost always on the right.

He started 21 league games as the title was won for a third successive year, scoring seven times. Paterson had mixed success in matches against Celtic, scoring against them for the first time in a victory in the Inter-City League competition but also starting in a Charity Cup Final collapse when a 2-0 lead became a 3-2 defeat.

The only medal he won in 1913/14 would be the Glasgow Cup where Third Lanark were easily defeated in the final, but his six goals in 32 league appearances weren't enough to prevent the championship being surrendered to Celtic, and he suffered another Charity Cup heartbreak when Third Lanark sprang a semi-final upset.

Season 1914/15 had hardly begun when war was declared, Paterson now even more determined to complete his medical degree so he could then help the war effort. He still managed to start in 33 games over the season, hitting the net seven times including goals in three successive matches against Dundee, Clyde and Hamilton. Rangers won no trophies that season but that didn't prevent the Ibrox crowd taking Paterson to their hearts, his skill and effort making him a real fan favourite. He graduated in 1916, meaning that 1915/16 would be his last season in Royal Blue until able to return from serving his country. He made over 30 appearances again in another season where no trophies were lifted, although Paterson did score against Celtic in the Glasgow Cup Final in a 2-1 reverse. He also starred in a terrific 3-0 win over the Parkhead men in the league in October 1915, giving a man-of-the-match display on the left wing when he again scored. Paterson had switched back to the left wing after the retirement of Alec Smith, striking up an excellent partnership with inside-left Tommy Cairns, a player who would go on to enjoy a magnificent Ibrox career.

After his graduation, Paterson joined the 14th Battalion the London Regiment, the London Scottish, where he was appointed medical officer. Over the next couple of years he endured some horrendous times on the front line, earning the rank of major, but was known to his men simply as 'Doctor Pat'. In 1917, Paterson was awarded the Military Cross for conspicuous gallantry, with his citation reading,

'Under an intense hostile bombardment, he hastened to the spot, dressed the wounded and cleared them from the road, personally seeing to their removal to the aid post. He then returned and cleared the dead from the road, setting a fine example of coolness and disregard of danger.'

Once the fighting was over, Paterson returned to Glasgow to work in a local hospital, where his exploits in foreign fields had made him a household name. In September 1919 he made a surprise and unannounced comeback for Rangers at Ibrox against Raith Rovers. Despite the fact he had not trained for the match and was both overweight and unfit, Paterson entertained the adoring crowd, and he even scored a goal in the 3-2 win that easily brought the loudest cheer of the day from the 12,000 crowd.

He was back in the team to stay and quickly regained his fitness and match sharpness. The left-wing partnership with Cairns was now back in harness, and Rangers went from strength to strength in 1919/20. On 18 October, champions Celtic visited Ibrox and were soundly beaten 3-0 in a match that most observers would report as Paterson's finest 90 minutes as a Rangers player. Before a crowd of 76,000 he tormented the Celtic defence, and capped his day by scoring the final goal. Paterson started in 36 of the 42 league games Rangers played, his 11 goals representing his best return as William Wilton's side won the title by three points. He also started in the Scottish Cup quarter-final with Celtic at Ibrox, which attracted a record crowd to the stadium – reported as being 85,000 – and was won 1-0 thanks to a Tommy Muirhead goal. Sadly there would be no Scottish Cup medal for Paterson, however, as he suffered semi-final defeat to unfancied Albion Rovers.

This was the last campaign of Wilton's Rangers as he tragically perished in a boating accident at the end of the season. The new era under Bill Struth would begin in 1920/21, but Paterson would not be a part of it. His brother-in-law John Scott was appointed the club doctor at Arsenal and invited Paterson to join with him in his London medical practice. Scott persuaded Arsenal manager Leslie Knighton to sign Paterson as an amateur player, fending off competition from several other London clubs. As an amateur, he was not paid a salary by the Gunners, but he did receive several 'gifts' from the club by way of recognising his contribution. These included a baby grand piano, a Venetian vase and a diamond tie-pin. The home he shared with his brother-in-law in Clacton must have been the envy of the neighbourhood, as on top of these gifts Paterson had also been given a solid silver coffee service worth over £100 as a farewell thank you from Rangers.

His Arsenal debut came on 30 October 1920 at Derby County, and he started 20 league games over the season, helping turn round the team's poor early results. His excellent form was rewarded by being selected to play for the English League against the Scottish League in March 1921 at Highbury. Paterson had never played international football, the rules of the time meant he did not qualify to play for Scotland as he was born in England.

Paterson visited the Scottish dressing room before the game, where he shook hands with every player, including two former Ibrox team-mates in Sandy Archibald and Andy Cunningham, as well as the man who replaced him at outside-left, the immortal Alan Morton. Just before kick-off, a fan presented him with a bunch of flowers, and it was reported that he played the first few minutes still holding them until a break in play allowed him to hand them over to someone on the touchline.

Paterson may have been great friends with the Scots, but that didn't stop him from creating the game's only goal when his teasing cross was finished by Sunderland centre-forward Charlie Buchan.

Paterson remained at Highbury until 1924, starting 73 times, when he then retired to concentrate fully on his GP practice. But he wasn't finished with football just yet. In February 1926, Arsenal manager Herbert Chapman was in the middle of an injury crisis with no fit recognised left-winger at the club. He persuaded Dr Paterson to make a comeback not long before his 35th birthday in a league game against Newcastle. Arsenal won 3-0 and Paterson scored. He then kept his place for a tough FA Cup tie at Aston Villa, which was drawn. Paterson then scored in the replay victory, with film of this available online from the old newsreel footage of the time. He then played his last senior football match when starting in the next round of the FA Cup at Swansea, which Arsenal lost 2-1. Incredibly these two goals scored in his brief comeback were the only goals he ever scored for Arsenal.

Dr Paterson moved to a new GP practice soon after this in Bramley, Surrey, and he remained there until his retirement, when he returned north to live in Ayrshire. On 31 August 1959 he died of a heart attack in his Newmilns home. He was 68 years old.

He is not in the Hall of Fame but his is a name that we should remember when talking of past heroes. A great player, and a great man.

- 41 goals in 168 Rangers appearances
- 2 league titles, one either side of the Great War
- A doctor on the front line
- A famous Arsenal signing
- Not in the Hall of Fame

50 JIMMY SHARP

The future P.O.W. sold to Rangers by Arsenal as they needed the money

JIMMY SHARP was born in the small Perthshire town of Alyth on 11 October 1880. He enjoyed a brief career in Junior football with first Edengrove then East Craigie, before signing for First Division Dundee in the summer of 1899. A tough-tackling and brave left-back, he quickly made his Dundee debut in an opening-day league win over Clyde in August.

Even though still a teenager, he became an immediate fixture in the Dundee team, virtually ever present during his five-year career at Dens Park. In 1902/03 Dundee mounted a title challenge, finishing second behind Hibs, and they also reached the Scottish Cup semi-final before falling to Hearts. In March 1903 he was selected to play for the Scottish League against their English counterparts, where he enjoyed a fine 3-0 victory, and he also scored a rare goal from the penalty spot in an important 2-0 win against Celtic.

Now the club captain, Sharp was given the honour of skippering the Scotland international team the following season in March 1904 when Dens Park was chosen to host the annual match against Wales. The 1-1 draw would be his first and last Scotland appearance of his Dens Park career as he decided to move south that summer, joining Southern League club Fulham. He remains the last Dundee player to captain Scotland, and played 114 times for them, scoring five times.

It seemed a strange move for an international player reaching the peak of his career, and he only lasted one season at Craven Cottage before moving to Woolwich Arsenal in 1905. Sharp was a regular from his winning debut against eventual champions Liverpool on the opening day, starting 35 of the 38 league matches as Woolwich Arsenal finished 12th. He also played his part in a fine FA Cup run, which ended when they lost to Newcastle in the semi-final.

His second Highbury season was interrupted by injury, but he was the first-choice left-back when available, playing 26 league games in a top-ten finish and again suffering FA Cup semi-final heartbreak, this time to The Wednesday. In 1907 his consistent form was rewarded with a return to the Scotland team, playing against both Wales and England. Sharp remained a regular in 1907/08, adding to his cap collection on 4 April 1908 in a draw with England. But behind the scenes Arsenal had serious financial difficulties. They were desperate to reduce running costs, and even though Sharp had started 32 league games during the season, the board had made it known that all players had their price, and Rangers enquired what that price would be. After a brief negotiation, Sharp was on his way to Ibrox for a bargain fee of £400. His Arsenal career had 116 appearances and five goals, all of them penalties.

What an introduction Sharp was to get in Royal Blue. Great rivals Celtic were one win away from a fourth successive title, with their next match at Ibrox. Sharp made his debut at left-back in front of 40,000 fans and despite impressing in his new surroundings the day ended dismally, with future Rangers regular Alec Bennett scoring the game's only goal for the visitors. Sharp's only other appearances before the season's end were in an unsuccessful Charity Cup campaign, and it was not the start to his Rangers career he would have been dreaming of.

Season 1908/09 saw Sharp start the first 18 league games, but he had never settled back in Scotland and made it known he would prefer a return to London. His last Rangers appearance was on 19 December 1908 in a home draw against Kilmarnock at right-back, and two weeks later the club accepted a £1,000 bid from Sharp's former club Fulham. His Rangers career had lasted for less than nine months, with 22 games and no goals.

Fulham were now a league club in the Second Division, and Sharp won his fifth and last Scotland cap just a couple of months after his move back, a 3-2 loss to Wales. Sharp made 108 starts for Fulham over the next three and a half seasons, a model of consistency as the London club finished mid-table every season. In November 1912, near neighbours Chelsea paid the huge sum of £1,750 for the 32-year-old as they fought a relegation battle in the First Division after being promoted the previous season. He made his Chelsea debut against Blackburn in a 1-1 draw at Ewood Park, then became the regular left-back. Sharp played 23 league games before the season ended and was a big part of Chelsea just avoiding the drop. By April 1915 Sharp had racked up 63 starts for Chelsea, and when football was suspended due to the Great War he returned to his home area in Dundee and played as a guest for a brief time for Dundee Hibernian.

Even though now well into his 30s, Sharp was determined to play his part in the conflict. He joined the Black Watch regiment in 1916, and saw active duty on the continent. On 28 April 1918, the *Sunday Post* printed this worrying article, 'Lance-Corporal James Sharp, Black Watch, the well-known Dundee, Chelsea, Fulham, and Scottish International footballer, is officially notified as wounded and a prisoner of war in Germany.

His parents, who reside at Park Avenue, Dundee, have received word to that effect.

For some time back much anxiety had been as to Jimmy's fate. He has been in France with the Black Watch for a considerable time.'

Happily, when the war ended, he was repatriated and fully recovered from his injuries. In 1919 he returned to Fulham for a third time, this time in the role of trainer. On 17 April 1920 Harold Crockford missed the team bus for the trip to Bury, meaning only ten players travelled north. Sharp, now 39, stepped in, played inside-left and amazingly scored his last senior goal in a 2-2 draw.

Sharp would later be trainer at Walsall in the Third Division North, and also in Northern Ireland with Cliftonville. He died in November 1949 at the age of 69.

- A dependable and consistent full-back
- Last Dundee player to captain Scotland
- Sold by Arsenal as they needed the money
- A brief Rangers career with a debut against Celtic in a league decider
- Helped Chelsea avoid relegation
- Had three spells as a player for Fulham
- A prisoner of war
- A trainer who scored for the first team aged 39

51 JIMMY SPEIRS

The Rangers forward and English FA Cup winner killed in the Great War

JAMES HAMILTON Speirs was born in Govan on 22 March 1886, one of six children. The family moved to Govanhill near the start of the 20th century, where young Jimmy started to show his footballing talent for local club Anandale while working as a clerk. A clever inside-forward, he made the move to Maryhill Juniors in the spring of 1905 where he helped the club to several local trophies, including the Glasgow Junior Cup, Speirs scoring the final winner against Ashfield. It wasn't long before he was attracting the attention of senior scouts, and in the summer of 1905 the 19-year-old signed for Rangers.

Rangers had suffered a trophyless season in 1904/05, losing the league title in a play-off against Celtic, and manager William Wilton was starting to reshape his team in search of a return to the club's dominance of the earlier 1900s. But Speirs endured a dismal debut, playing at centre-forward in a 5-0 Ibrox humiliation by Hearts on 25 September. Despite this, he retained his place and scored his first Rangers goal in his next game, a consolation effort in another painful defeat, this time 3-1 at Third Lanark in the Glasgow Cup. Rangers ended the league season in a disappointing fourth place but Speirs could be relatively happy with his contribution of six goals from 18 starts in the league.

But it was in cup competitions that he seemed to save his best. He scored a hat-trick in the Scottish Cup first round win over Arthurlie, although was unable to prevent a third-round exit at the hands of Port Glasgow. He also played a huge part in a thrilling Charity Cup semi-final win over champions Celtic in early May 1906, opening the scoring at Parkhead after just three minutes and later adding another as Rangers powered to a 5-3 victory. Speirs then scored the first goal in the final at Hampden against Queen's Park and also hit the winner in a 3-2 triumph that saw him collect his only winners' medal as a Rangers player. His form at the end of his debut season was hugely impressive, he had already scored a double at Parkhead in a Glasgow League win on 31 March.

The late-season successes had given Rangers some confidence that 1906/07 could finally see the good days return, but it wasn't to be despite another solid return from Speirs. He scored 13 league goals from 22 appearances, including five in his first five starts, but the title challenge never looked convincing and the team ended the season third, with Celtic champions again. The bitter rivals also ended Rangers' Scottish Cup dream for the season in the quarter-finals. Speirs scored in the Glasgow Cup semi-final against Queen's Park but the amateurs prevailed after a replay, so again it was the end-of-season Charity Cup that represented the last hope of silverware. Unfortunately, Speirs suffered an injury in a league game against Kilmarnock and missed the rest of the campaign, sitting out the Charity Cup Final and watching his team-mates battle to a superb 1-0 win over Celtic.

Season 1907/08 was a forgettable one for Speirs but memorable for three reasons elsewhere. Niggling injuries and the excellent form of his replacement in the team, Bob Campbell, meant Speirs was restricted to just 13 league starts. His five goals included a double in a 4-2 win over Motherwell as Rangers again stumbled to third place at the end of the season. Celtic won all four trophies, but Speirs got a surprise call-up to the international team in March 1908, starting at centre-forward in a 2-1 win over Wales. It would be his only cap. That same month, Speirs was initiated into the Freemasons at Lodge 553 in Glasgow, something he took very seriously for the rest of his life, rising to the status of master mason by 1913. The third momentous occasion for Speirs had happened a few months earlier, the birth of his son James in December 1907.

After another blank season, Rangers were looking to rebuild and decided that Speirs was no longer part of their plans. He left Ibrox in the summer of 1908 and joined Clyde, who he helped to a massively improved season. Speirs hit ten goals in 20 starts as Clyde went from second-bottom to third in the league, finishing just three points behind champions Celtic. He also helped them to a Scottish Cup semi-final, which they lost to the Parkhead men. His excellent form at Shawfield earned him a move to the English First Division when Bradford City signed him in the summer of 1909. Speirs would then write himself into Bradford folklore.

His debut on the opening day of the new season ended in a 1-0 loss to Manchester United. But by the time he scored his first Bradford goal three months later in a win over Sunderland, the Yorkshire team were looking like a side capable of a high league finish. Speirs played every game of 1909/10 and scored seven goals to help Bradford to seventh in the table, at the time their record league placing. He became captain and scored another seven league goals in 1910/11 as they improved to fifth, which remains Bradford's best season in the top flight. Despite this, it was in the FA Cup that history was made.

Speirs led his side to the final with impressive wins over Burnley in the last eight and Blackburn in the semi-finals. Lying in wait were Newcastle United, one of the powerhouses of the game who had won three league titles in the previous seven years and who were cup holders after beating Barnsley the previous year. The match was held at the Crystal Palace in London, and 69,000 fans watched a tense and dour struggle that ended goalless.

Four days later, the teams met again at Old Trafford for the replay, with nearly 67,000 in attendance this time. Speirs must have felt very much at home in that Bradford team as eight of the side were Scots, a record to this day. After 15 minutes, a shot by half-back George Robinson was deflected across goal and met by the head of Speirs. It should have been a comfortable save for Newcastle goalkeeper Jimmy Lawrence, but he somehow let it squirm into the net. There was no further scoring, and at the final whistle Speirs was one of a rare band of footballers, an FA Cup Final captain who also scored the winning goal. He lifted aloft the new trophy, which had been made by the jewellery firm Fattorini and Sons, who ironically were from Bradford. This remains the club's only major honour.

Speirs remained at Bradford for one more season, and after 33 competitive goals for them he joined Leeds City of the Second Division for the enormous fee of £1,400 under the famous manager Herbert Chapman. After being mainly a centre-forward at Bradford, Chapman saw Speirs more as a creative inside-forward, and he made his first Leeds start against Fulham in a 3-2 home defeat. City had finished second bottom of the table the previous season, only retaining their league status via the re-election process, and were determined to avoid a repeat. Speirs scored his first goal for his new club against the other Bradford team, Park Avenue, and quickly became a central figure in their vast improvement. He ended the league season in great form, scoring eight times in the last seven games including a double against promotion-chasing Birmingham City as Leeds ended 1912/13 in fifth.

Speirs maintained his excellent form in 1913/14, scoring 11 goals as Leeds improved to fourth. But as war began to overshadow everything else, his last season at Leeds ended in a disappointing 15th-place finish despite him hitting double figures again. In total, Speirs played 78 times for Leeds and scored 31 times, a very good rate for a player who was deployed off the front.

English football was put on hold at the end of the season and Speirs returned to Glasgow with his young family, which now included daughter Betty. He could have continued in Scottish football, where the game carried on, but despite being exempt from military service due to the young age of his family he decided to enlist in the war effort by joining the Queen's Own Cameron Highlanders on 17 May 1915. After his initial training in Inverness, he was appointed as a lance corporal, and was transferred to mainland Europe for the first time in May 1916. During that year, Speirs suffered a wound to the elbow which briefly sidelined him from action, and he also was promoted to the rank of corporal.

In 1917 he was again ready for battle, and he took part in the Second Battle of Arras in April, with his bravery rewarded by the award of the Military Medal the following month. The scale of loss during this battle was horrific, with 158,000 dead. Speirs and his comrades buried their deceased comrades in between the bursts of gunfire and shells. As a mark of the respect he held, Speirs was again promoted in May 1917 to the rank of sergeant, and after a brief home leave in Glasgow he was back on the front line in August. During the early part of that month, the bloody Battle of Passchendaele was raging, and it was in this Belgian field he lost his life on approximately 20 August 1917. Speirs suffered a gunshot wound to the thigh during a regimental advance on enemy lines, with his colleagues unable to bring him back from the battlefield due to heavy shelling. He was reported missing, presumed dead, to his wife Bessie, but his body was not retrieved until October 1919, long after the guns had stopped.

James Hamilton Speirs is buried at Dochy Farm New British Cemetery at Ypres in Belgium.

In August 2017, a memorial silhouette was unveiled at the Scottish War Memorial at Passchendaele. It was funded by the Rangers supporters' group Club 1872, and the ceremony featured a short tribute speech by the great winger Willie Henderson. The Rangers family will never forget the ultimate sacrifice made by Speirs.

- A cup final winner against Celtic
- 3 seasons in Royal Blue
- Scotland international
- FA Cup-winning captain and goalscorer
- A father, a husband, a captain, and a hero

52 JOCK BUCHANAN

The war hero who was the first player sent off in a Scottish Cup Final

JOHN BUCHANAN was born in Paisley in March 1894, and was known to friends and family as Jock. He came from a footballing family, his father being a professional with Abercorn, and his elder brother George was signed by Morton. His playing career started at Johnstone FC, who at that time were a senior club, but everything went on hold when he enlisted with the armed forces during the Great War. Although still in his early 20s, he rose to the rank of lance corporal, and in 1917 was awarded the Distinguished Conduct Medal for Gallantry during the conflict in Mesopotamia. He had previously suffered a gunshot injury during the conflict, and when he left the Forces at the end of the war he could look back on his service to his country with great pride.

Buchanan resumed his career at Johnstone, before being signed in 1919 by his home town club St Mirren. He was a versatile player, at home in attack or defence, and he scored a decent total of 17 goals in 48 league games for the club. However, that couldn't save St Mirren from relegation in May 1921, and Buchanan was on the move again to local rivals Greenock Morton.

Buchanan mainly played at half-back and Morton went on an impressive Scottish Cup run in his first season. A hard-fought away win at Motherwell in the quarter-finals saw them face Aberdeen at Dens Park in the last four, where a 3-1 win meant a final date on 1 April 1922 against hot favourites Rangers. Morton's preparations were dealt a blow when regular centre-forward George French was declared unfit, and in the resulting reshuffle

Buchanan played up front. It was to be a day to remember for him, and another Scottish Cup day to forget for all associated with Rangers, who hadn't won the competition since 1903 and had sensationally lost the previous final to unfancied Partick Thistle.

Morton's Jimmy Gourlay opened the scoring with a free kick on 12 minutes, after Rangers keeper Willie Robb was harshly ruled to have handled outside his penalty area. From then on it was a constant Rangers onslaught, Buchanan having to help out in defence more often that leading attacks on the opposition goal. Rangers suffered another blow on the half hour when forward Andy Cunningham had to leave the field with a broken jaw but the ten men still dominated, passing up chance after chance. When the final whistle sounded, most of the 75,000 crowd could scarcely believe the outcome as Morton won the cup for the first, and still the only, time. This would not be Buchanan's last cup final.

Buchanan spent a further five years with the Greenock club, but that first season was to be as good as it would get for him at Cappielow. Morton were steady mid-table performers, doing enough to stay clear of the drop zone but without threatening a high finish. Then in 1926/27 a disastrous run of form saw them end the campaign in 19th place and they were relegated to the Second Division.

Despite this, Buchanan had impressed the national team selectors and he was chosen to go on an official SFA tour of Canada in the summer of 1927. These matches were not official Scotland internationals, so no caps were awarded, and he showed his versatility again when he was selected in both defence and in attack in different matches. He even scored a first representative goal in a 7-1 hammering of Northern Ontario on 1 July.

Buchanan started the season still with the Greenock men, but in December 1927 Morton accepted an offer from Bill Struth's Rangers who had lost the services of stalwarts Tommy Cairns and Arthur Dixon earlier in the year and who were looking to strengthen the playing squad. After 200 league appearances for Morton, and 31 goals, the 33-year-old Buchanan became a Rangers player.

His debut came on Christmas Eve 1927 playing at right-half, and it was a day to remember as table-topping Rangers thrashed Aberdeen 5-0. But it wasn't until late February that Buchanan became a first-team regular, and by the time March was over he had played in a winning Scottish Cup semi-final against Hibs and also scored his first Rangers goal, against Falkirk. Rangers were clear at the top of the table and looking certain to retain their league title, but the prize the club wanted more than any was the Scottish Cup, and on 14 April 1928 they had a final date with old foes Celtic. It was now 25 long years since the national cup was in the club's possession, and Buchanan lined up that day in front of a massive 118,000 crowd as Rangers finally put the hoodoo to bed in style. After a goalless first half, Rangers were awarded a penalty in the 55th minute after Celtic's McStay saved a goalbound Jimmy Fleming shot on the line with his hand. Captain Davie Meiklejohn took on the responsibility of this most high-pressure spot-kick, and when he scored the men in Royal Blue were inspired. Further goals from Bob McPhail and Sandy Archibald (two) saw the cup won in emphatic style, and the celebrations of the Ibrox supporters could be heard long into the night. Buchanan had his second Scottish Cup winners' medal.

Just a week later, Buchanan lined up at Ibrox against Kilmarnock, with a win guaranteeing the title and the first double of league and Scottish Cup in club history. The result was never in doubt, Rangers cruising to a 5-1 win. In all, Buchanan started 13 league games that season, scoring that solitary goal against Falkirk. He didn't start in the Charity Cup Final, which was won against Queen's Park, meaning Rangers had won three of the four main competitions for the season.

That domination looked to continue in 1928/29 with Buchanan now a regular. He played in 32 of the 38 league games, scoring twice as Rangers only lost once in the league, at Hamilton in March 1929 after the title was officially wrapped up. Celtic were defeated home and away, although they did win the Glasgow Cup tie between the sides in early September, a match Buchanan missed. Another double was looking likely as Rangers eased into the Scottish Cup Final, with Kilmarnock the opposition. The Ayrshire team had lost home and away to Rangers in the league, conceding seven goals in the process, and another enormous crowd turned up at Hampden on 6 April expecting to see a routine Royal Blue win. It was to be another reminder to the club just how unpredictable cup football can be.

The attendance was given as 114,000, which was 4,000 fewer than the previous year, but the Hampden gates had been closed with thousands still outside vainly trying to get entry. With Buchanan in his usual right-half position, Rangers started strongly, and the Kilmarnock goal had a charmed life before a penalty was awarded in the 16th minute. Tully Craig took the kick only to see it brilliantly saved by the Kilmarnock goalkeeper Sam Clemie. The final somehow remained goalless at half-time, but with the wind at their backs in the second half Kilmarnock were a different team and a quick break in the 48th minute ended in Aitken scoring for the Ayrshiremen. The goal rattled Rangers, who never recovered their earlier fluency, and a second goal by Williamson effectively ended the contest.

Then with just two minutes remaining, Buchanan wrote himself into Scottish Cup Final history in a way he would not have wanted. His frustration at several questionable decisions caused him to direct his anger at the referee, Mr Dougray of Bellshill. What exactly he said to the official has never been reported, but it was enough for Dougray to send Buchanan from the field, an ignominious end to the day for a man who had enjoyed previous final triumphs. Buchanan became the first player sent off in the national cup final, and he would remain the only man so punished for over half a century, until Celtic's Roy Aitken was sent off against Aberdeen in 1984.

These were the days before automatic suspensions, and Buchanan started all of the remaining three league games and also played in the Charity Cup Final in mid-May against Celtic at Ibrox. Two goals each from Tommy Muirhead and James Marshall gave Rangers a convincing 4-2 win, and Buchanan had his first winners' medal in the competition.

By now Buchanan was a Scotland international, making his debut in April 1929 against England at Hampden close to his 35th birthday, a game won 1-0. He only was selected once more for Scotland, in a painful 5-2 loss to England the following year.

Season 1929/30 would be a momentous one for Rangers and Buchanan. Never before had the club won all four of the competitions entered, but this was the year it finally happened. The league title was won by five points from an excellent Motherwell team in second place. This was despite some significant selection problems during the campaign, most notably the first Old Firm league match of the season in October when no fewer than seven regulars were absent. Tully Craig, Dougie Gray, Alan Morton and Tommy Muirhead were away on international duty with Scotland in Wales, and Buchanan was on the injured list along with Davie Meiklejohn and Bob Hamilton. Unfamiliar names such as Jim Purdon and Bob Ireland started at Ibrox and rose to the occasion, beating Celtic 1-0 with a goal by reserve left-winger Willie Nicholson.

By this time, the first trophy of the season had been won. The Glasgow Cup Final against Celtic went to a replay which was handsomely won 4-0. Buchanan played, but the star was prolific centre-forward Jimmy Fleming who scored a hat-trick. In all Buchanan played in 25 league games that season, and he also started in seven Scottish Cup ties, including the final on 12 April 1930 against Partick Thistle. The match ended in a dour 0-0 draw before 107,000 spectators, and Buchanan picked up a slight knock causing him to miss the midweek replay. Bob 'Whitey' McDonald took over at right-half as a late Tully Craig winner won the match 2-1 and secured the third leg of the quadruple.

All that remained for a clean sweep was the Charity Cup, and the final was against Celtic on 10 May. Buchanan lined up in an unfamiliar right-back role with regular Dougie Gray absent, and the trophy looked Ibrox-bound with Rangers leading 2-1 going into the 90th minute. This was despite Rangers playing with just ten fit players for the entire second half as Bob McPhail had been involved in a nasty clash of heads just before the interval, and he missed the start of the second half before playing as a token left-winger once deemed fit enough to return to the field. In the last minute, however, a defensive mix-up allowed Celtic to equalise, and there was to be no further scoring after an extra 30 minutes extra time. The rules of the competition meant the winners were then decided by the team who had won the most corners, but this was also level. So the final piece of silverware in 1929/30 was decided by the toss of a coin, and Rangers captain Meiklejohn correctly called 'heads'. Buchanan had his second Charity Cup medal, and Rangers were the undisputed kings of Scottish football.

The following season would be Buchanan's last as a Rangers player. He started 26 times in the league, and the title race was to be a close-run thing with Celtic. It took an impressive run of form in the run-in to finally get in front, Rangers winning 11 and drawing two of their last 13 matches with Buchanan featuring in the majority. He experienced disappointment in both the Glasgow Cup and Scottish Cup, playing in the 2-1 Glasgow Cup Final defeat to Celtic and in the surprise 2-1 home loss to Dundee in the Scottish Cup. And although Rangers did retain the Charity Cup against Queen's Park, he wasn't selected for the final match. Still, in a four-season Rangers career of over 120 first-team appearances, he had won four league titles, two Charity Cups, one Glasgow Cup and one Scottish Cup.

In the summer of 1931 Buchanan, now aged 37, moved to Northern Irish football by joining Linfield, where he added another league medal to his collection. He returned to Scotland after just the one season, playing for East Stirling for a year before retiring.

After football, Buchanan ran a successful grocery business, but passed away at the age of just 53 on 3 October 1947.

- A decorated war hero
- Upset Rangers in the Scottish Cup Final with Morton
- Played in the most famous of all Rangers Scottish Cup Final wins
- 4 league titles in four seasons
- The first man to ever be sent off in the Scottish Cup Final

53 JOE HENDRY

The Rangers defender who started match commentaries for blind supporters

JOE HENDRY was born in Greenock in 1886, and he spent the vast majority of his life living in the town. He was a talented young footballer and started his career in the local juvenile side Garvel United before moving to Junior team Maryhill Juniors in late 1906. He immediately became their first-choice left-half, and made such an impression that within a year he moved to the senior game with local club Morton, who he joined in December 1907.

Hendry immediately became a fixture in a Morton team struggling towards the wrong end of the First Division, eventually finishing 13th out of the 18 clubs. His second season there saw his first appearances against Rangers, which were occasions Hendry would have rather forgotten as he lost 8-0 and 7-1 in the two league games against them. These weren't the only heavy defeats suffered in 1908/09 as Morton ended the season second from bottom, which at that time did not mean automatic relegation. Despite the team struggling to compete, Hendry stood out in a poor side, and in 1909/10 Morton were again toiling near the bottom towards the end of the season when they accepted an offer from Rangers for him. After 73 Morton appearances and two Morton goals, Hendry became a Rangers player.

He started in the last two league fixtures of the season and made his debut a 1-0 win over Clyde on 23 April 1910, the goal scored by Jimmy Gordon. The season had ended in massive disappointment for Rangers, who had hoped to finally end their long run without the title after signing big names Billy Hogg, Herbert Lock and Willie Reid, but third place was how it had ended. Hendry immediately became a regular starter as 1910/11 got under way, Rangers looking to end a run of six successive Celtic title triumphs. He started in all but three league games that season as Rangers finally mounted a real challenge for the major honours after an inconsistent start. By Christmas, five league games had been lost, including a scarcely believable 5-1 Ibrox defeat to Hendry's old club Morton, but there were signs the balance of power was shifting as Hendry won his first winners' medal in a fine 3-1 Glasgow Cup win over Celtic in early October. The league was decided by a long unbeaten run from Christmas, with 12 wins and four draws in the last 16 games. This included Hendry's first Rangers goal in a 4-0 win over Hamilton at Ibrox on 14 January 1911. That unbeaten run powered the team to the title, winning it by four points from second placed Aberdeen. Hendry didn't play in the Charity Cup Final win over Celtic at the end of the season as three of the four trophies ended 1910/11 at Ibrox, the only exception being the Scottish Cup after a second-round loss to holders Dundee.

It was during his first full season at Ibrox that Hendry won his only representative honour, playing for the Scottish League against the Southern League in October 1910.

Hendry's second full season was another story of success. He started in 32 league games, chipping in with one goal again, this time against Motherwell. He also scored in a Glasgow Cup win over Queen's Park then played in the winning final against Partick Thistle to earn a second medal in the tournament. The league was also retained, this time by a convincing six-point margin from Celtic. Sadly it was also another season where the Scottish Cup run ended early, this time in a 3-1 second-round defeat to a Clyde team and their trainer Bill Struth despite Hendry scoring Rangers' goal. Clyde also ended Ibrox interest in the 1912 Charity Cup in Hendry's 39th and final appearance of the campaign.

Season 1912/13 saw Hendry start far fewer games, mainly due to an injury he picked up against St Mirren in December. However, he did play enough times to earn a third successive league championship medal, starting in 13 league matches without scoring. He played in a hard-fought Glasgow Cup semi-final win over Partick which took three matches to decide, but missed the final which was won 3-1 over Celtic with Jimmy Gordon filling in at left-half. By the time Hendry had recovered from his pre-Christmas injury in March 1913, Rangers were again out of the Scottish Cup after a dismal loss to Falkirk at Ibrox the previous month. He missed the final few weeks of the season with another injury, sitting out the Charity Cup Final against Celtic, which was lost 3-2.

Three full seasons at Ibrox, and three times a league champion, and Hendry was back to full fitness for the beginning of 1913/14. He started 29 of the 34 league games, scoring twice including a vital goal against Kilmarnock in a tight 1-0 win in March. But he played in the two league defeats to Celtic that proved decisive in the title race, Rangers ending the season in second place. The second of these defeats saw Hendry leave the field injured with a bad head wound after just 15 minutes, and his ten colleagues were then swamped 4-0. The only cup competition won during the season was the Glasgow Cup, for a fourth successive year, but Hendry missed out on a medal as he had to sit out the final win over Third Lanark. He also missed the club's latest Scottish Cup disappointment, an early exit this time to Hibs. This was to be the last season of Scottish football before the declaration of war in the summer of 1914.

Hendry continued to play for the club during the conflict, with 20 starts in 1914/15, 20 more in 1915/16, and six appearances in 1916/17. All three of these titles were won by Celtic by comfortable margins. Hendry managed to get on the score sheet twice during these wartime years, scoring against Aberdeen and Raith Rovers. The closest he got to adding to his winners' medal collection was the 1915 Charity Cup Final, when he started against Celtic. Despite goals by future legendary players Andy Cunningham and Tommy Cairns, he had to settle for a runners-up medal after a close 3-2 defeat. His last game for Rangers came on 21 April 1917, not a fitting occasion as it was a dismal 3-1 home defeat to Hamilton. Hendry had played a total of 172 games for the club since his debut seven years previously, scoring eight Rangers goals.

He remained a registered Rangers player until 1919 and was loaned to Dumbarton for the final season of wartime football in 1918/19, where he played 23 times and scored twice as the Sons finished 15th in the First Division. Once released by Rangers, Hendry signed for Glasgow rivals Third Lanark at the age of 33 and played at Cathkin for a single season, starting 20 times and scoring once. His last two seasons in Scottish football were played in Perth, although St Johnstone at that time were not part of the league structure. In the summer of 1922 he moved to Belfast Distillery and his highlights in a single season 'across the water' were scoring a winning goal against Linfield and winning an Irish Cup medal, ironic after failing so often in the Scottish competition. He also was chosen to represent the Irish League in 1923 against the Scottish League, something he must have looked forward to, but then had to pull out after picking up an injury.

In 1923 Hendry retired from football and returned to his native Greenock. He was a regular at the home matches of Morton, the club he told friends would always be his first love. And within a short time he had the idea of accompanying blind supporters and describing the action to them so they could get some better enjoyment out of the matchday experience. This service is a feature of countless football stadia in modern times, but it is thought that Hendry was the first to provide this service anywhere in the world. Hendry formed The Greenock Morton Blind Club in 1927, recruiting other volunteers to help provide this simple but life changing service. In later years, he started broadcasting Morton home games to local hospital radio.

Hendry died in 1966, and his obituary in the *Greenock Telegraph* stated, 'Football was his abiding love. He was never happier than when watching Morton at Cappielow or relating the kick-by-kick story of the games to his great admirers, the Morton blind fans, a happy coterie who owed Joe a great deal for what he did for them in various directions.'

He involved his son Joseph in the work of the Blind Club, and his son also carried out match commentaries for many years, as well as serving on Greenock Corporation as a Liberal councillor from 1961 to 1972, then on Inverclyde District Council from 1977 until his death in 1989.

In 2019, the Hendry family put up his 1911 league championship medal for auction. It was sold for £2,400.

- Three time-league winner with Rangers
- Winner of cup competitions in Glasgow and Belfast
- Founder of the first matchday commentary service for blind supporters

54 JOHN BARKER

The first man to score a hat-trick for Rangers against Celtic

BORN IN Govan on 28 June 1869, John Barker was to call the burgh his home all his days. The son of a shipyard worker, he started his football career with local club Linthouse in 1889. A strong running left-winger with an explosive shot, he quickly became a fixture in their first 11.

Linthouse were one of several clubs who took part in the inaugural Glasgow Cup in 1887. Although they usually fell to heavy defeats if drawn against one of the bigger city clubs, in 1891 they received some favourable draws and reached the semi-finals. Pollokshaws and Whitefield had been defeated, but the last-four tie represented a whole new level when the Govan team were paired with Celtic at Parkhead. This was to be Barker's first competitive match against them, and one he would want to forget as the left-winger was helpless to prevent a 9-2 defeat. It was a game Barker would use as motivation in future years.

Linthouse by now were founding members of the Scottish Football Alliance, a brief competitor to the Scottish Football League, coming up against the likes of Partick Thistle, Kilmarnock, Morton and Airdrieonians in a competition that would become the Second Division a few years later. With Barker starring on the left wing, Linthouse would go on to become champions in that first 1891/92 season, although he was no longer a Linthouse player by the conclusion and in February 1892 he made the short move to Rangers.

Barker made his Rangers debut on 13 February 1892, one week after a heavy Scottish Cup defeat to Celtic, and he scored in a 7-0 home league rout of Vale of Leven. The following month he netted his first hat-trick in Royal Blue in a 5-2 victory over Renton. In all, Barker made nine starts before the end of the season, scoring six times, but the club were unable to defend the league title they had shared the previous year with Dumbarton, only finishing fifth.

Rangers started 1892/93 well, with Barker a key player. They remained unbeaten in league and cups past the turn of the year but then suffered an unexpected setback in late January when despite a Barker goal they were knocked out of the Scottish Cup 3-2 at St Bernard's. Just three weeks later, on 18 February 1893, came the first cup final of the season, a Rangers v Celtic Glasgow Cup encounter at Cathkin Park. Barker was determined this tie would be very different from his embarrassing experience with Linthouse. In driving rain and on a sodden surface, Barker terrorised the holders' defence throughout. He opened the scoring with a fine shot and fully deserved to be on the winning side as further goals from Neil Kerr and John McPherson gave Rangers their first Glasgow Cup triumph in a 3-1 success.

This was to be the high point of the season as a late slump in the title run-in with successive three-goal defeats to Dumbarton and Celtic, saw Rangers slip to a second-place league finish by a single point. Overall in 1892/93, Barker scored five goals from 19 starts.

Season 1893/94 saw Rangers drop early points with two draws in their first three games. The fourth game of the season, on 2 September 1893, was at home to Celtic. A crowd of 10,000 saw a Rangers team fired up for revenge after blowing the title a few months earlier. And this was to be the day Barker made history. After an end-to-end opening spell where both goalkeepers were tested, Barker made a fine run on the left and his perfect centre was finished expertly by John McPherson. Rangers now scented blood and piled relentless pressure on their opponents. Barker fired a thunderous shot past the helpless Cullen to double the lead, and the game was over just before half-time when a flowing move was finished by a clinical John Gray header. Rangers were in no mood to settle for three. The second half was a continuation of attempts on the Celtic goal, with Cullen making several outstanding stops. But he was helpless to prevent Barker adding a fourth with an easy finish then was again beaten near the end when Barker completed his treble with another fierce drive.

Barker became the first Rangers player to score a league hat-trick in the fixture, and even to this day it is a feat rarely achieved. Only R.C. Hamilton, Torry Gillick (in the wartime Southern League), Jimmy Duncanson and Johnny Hubbard have ever managed to equal Barker's memorable feat.

Rangers were to suffer from too much inconsistency to mount a serious league challenge but they found their best form in the Scottish Cup. Winning the trophy had been the club's biggest ambition ever since their first final heartache in 1877, and bringing the cup to Ibrox was the Holy Grail for all at Rangers. After sweeping into the last four, a home 1-1 semi-final draw with the mighty Queen's Park looked to be a fatal slip as the replay would be at their Hampden fortress. But a magnificent 3-1 win meant a final date with Celtic on 17 February 1894.

The first half was goalless, Rangers coming close in the opening minutes when McCreadie shot narrowly past when well positioned, but Celtic came even closer just minutes before the interval when Blessington struck the crossbar with Rangers goalkeeper Haddow well beaten. The second half was to prove to be the finest 45 minutes of the club's history until that point. In a remarkable and devastating 13-minute period, Rangers overpowered their opponents with a superb display of attacking football and the destination of the cup was decided. It started on 55 minutes when Hugh McCreadie controlled a David Mitchell free kick 12 yards from goal and lashed the ball beyond Celtic keeper Cullen and into the net. On 65 minutes it was 2-0, and it was a goal fit to win any trophy. Barker received the ball 50 yards from the Celtic goal, then weaved his way past several despairing challenges before crashing home his shot from just inside the penalty area for an unforgettable solo goal. If there remained any doubt about the outcome, that lasted only three more minutes when John McPherson pounced on a defensive error to beat Cullen from close range.

Celtic were a beaten team but refused to throw in the towel, and were rewarded with a consolation goal after 75 minutes when Willie Maley converted a McMahon corner from three yards out, the only moment of slack defending in the entire second half. The final whistle sparked joyous scenes both among the Rangers players and their supporters, and the roar could be heard back at Ibrox when captain Mitchell lifted the Scottish Cup for the club's first triumph in the competition.

Barker ended the season with eight goals from 19 starts, with five of those goals against Celtic. He was also by now an international player, featuring against Wales in both 1893 and 1894. Incredibly, these were to be his only appearances for Scotland although he scored four times, including a debut hat-trick.

In 1894/95 he remained a Rangers regular. He scored against Celtic again in his next appearance against them in September but the game ended in defeat. It was this season when Barker's run as an automatic choice ended as Rangers had unearthed a young left-winger from Darvel called Alec Smith whose initial appearances were so impressive he simply had to play. Barker played on the right wing, at inside-right and at centre-forward as manager Wilton tried to find a way to accommodate both. The writing appeared to be on the wall by May 1895 when Barker scored from centre-forward in the Charity Cup semi-final win over Third Lanark but he was dropped for the final against Celtic despite his great record against them.

But Barker still was regularly selected in 1895/96, but only on the left wing when Smith was unavailable. He kept a reasonable scoring record and even played in defence in one game. His 84th and last Rangers appearance was at centre-forward in a 2-1 win over Queen's Park in the Glasgow League on 18 April 1896. In those 84 matches he scored 34 goals. These included seven in 11 games against Celtic.

In the summer of 1896, Govan-born-and-bred Barker returned to Linthouse, now a Second Division club. A qualified draughtsman, he balanced his football with his job at the shipyard. Despite Linthouse finishing bottom of the table, he scored 13 goals in 18 intermittent starts before retiring in 1898 at the age of just 29 to concentrate fully on his shipbuilding career. After Barker and local girl Ellen were married they set up home in Govan with their daughter, also Ellen. Barker died of lymphoma the day after his 72nd birthday on 29 June 1941.

The name of John Bell Barker is carved into Rangers history.

- 34 goals in 84 appearances
- Scored in the first Glasgow Cup final win
- Scored in the first Scottish Cup final win
- Scored the first hat-trick against Celtic

Back Row (left to right)—Dawson, Lynas, Smith, Munro, Simpson, McDonald, Winning, Cheyne, Jenkins. Middle Row—Turnbull, McKillop, Ross, Galloway, Duncanson, McPhail, Woodburn, Main. Front Row—Gray, Harrison, Venters, Little, Brown, Thornton, Shaw, Fiddies, Kinnear.

A 1938-39 picture including Tom McKillop, Jimmy Duncanson, Adam Little and James Fiddes.

ALEX. BENNETT,
GLASGOW RANGERS F.C.

Alec Bennett.
(Courtesy of The Founders Trail)

The 1907 team with Alex Craig, Sandy Newbigging, Jimmy Galt, David Taylor, George Livingstone, Robert Campbell and Archie Kyle. (Courtesy of The Founders Trail)

A second 1907 team picture which also features Jimmy Speirs.

langers in 1907-08. Back row (left to right): J.Wilson (trainer), G.Wallace, G.Livingstone, A.Barrie, J.Macdonald, .T.Butler, R.C.Hamilton, J.J.Dunlop, A.Newbiggin, J.Spiers, G.Law, J.Gordon. Front row: A.Craig, Jo.Bell, J.Galt, J.Dickie, I.G.Campbell, J.Currie, A.Kyle, G.R.Watson, A.Smith. On ground: J.May. W.Henry.

Rangers at Dundee, 1893. Andrew McCreadie and John Barker are the last two players seated and David Mitchell stands over them. (Courtesy of The Founders Trail)

Taken to celebrate winning three successive Scottish Cups from 1948 to 50. Billy Williamson and Jimmy Duncanson are first and fourth in the front row.

D. Mitchell, Rangers F.C.

A sketch of Charles Heggie from a
newspaper of the time.
(Courtesy of The Founders Trail)

David Mitchell.
(Courtesy of The Founders Trail)

A 1921 tour picture. Trainer George Livingstone stands on the left, while Geordie
Henderson sits third from last at the front.

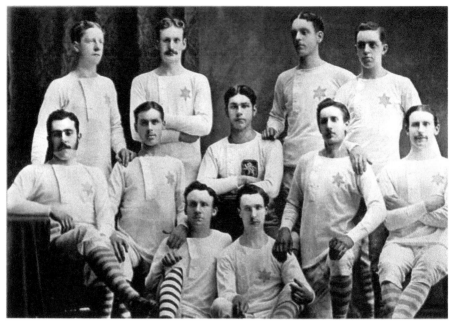

George Gillespie is top left in the iconic Gallant Pioneers picture from 1877.
(Courtesy of The Founders Trail)

A sketch of Harry Rennie from a
newspaper of the time.
(Courtesy of The Founders Trail)

Herbert Lock.
(Courtesy of The Founders Trail)

A 1928 group picture. The back row includes James Marshall (second from left) and Jock Buchanan (extreme right).

*John Barker.
(Courtesy of The Founders Trail)*

*Rangers in 1897: (Back) Low, Matt Dickie,
N. Smith, Jimmy Millar, Tom Hyslop,
A .Smith, Oswald, Bobby Neill (Front)
McPherson, Gibson, David Mitchell,
Andrew McCreadie, Turnbull.*

THE GLASGOW RANGERS FOOTBALL TEAM.

Commemorating the 1898–99 Invincibles. (Courtesy of James Lepick)

This 1911 team includes Joe Hendry, Jimmy Patterson, John Robertson, Robert Campbell, Billy Hogg, Jimmy Galt, Willie Reid, Herbert Lock, Alec Bennett and Bobby Parker.

LEFT TO RIGHT - BACK ROW :- RIDDELL, HENDRY, PATERSON, ROBERTSON. MIDDLE ROW :- J.WILSON (Trainer), MONTGOMERY, ORMOND, CAMPBELL, FARRINGTON, HOGG, FERGUSON, GALT, LAWRIE, GORDON. SITTING :- BODEN, REID, R.BROWN, BOWIE, LOCK, BENNETT, PARKER, SMITH. ON GROUND :- A.BROWN, GOODWIN.

The 1932 Scottish Cup winners. Director Robert Campbell is the first man standing in the back row. James Marshall stands third from right.

Matt Dickie.
(Courtesy of The Founders Trail)

A sketch of Neil Kerr from a newspaper of the time.
(Courtesy of The Founders Trail)

Jimmy Duncanson (second right) watches on as captain Jock Shaw holds the Scottish Cup in 1950.

Sandy Newbigging, aged 97, at the Rangers centenary celebrations in 1973.

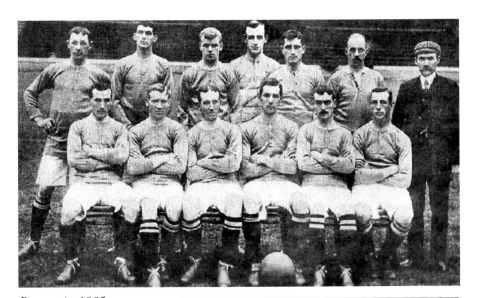

Rangers in 1905.
Back row: Tom Sinclair
(second).
Front row: R.S. McColl
(third), Archie Kyle (fifth).

Willie Reid.
(Courtesy of
The Founders Trail)

WILLIAM REID, RANGERS F.C.

Rangers 1899/1900. The back row includes Matt Dickie, Bobby Neill and Jacky Robertson. The front row includes Johnny Campbell. Insets are Jimmy Millar, David Mitchell, John Wilkie and Tom Hyslop.

The first Rangers team to lift the Scottish Cup in 1894.

FIRST RANGERS TEAM TO WIN THE SCOTTISH CUP 1893–94

J. Taylor (*Trainer*).
Back Row—H. McCreadie, J. Steel, N. Smith, D. Haddow, D. Mitchell.
Sitting—A. McCreadie, D. Boyd, W. Wilton (*Secretary*), J. Drummond, J. MacPherson, J. Barker.
Front Row—R. Marshall, J. Gray.

Scottish Cup.   Glasgow Cup.

55 JOHN ROBERTSON

The injury-jinxed Rangers player who suffered a career ending spinal injury

JOHN NICOL Robertson was born in the South Ayrshire village of Ochiltree on 7 May 1883. A talented left-sided footballer, he spent some time training with Rangers as a teenager but was not offered a playing contract. Aged 18, he agreed to move to England and join Bolton Wanderers in 1902.

He struggled to force his way into Bolton's first team, despite the club struggling at the foot of the First Division and ultimately being relegated. And he saw very little first-team action in the Second Division either, with only very occasional appearances at left-back when regular starters were unavailable. After only 15 league appearances in four years, he left Lancashire and joined Southern League side Southampton in May 1906.

His Southampton debut came on 8 September against Norwich at The Dell. Fans and team-mates were impressed with the new left-back despite Southampton only managing a 2-2 draw. It was in his second appearance against Crystal Palace when his injury curse first struck. The game was a fiercely competitive 1-1 draw, and Robertson suffered a bad enough knee injury to force him to leave the field. He missed several weeks thereafter but returned to the side before the end of the year. In all, he played 26 times in his first Southampton season in the league and FA Cup.

He played for Southampton for six seasons, and in every one of them he missed spells due to a recurrence of that same knee injury. Every season saw him start more than 20 but only once more than 30 times. When fit, however, he was a key player in the team, the *Southampton Echo* describing him as 'a classy half-back and an exceedingly capable player'. He only ever scored twice in senior football, both for the Saints, the first one a very important strike as it was the only goal in an FA Cup tie against West Bromwich Albion in February 1908. Non-league Southampton enjoyed a great cup run that season, beating the mighty Everton on the way to reaching the semi-finals where Robertson tasted disappointment in a 2-0 loss to Wolves.

Season 1909/10 was his most consistent, playing in six different outfield positions and only missing six games, and his influential and impressive displays were rewarded by being selected twice for the Southern League representative team. His last Southampton appearance was on 16 March 1912 in a 3-1 win at Crystal Palace, the opposition on that fateful day when his knee problems began. After 194 games on the English south coast, Robertson returned home to Scotland to sign for champions Rangers.

William Wilton's men were short of full-back cover, youngster George Ormond filling in, and the manager needed experience in that area. The 1911/12 title was already won when Robertson made his debut on 30 March against Kilmarnock at Rugby Park, when an experimental team lost 3-2. He started just one other game before the season ended, a defeat at Hearts.

Robertson began 1912/13 as the first-choice left-back. His old knee injury kept him out for a few weeks in September, but he was back in time for three hard-fought games against Partick Thistle in the Glasgow Cup semi-final, a 2-0 win in the second replay putting Rangers through for a final clash with Celtic. On 12 October 1912, Robertson made his first appearance in a cup final and in an Old Firm game. It was to be a day to remember, Rangers winning 3-1 with goals from Billy Hogg, Alex Bennett and Alec Smith in front of 90,000 fans at Hampden. Typically, Robertson failed to finish the match after leaving the field with another serious injury, ligament damage that kept him on the sidelines for two months. Incredibly, Celtic had been leading 1-0 when he went off.

The 1912/13 title race was a close affair between the Glasgow clubs. Robertson tasted defeat in his next appearance against Celtic at the turn of the year and three days later lined up at Ibrox against Hibs in a vital match on 4 January 1913 which would be his final appearance. Rangers won 5-3 in a magnificent end to end encounter, but the day was spoiled when Robertson suffered a sickening injury in a full-blooded collision during the second half and suffered significant damage to his spine. He spent the rest of the season in hospital, and although his 12 league starts qualified him for a medal, this seemed irrelevant as he faced a fight to see whether he would ever walk again.

Robertson faced his painful battle with the same determination that he showed in overcoming his knee injuries. He slowly progressed, and eventually was able to regain some mobility. He would, however, need walking sticks for the rest of his life. With his football career over at just 30 years old, Robertson had to face up to a life of disability.

Incredibly, this still wasn't the last serious injury he suffered. Ten years after his back injury, in October 1923, he was crossing the road near his Maybole home when he was struck by a car. Robertson suffered fractures to both arms and both legs, meaning another very lengthy hospital stay.

During his recovery, Robertson was kept informed on the football career of his nephew Tom. The young Tom was a skilful right-back at local club Ayr United, and then became a goal scoring winger with Dundee before moving to Clyde in 1936. His uncle was proud of him, trying to attend matches to watch him as his health allowed. But on 23 January 1937, John suffered a catastrophic and fatal brain haemorrhage, passing away after years of pain at the age of 53.

He wasn't alive to see his beloved nephew's greatest moment, when Tom starred in Clyde's Scottish Cup Final win over Motherwell in April 1939.

- A dependable full-back
- 18 appearances
- Won the Glasgow Cup and the league title, but injured before either were lifted
- A life of pain after football due to serious injuries on and off the field

56 AND 57 JOHN WILKIE AND
            JOHNNY CAMPBELL

The inseparable 'Babes' who helped Rangers to an invincible season

SOMETIMES IN football there comes along a partnership that just seems right. Over the years, Rangers have had many great pairings in both defence and attack. One such link-up involved two players whose telepathic understanding on the field meant several clubs brought them together in search of success. Their names were Johnny Campbell and John Wilkie.

Campbell was born in Govan on 2 October 1877. Like so many others, his football career started in the Junior game, at Renton United, before he joined Govan club Linthouse in 1893 aged just 16. A quick left-footed winger with an eye for goal, he was soon being watched by bigger clubs and in 1894 he joined Second Division Partick Thistle. His debut came in the opening match of Thistle's league campaign, scoring in a 5-2 win over Dundee Wanderers. The inside-forward beside him that day also making his debut was John Wilkie.

Wilkie, also known as James or Jack, was another Govan boy, born the November before Campbell. He started out at Summerton Athletic before joining Thistle also in 1894. Although Partick finished only eighth in the ten-team league, the two teenagers immediately formed an entertaining and productive partnership for them and were given the nickname 'The Babes' by the Thistle supporters. Neither player missed many matches that season, Wilkie being the more productive with nine goals from his 21 starts.

But the partnership was to be broken up after only one season when Blackburn Rovers of England's First Division took Wilkie down south in the summer of 1895. Wilkie enjoyed a solid eighth-place finish in his debut season with them, while Campbell helped Thistle to an improved fifth in the Scottish second tier. But neither player seemed to hit their consistent best, and in the close-season of 1896 Rovers decided to reform The Babes to see if this would improve their fortunes. The partnership made their first league appearance in over a year against West Brom, and over the following two seasons the Rovers line-up invariably ended with 'Wilkie and Campbell'. But despite their efforts, and a fair goalscoring return, Rovers were a shadow of their former glories as they had a defence that leaked a serious number of goals. As a result, they finished 1896/97 just above the relegation play-off places, and were in serious relegation trouble again in the following season, only surviving when the league was expanded.

By now, Campbell had ten goals in 56 Rovers starts, while Wilkie had 17 in 75. Neither player was enjoying their football in Lancashire, and Campbell and Wilkie were given their chance to return north in August 1898 and both signed for Rangers. This was a Rangers on the verge of becoming the dominant team in the country, but despite winning the last two Scottish Cups they hadn't been crowned champions since the first season of league football in 1980/91.

Both players made their debuts in Royal Blue on 27 August 1898, the second league game of the season. It was to be a second victory, club legends Alec Smith, R.C. Hamilton and John McPherson all scoring in a 3-1 success away to St Mirren. Smith was still the first-choice left-winger so Campbell played on the right, meaning that the partnership was not quite the same as before. Both lined up again the following week when Wilkie got his first Rangers goal in a 3-2 win at Hearts. Three wins from three, but nobody could have thought just what a historic season was beginning to unfold.

Previously injured inside-forward Jimmy Millar regained his place in the side after the Hearts game, meaning Wilkie only featured occasionally. Campbell, who was to enjoy far greater success of the two across the season, scored his first Rangers goal the following week in a comfortable home win over Third Lanark, and his displays attracted the national team selectors before the season ended. Campbell played in 16 of the 18 league games in 1898/99 as Rangers incredibly went through the entire campaign without dropping a single point. He scored in a 4-0 hammering of Celtic at Parkhead, he got four in a 5-2 rout of St Bernard's, and he scored again in the return Old Firm fixture on 2 January at Ibrox when Hamilton claimed a hat-trick. On 7 January 1899, Rangers defeated Clyde 3-0 to win their 18th and final league game of the season and make history, with Campbell starring on the right wing. Meanwhile, Wilkie was a patient and able deputy, returning to the team for the Glasgow Cup semi-final win over Celtic and scoring a crucial league goal in a hard-fought 2-1 win at Dundee. He was to feature in the end-of-season Glasgow League fixtures, and scored his first goal against Celtic in a defeat in that competition in May 1899.

Campbell made his Scotland debut on 18 March of that year, scoring twice in a 6-0 thrashing of Wales. He scored another double the following week in a 9-1 rout of Northern Ireland, before tasting defeat against England in April in a 2-1 reverse. He would only win one more cap, and scored two more goals in February 1901 in Scotland's record win, an 11-0 embarrassment over Ireland. His international career read played four scored six, and in those four games Scotland scored a scarcely believable 27 goals.

Despite the incredible 100 per cent league record, Rangers would fail to bring home any of the cup competitions, with Campbell playing in losing finals against Queen's Park in the Glasgow Cup, and Celtic in both the Scottish and Charity Cups.

Season 1899/1900 saw Rangers retain the league title, and also saw the old Campbell-Wilkie partnership starting more often. Wilkie played more games this time, mainly due to an injury to Campbell, and in several matches they played at right wing and inside-right together. Campbell had started the season on fire, scoring five times in the first four league games, but he missed almost all of October to March. Meanwhile, Wilkie was showing what he was capable of when given a run in the team. He scored a vital goal in a 1-1 draw against Celtic in the Glasgow Cup Final in November, and claimed a winners' medal in the replay thanks to a Bobby Neil penalty. He hit 18 goals in just 23 appearances that season, with hat-tricks against Hearts in the Inter-City League and against Maybole in the Scottish Cup. His six goals in 11 league games meant he thoroughly deserved his winners' medal as Rangers retained their crown.

Campbell, however, only played in seven league matches, also scoring six times. He missed the Glasgow Cup success but played in the end-of-season Charity Cup Final, scoring in a memorable 5-1 hammering of Celtic.

Season 1900/01 was something of a disappointment for the players, although the club again brought the title back to Ibrox. Campbell suffered an injury and was unable to reclaim his place in the team when fit, and Wilkie was sent on loan to new English Second Division club Middlesbrough. Wilkie then claimed a place in their history when on 2 March 1901 he scored the club's first league hat-trick, bagging five goals in a 9-2 win over Gainsborough Trinity. But the following season Campbell was back fit, Wilkie was back at Ibrox and they had one last successful season together at Rangers.

Campbell started 12 league games and 21 overall, scoring five times. The highlight was a terrific strike in a memorable 4-2 win at Parkhead on New Year's Day 1902. Wilkie started 14 league games, and 22 overall, scoring six times. His included a goal in the drawn Glasgow Cup Final against Celtic, although he missed the replay. By the summer of 1902 both players had three league medals, and both had enjoyed cup final wins over Celtic. But 1902 saw the terrible tragedy of a disaster and loss of life at the stadium during a Scotland v England international, and the club, desperate for funds to both rebuild the stadium and also to pay compensation to victims' families, put every player up for sale.

Campbell, after 70 appearances and 32 goals, was sold to West Ham United. Wilkie, after 29 goals in 61 appearances, was sold to his old club Partick Thistle. They had started together 35 times for Rangers. It seemed that was the end of 'The Babes' together, almost a decade after they first took to the field in the same team.

Campbell scored once in 18 starts for Southern League West Ham before returning to Scotland in 1903 to play for newly crowned champions Hibernian. He stayed there for three seasons. Wilkie scored 11 times in 31 further Partick Thistle appearances before in the summer of 1905, he was also signed by Hibs. The old partnership would be together one last time. They only played five times together for Hibs as both players were now reaching the end of their top-level careers. But they did feature together against Rangers on 11 September 1905, when Campbell scored but couldn't prevent their old club winning 2-1. Their last game together was the following month, a drab and dismal 2-1 defeat to Falkirk, with Wilkie scoring the consolation goal. Hibs were struggling for consistency and sold both players soon afterwards.

Campbell went back south to play briefly for New Brompton (now known as Gillingham) before an emotional return to Partick Thistle in 1906. He had just been married and stated that this was him now 'returning home'. But time had caught up with him, and he drifted out the game after spells with Bo'ness and Dumbarton Harp, finally retiring in 1910.

He then embarked on a whole new career, becoming a ship's steward and sailing the high seas. Sadly, this was not for as long as he had hoped, as in January 1919 he contracted tuberculosis and died aged just 41.

Wilkie left Hibs under a cloud, suspended and transfer listed for indiscipline at training. He left to join Ayr Parkhouse before also drifting out of the game.

He married twice, the second time in 1918 when the marriage certificate gave his occupation as a shipyard labourer. Sadly he also died at a young age, passing away in 1922 aged only 45.

- Two sons of Govan born less than a year apart
- A partnership at four different clubs, after making their professional debuts the same day
- Goalscorers in both divisions in Scotland and in England
- Contributed to the legendary Rangers 100 per cent league season
- Both scored against Celtic in cup finals
- Both passed away in their 40s

58   JOHNNY WALKER

The ex-Ranger who scored the goal that won Liverpool their first league title

HIS NAME might sound like a famous whisky, but footballer Johnny Walker was born in Shotts in August 1873. Mostly an inside-forward and capable of playing in any position across the forward line, Walker began his career with local side Armadale Thistle in 1891. But it wasn't long before senior clubs were watching the youngster, who combined pace and deceptive strength with an eye for goal. In February 1893 he was snapped up by Hearts, beginning an impressive 13-year career in the senior game.

Despite Hearts having one of the best teams in the country, the teenage Walker was given his league debut within a fortnight of joining when he lined up against St Mirren on 18 February 1893 at Westmarch Park in Paisley. It wasn't the happiest of starts as the Paisley team ran out 3-1 winners. But Walker had impressed, and over the next five years he established himself as not just a key player with his club but also made his international debut.

This was to be a period of great success for Hearts. They won their first Scottish league title in 1894/95, dropping just five points in 18 matches. With Walker now captain, and a Scotland international too after a scoring debut against Ireland at Parkhead in March 1895, they added to their trophy haul the following season by lifting the 1896 Scottish Cup. This was an especially satisfying win as they defeated local rivals Hibs 3-1 at New Logie Green, in the only final ever played outside of Glasgow. Walker led his team to another league title the following season, overtaking Hibs in an impressive run-in when Hearts won their last seven games. On 2 April 1898, Johnny Walker played his last game in a Hearts shirt, a 3-1 win over St Bernard's in the East of Scotland League. Including such competitive games as these, he played 135 times for Hearts and scored 60 goals.

In April 1898 he signed for Liverpool in a £350 double transfer along with team-mate Tom Robertson. Walker made his debut on 11 April at Anfield, playing at outside-right in a 4-0 win over the Wednesday, and he appeared in two more league games before the season ended, scoring in both. His first goal came in a defeat to Derby County at the Baseball Ground.

His first full season at Liverpool was an eventful one. On the pitch, Walker made the inside-right position his own, missing only two matches all season. He scored 11 times in 32 league starts as Liverpool mounted a title challenge but ultimately ended second behind Aston Villa. Off the pitch, in November 1898, Walker found himself on the front pages of the local press, arrested for breach of the peace along with fellow Scottish team-mates Hugh Morgan and John Allan after a drunken night out ended in an argument with a police constable.

Walker started the following season in brilliant form, scoring seven times in his first ten games, although inconsistency blighted both the player and the team, meaning they dropped too many points to be serious contenders. But season 1900/01 was to be different.

Walker started 29 times in the league, again scoring regularly early on. Liverpool remained in contention, but it appeared they were destined for another second place as Sunderland sat on top going into April. But the Roker Park men stumbled in the run-in with a defeats to Everton and then The Wednesday. Despite winning their final game against Newcastle, it left Liverpool only behind on goal average, and they still had a game to play. A point against already relegated West Bromwich Albion at The Hawthorns would give the Anfield club their first championship.

In front of 4,000 fans, Liverpool started the match with Walker in his usual inside-right position, and with plenty of Scottish company as fellow Scots Tom Robertson, Billy Dunlop, Bill Goldie and Tommy Robertson all lined up. In the 20th minute came the moment of destiny. West Brom were on the attack and their forward Garfield looked certain to score. But a desperate tackle started a swift counter attack, which was finished off by Walker. In a game of few chances, that one goal was enough for the victory and Liverpool were champions of England.

Walker had one more season at Liverpool, playing his 120th and final game for the club in a 1-1 draw at Blackburn in April 1902. Fittingly he signed off with a goal, a 75th-minute equaliser to rescue a point. In those 120 matches he had scored 30 times. On 1 May 1902 Walker's contract at Anfield expired and he returned north to sign for Scottish champions Rangers.

Although Rangers had just won their fourth consecutive league title, this was a time of great sadness at Ibrox. The terrible tragedy of the stand collapse in early April in the Scotland v England international that claimed the lives of 25 supporters had cast a dark shadow over the club. Every player was up for sale, and the club were determined to raise as much money as possible to help affected families as well as rebuild their stadium. It was perhaps unimportant that fixtures still had to be played, one of which was a debut for Walker in a 1-1 draw against Queen's Park in the Inter-City League on 10 May at Hampden. He scored Rangers' goal.

Walker played at Ibrox for the next four seasons, often as an outside-right. It was a period of little success, although the player himself gave some outstanding displays. In a classic New Year's Day match in 1903 he scored twice in a minute against Celtic in a 3-3 draw. He played in the first two drawn matches against old club Hearts in the 1903 Scottish Cup Final, but missed the decisive 2-0 second replay victory that brought the cup back to Ibrox on a day of high emotion. This was to be the last Rangers success in the competition for a quarter of a century.

Walker gave another man-of-the-match display in the first round of the cup the following season, scoring twice in a thrilling 3-2 Ibrox win over their Tynecastle rivals. He scored another double in the semi-final against Morton, but suffered final heartbreak when Celtic came back from two behind to win 3-2. A few weeks later he played in his only winning cup final in Royal Blue, a 1-0 win over Third Lanark in the Charity Cup.

The final seasons of Walker's Rangers career were hampered by knee problems, meaning he missed significant spells. Maybe fittingly, his last league start was at Tynecastle, which ended 2-2, and his final competitive appearance was on 1 May 1906 in a 3-0 win over Queen's Park in the Glasgow League. Overall, he played 92 times for Rangers, scoring 35 goals.

Despite the club seeing little success, his form in spells had been enough to see a recall to the Scotland team in 1904 for matches against Wales and Ireland. He won five caps overall, scoring three times.

Walker left Ibrox for Greenock Morton in the summer of 1906, playing 28 times before a serious knee injury forced his retirement. In 1910, he emigrated to Canada, becoming an engineer with Manitoba Telephones. Then, like everyone else, his life changed significantly in 1914 with the outbreak of war. Walker enlisted in 1916, serving with the Canadian Signal Corps. After the conflict he returned to his telephone company job, until 1937.

On 17 February at the age of 63, Walker was killed in an accident with a power saw while cutting wood in the village of Louise, Manitoba.

There are some great names who have represented Liverpool and Rangers. But there will be few supporters of either club who know of the former Ranger who scored the first title-winning goal in Liverpool's history.

- Rangers career: 1902–1906
- Scorer of Old Firm goals
- Won the Charity Cup
- League- and Scottish Cup-winning captain of Hearts
- Scored the goal that won Liverpool their first league title

59 KARL PEKARNA

The first overseas player to play for Rangers

IN MODERN times, Rangers fans have enjoyed watching some magnificent players who came from outside Britain. Brian Laudrup, Jorg Albertz, Arthur Numan, Nacho Novo and Alfredo Morelos are just some of those who have worn the shirt and captured the hearts of the support. Players signed from overseas are now as much part of the game as pie and Bovril. But at the turn of the 20th century, foreign footballers were non-existent in the Scottish game, and this is the story of the first overseas player who signed on at Ibrox.

Karl Pekarna was born on 7 July 1881 in the lower Austrian municipality of Oberlaa. He enjoyed playing football in his youth, even though the game was still in its infancy in the country. On leaving school he got a job as a postman, and the teenager turned out in goal for the small Viennese outfit FC Sevilla (not to be confused with the famous Spanish club). His all-action style and eye-catching diving saves saw him gain rave reviews, and at the age of 18 he joined First Vienna. Initially a deputy to their regular goalkeeper Karl Mollisch, Pekarna got his big chance in May 1900 when Mollisch suffered an injury, and he made his debut against Weiner FC. Once in the side he was there to stay, the teenager commanding his penalty area like a player well beyond his years.

First Vienna were founded in 1894, so in 1904 they decided to hold a close-season tournament to celebrate their tenth anniversary, inviting Boldklub 1893 of Copenhagen and Glasgow Rangers to take part. Rangers agreed to the trip, and combined the tournament with a wider Austro-Hungarian tour, which would include matches in Vienna and Prague (the country that was to become Czechoslovakia was at that time part of the Austro-Hungarian Empire). Rangers kicked off the tournament on 22 May with a thumping 7-2 win over First Vienna, and would go on to record other similar huge scores against opposition that was still amateur. As a sign of just how easy these tour games were for the Scottish professionals, there was a report of the Rangers goalkeeper writing postcards for his family back home while a match against Weiner FC was being played, such was his boredom. Rangers won that game 8-0.

But it was in the First Vienna tournament that events unfolded to create club history. The Danish goalkeeper suffered an injury against Vienna, meaning they were without a keeper for the next match against Rangers, so the hosts allowed them to borrow Karl Pekarna. Rangers had already beaten Boldklub 1893 9-0 in their first meeting of the competition, but it had been played in horrendous weather, and the teams agreed to a rematch in order for the spectators to see a better spectacle. On 26 May, Pekarna lined up for the Danes against the Rangers firepower and made a series of brilliant stops. He couldn't prevent the Scots winning 5-3, but his display had hugely impressed the Rangers players and management.

Rangers went on to complete their tour with two thumping victories in Prague, the final fixture being a 5-0 hammering of Slavia Prague. On returning home, Rangers kicked off 1904/05 with Willie Allan and John Watson vying for the starting position and new signing Tom Sinclair in the reserves. Neither of the two keepers who started the season were impressing, and by late October it was the inexperienced Sinclair who was in the team. He was doing well, but William Wilton was concerned he had no depth in his squad, and Rangers were in a tight league race with Celtic. Remembering the brilliant young Austrian from the overseas tour, he contacted Pekarna in December and offered him a contract to sign on at Ibrox for the remainder of the season. He agreed to the terms on offer, said to be £3 10s per week, and made the trip to Glasgow where he signed the contract at the end of January 1905.

Pekarna became the first overseas player in the history of Rangers, and the first professional footballer to come from Austria. By now he was an international, starting in two matches between the city teams of Vienna and Budapest which were then recognised as full international matches, being justified as such by the description of 'games between the representative teams of the Austrian and Hungarian football associations'. His first match in Rangers colours was a reserve Old Firm clash, and he did well enough to keep his place for virtually the rest of the season.

Sinclair, however, was still performing consistently in the first team, in a season where Rangers reached both the Scottish Cup Final and a play-off to decide the league title. He played in both, but both were lost. This meant the impressive Pekarna was used only in reserve matches and friendlies, until 8 May 1905 when he was selected for the first team in a Glasgow League match against Queen's Park at Hampden. Pekarna kept a clean sheet in front of 3,000 spectators as Rangers won 2-0 with goals by two great international forwards, Finlay Speedie and Alec Smith. This would be Pekarna's only first-team appearance for the club.

Despite his lack of first-team action, Pekarna had impressed the manager and he was offered another contract for 1905/06 on similar terms. But he opted to return to Vienna, a combination of homesickness and lack of first-team football driving his decision.

On his return home, Pekarna had to reapply for amateur status having been a paid professional for the preceding months. The football authorities were reluctant to agree to this, and it took a threat by First Vienna to resign their association membership for the request to finally be accepted. This issue of past professionalism was to recur in May 1908 when Pekarna left First Vienna to sign for FC Wacker in the Bavarian city of Munich. Again, his debut was delayed until he could prove his amateur status. Once he was given the go-ahead he certainly impressed at his new club, as in 1910 he was offered a 'not inconsiderable payment' to move to Bavarian champions Bayern Munich, where he replaced German international Ludwig Hofmeister as their first-choice goalkeeper.

He remained at Bayern until the outbreak of war in 1914, winning the league title in 1911, and combining his football career with a job as a supervisor in a sporting goods shop. He returned to Austria with his wife and daughters on the cancellation of football during the war, and his playing career ended in 1919 with a brief comeback spell at SK Slovan in Vienna.

Pekarna briefly moved into coaching, first at SG Duren in Germany and then at Alemannia Aachen. Once leaving the latter role, he became a teacher.

In 1920, Pekarna's younger brother Ludwig was killed while playing in goal in a match in Vienna after a collision left him with a fractured spine. This tragedy may have contributed to his decision to leave football, but his teaching life was cut short in 1926 when Karl suffered a significant stroke that left him confined to a wheelchair. He was rarely seen in public after this, and died in Vienna on 23 January 1946 at the age of 64. When his death was made public, the former Germany national team coach Otto Nerz described Karl as 'the best goalkeeper of his time'.

Pekarna spent just a few months at Ibrox and made only one appearance. But he will forever be the first foreign player to wear the Rangers colours, and that makes him a man worth remembering.

- Teenage goalkeeping sensation in Austria
- First overseas player to sign for Rangers
- Also played for Bayern

60 MATTHEW DICKIE

The Invincible Rangers goalkeeper

THE DUNBARTONSHIRE village of Rhu holds a special place in the history of Rangers, with the Gallant Pioneers Moses McNeil, Peter McNeil and Peter Campbell being born there. For those who remember the Rangers teams of the 1970s, one of the great players of that decade, Derek Parlane, also hailed from the village on the east shore of the Gare Loch. All four of these men are members of the Hall of Fame.

But there is another son of Rhu who is less well known, but who also played his part in a historic era for Rangers. He was born in the village on 19 August 1873, just as the McNeil brothers and their friends were trying to grow their new football team. His name was Matthew Dickie.

Dickie's football talents were as a goalkeeper and he played for several amateur teams in the Helensburgh area as a youngster before signing for Renton FC in 1889, based at Tontine Park in West Dunbartonshire and one of the leading clubs in the early years of Scottish football. The teenager had joined a team who had won the Scottish Cup twice in the previous four seasons, and who had beaten English FA Cup holders West Bromwich Albion in 1888 in a match billed as deciding 'The Championship of The United Kingdom and the World'.

The young keeper had to bide his time, learning from more experienced goalkeepers such as Scottish international John Lindsay, and it wasn't until 1894 that he became the regular custodian. It didn't help that the club were suspended for several months by the SFA for playing an unauthorised friendly match, and on their reinstatement into the game

Renton never hit their previous heights again. By the time Dickie was the first-choice goalkeeper, Renton had suffered relegation to the Second Division Two, and despite a good Scottish Cup run in season 1894/95 that saw them reach the final they never played in the top tier of Scottish football again.

Dickie kept goal in that 1895 final, where he suffered a 2-1 defeat by St Bernard's at Ibrox. In all, he started in almost 40 league and cup games for Renton, but he wanted to play at a higher level, and he got his wish in the summer of 1896 when his club agreed to a transfer to Rangers.

William Wilton's team had failed to win any trophies in the previous two seasons despite some excellent players and winning the Scottish Cup in 1894 and the Glasgow Cup in both 1893 and 1894. One reason for the lack of success was a shocking inconsistency, and that was reflected in the goalkeeping position which had been filled by three different players in the second half of 1895/96 in John McLeod, Jim McAllan and Jimmy Yuill. The defence needed the presence of a regular and reliable custodian, and the manager saw Dickie as that man. How right he would prove to be.

Dickie's Rangers debut came on 15 August 1896 at home to St Mirren, and he enjoyed a fine start to his Ibrox career with a thumping 5-1 win. Dickie slotted in behind regular full-backs Nick Smith and Jock Drummond, with the likes of the experienced Andrew McCreadie and former captain Davie Mitchell at half-back. He quickly gained the trust of his team-mates with his solid shot-stopping and command of the goalmouth, and the team saw an almost immediate improvement. As well as ability, Dickie's biggest strengths were his concentration and his consistency, and he became a player Wilton relied upon. This was shown by the incredible statistic that Dickie played in 124 of the next 132 league games that Rangers played, only missing matches either for international duty or injury.

Despite the team's obvious improvement, the ever-present Dickie wouldn't win a league medal in his first season, the team stumbling in the run-in and ending up third, just three points behind winners Hearts. But he did collect plenty silverware as his arrival coincided with an amazing period of success for the club. His first triumph came in November 1896 when he played in the 2-1 Glasgow Cup Final win over Celtic, and by the end of the season he had added winners' medals in both the Scottish Cup and the Charity Cup. His second Scottish Cup Final appearance came in late March when Dumbarton were thrashed 5-1, and the last game of his memorable debut season was a 6-1 rout of Third Lanark to win a first Charity Cup for the club. Dickie had all three cup medals after only one season at Rangers.

Dickie capped off a fairytale first season by winning his first Scotland cap in March 1897 when he was selected for the match against Ireland at Ibrox. Not only was it his home ground, but club-mate Jock Drummond was team captain, and three of the Scotland goals in the 5-1 success were scored by fellow Rangers men Neilly Gibson and John McPherson. Dickie played for Scotland just twice more, with the incredible aggregate score of 19-4 in those three games, the highlight being a 9-1 annihilation of Ireland in 1899. He also played once for the Scottish League, a 2-1 win over their English counterparts in 1898 at Villa Park.

He missed just one league game in 1897/98, the team finishing second behind Celtic. But it was again the cup competitions that saw Rangers dominate. Dickie kept clean sheets in both the Glasgow Cup and Scottish Cup finals, which were won against Queen's Park and Kilmarnock. The Glasgow Cup Final in late November started off a brilliant run for both player and team, Rangers putting together seven successive wins that saw Dickie concede just once while the forwards plundered a total of 49 goals. This sequence included a magnificent 5-0 beating at Easter Road of a very good Hibs team who finished the league season in third place. After another clean sheet in a Charity Cup semi-final success against Celtic, it looked like another cup clean sweep was on the cards but the season ended with a surprise 1-0 loss to Third Lanark in the final.

All that was missing now for Dickie was a league title. And despite Celtic's success the previous season, which saw them become champions without losing a game, confidence was high at Ibrox that Rangers had the team to win the title for the first time since the opening season of league football in 1891. As well as the excellence of a defence with Dickie, Nicol Smith and Drummond, the Rangers support got to watch a team with the creative talents of Gibson, Alec Smith and McPherson in addition to the scoring exploits of Hamilton and Millar. It all came together in 1898/99 as Dickie and his team-mates made football history.

Eighteen wins from 18 league games played was the final record as Rangers took the title in prefect fashion. Dickie started in all of the matches, only conceding 18 goals in an era when all teams played with five forwards. Among the clean sheets, there were probably three that stood out. In a handsome 4-0 win at Parkhead in September, Rangers dominated from start to finish but still needed their star goalkeeper to pull off important saves. On Christmas Eve came a 10-0 home win over a Hibs team who had very nearly won their home fixture earlier in the campaign, this result clinching the title with three games to play. Then on 7 January 1899, a 3-0 win at Clyde completed the league fixtures and confirmed the first 100 per cent invincible league season in world football.

Rangers went on to prove themselves the best team in the country by retaining their league crown in each of the next three seasons, with Dickie the ever-reliable last line of defence. He started in the first 17 league games of 1899/1900, only missing the final one due to international duty against Wales. The title was won by a massive seven points, although Dickie did taste league defeat for the first time in almost two years when he played in a slightly unlucky 3-2 reverse at Parkhead on New Year's Day 1900. He did keep a clean sheet in the Old Firm Glasgow Cup Final, which was settled by a Bobby Neill penalty, and added another Charity Cup medal to his growing collection when in goal in a 5-1 battering of Celtic in the final. As in the previous season, the Scottish Cup run was ended by their great rivals, however they had a very good team during this time and it took an exceptional Rangers side to consistently finish above them.

The margin of victory in the 1900/01 league season was six points, Dickie ever present in the 20 matches. The only cup success was in retaining the Glasgow Cup, the first round memorable for two classic games against Celtic with the replay won 4-3 after an initial 3-3 draw. That first match included a real collector's item, a horrendous Dickie error where he misjudged a floated free kick and could only palm the ball into his own goal. He still ended up smiling, though, playing in the final win over Partick.

Season 1901/02 saw Dickie miss a few weeks with an injury, but he still played in 15 league games as the title destination was massively influenced by a 4-2 victory at Parkhead in the third-to-last fixture in front of 40,000 fans. Dickie added yet another Glasgow Cup success, playing in the drawn final against a Celtic team who scratched from the replay in protest at the venue selected. Despite yet another title, that season ended with a massive cloud of despair over the club due to the terrible loss of life at the Scotland versus England match at the stadium. Off the field rebuilding and compensation to victims was the priority for the following season.

Dickie retained the goalkeeping position in 1902/03, starting in 21 league games as the title defence failed early on with three defeats in the first five matches while the club was still reeling from the disaster. But Dickie would be a star man in the team bringing the Scottish Cup back to Ibrox for the first time since 1898, an emotional triumph for all at the club. He kept out the Celtic attack in an excellent 3-0 quarter-final win at Parkhead before starting in all three matches in the final against Hearts. A 1-1 draw, then a 0-0 draw preceded the decisive meeting on 25 April 1903 at Parkhead, when Dickie gave an outstanding display as a ten-man Rangers team hampered by a first-half injury to Jock Drummond fought like tigers to win 2-0 thanks to goals by Alec Mackie and R.C. Hamilton.

Season 1903/04 would be Dickie's last as a Rangers player. Now into his 30s, he suffered the first significant injury of his Rangers career in the latter stages of the campaign, sitting out several huge matches. He had still started in 15 league games prior to this, in a season where Rangers finished a disappointing fourth. Dickie played in his last Old Firm league match in October, fittingly keeping a clean sheet in a hard-fought 0-0 draw. But he missed the entire Scottish Cup campaign through injury, his deputy John Watson in goal for the final where Celtic came back from two goals down to win 3-2. Dickie didn't play in the revenge Charity Cup Final win over them, his last game for the club coming in a low-key Inter-City League match at Ibrox against Third Lanark on 10 May 1904 that featured several fringe players. Rangers won 4-1.

In the summer of 1904, Dickie was allowed to leave after a magnificent eight years of service, joining Clyde where he enjoyed first-team football until his retirement in 1907.

After his playing days, Dickie retained an active interest in sports. He helped run Helensburgh Football Club for many years and followed them all over the country to watch them play. He was also a very keen and talented bowler, winning the championship of Helensburgh Bowling Club four times between 1921 and 1933. Such was his esteem at the club that in 1957 he was presented with a silver jack to commemorate his 50th year as a member.

Dickie was also a successful Helensburgh businessman, running a tobacconists shop in Sinclair Street, which was especially popular as it had a billiards room upstairs. He died on 30 December 1959 at the age of 86, his sons presenting a trophy to the local bowling club on his death to be awarded annually in his name.

But he will be most remembered as a truly great Rangers goalkeeper in a team who dominated Scottish football, and was the first Royal Blue custodian to win multiple titles. To the Rangers fans of the late 19th and early 20th centuries, Matt Dickie was simply 'The Goalie'.

Dickie, unlike many of his team-mates in that great Rangers side, is not yet inducted in the Hall of Fame. His incredible consistency and success must make him a worthy candidate for that honour in the future.

- Rangers career: 1896–1904
- 275 competitive appearances, 175 in the league
- 4 league titles
- 3 Scottish Cups
- 5 Glasgow Cups
- 2 Charity Cups
- 3 Scotland caps
- Ever present in the 'Invincible' season

61   NEIL KERR

The tragic tale of the man who starred in Rangers' first competitive win over Celtic

NEIL KERR was born in the village of Bowling in Dunbartonshire on 13 April 1871. A speedy forward at home on the right wing or through the middle, his career was somewhat nomadic at the start. He joined Cowlairs and played in the Scottish Cup in January 1890, then turned out for Hearts in the Roseberry Charity Cup in the April, and made a couple of appearances for Dumbarton soon after, before signing for Rangers in early August.

His Rangers debut was a historic occasion: the club's first league match, played at home against Hearts on 16 August. Right-winger Kerr scored twice in a fine 5-2 victory and he immediately became a fixture in the team as Rangers set out on that debut championship season. His first Old Firm appearance soon followed, a single-goal defeat in the Scottish Cup. But he was soon putting a smile back on Rangers fan faces when he became only the second Rangers player to score a league hat-trick in an 8-2 rout of St Mirren in early October.

Kerr was an ever present, scoring eight times in 18 league games, including a vital strike in a win over league leaders Dumbarton in April 1891. Rangers and Dumbarton ended the regular season level on points at the top, meaning a play-off match was arranged between the clubs to decide the first Scottish champions. On 21 May 1891 Kerr played at centre-forward in a thrilling 2-2 draw, after which it was decided the title would be shared. The first championship in Rangers' long history had been won, and Kerr was a big reason why.

He remained a mainstay of the team in 1891/92, although it wasn't a year the club took any honours. In total, he started 32 times, scoring 11 goals. Three of these were in the Scottish Cup as Rangers made the semi-finals, but despite scoring for the first time against Celtic, he again tasted defeat in a 5-3 loss. Kerr also lost in the Charity Cup Final to the same opponents, who enjoyed something of a hoodoo over Rangers in these early years. In March 1892 he was selected for Scotland A in a trial game but this was the closest he would come to international football.

In 1892/93, Kerr would at last get some revenge. He was still a regular starter and was in good form in the winter including a four-goal haul in the Scottish Cup against Annbank. He also scored an important goal in a 4-3 success over Abercorn in the league, then it was time to face Celtic in the Glasgow Cup Final on 18 February 1893.

On a historic day, Rangers ran out worthy 3-1 winners to claim their first win in the tournament as well as a first competitive success over their Parkhead rivals. After John Barker had opened the scoring in the first half, Kerr scored the crucial second goal in the second period with a brave header, and his strong running and clever play saw him named as the best player on the field in the newspaper reports that followed. The Rangers fans celebrated, with Kerr's name being sung loud.

The remainder of the season failed to live up to these heights. Kerr scored a crucial goal in the Charity Cup semi-final victory over Third Lanark, but least said about the final the better as he suffered a heavy defeat to Celtic who took some revenge for their earlier cup final reverse. The following season saw Rangers mainly prefer other forwards such as John Steel and John Gray, and Kerr missed out on selection for the club's first Scottish Cup Final success against Celtic, although he had scored in the opening round on the road to glory. He played his 87th and last game in Royal Blue in an end of season league defeat to St Bernard's. Kerr scored 34 times in those appearances.

On 4 June 1894, Kerr was transferred to newly promoted Liverpool, who were about to play their first season in England's First Division. It was a difficult season for the Merseyside club, who had only been admitted to the Second Division the previous summer. Kerr made his Liverpool debut on Thursday, 13 September, playing on the right wing in a 2-1 defeat to Bolton Wanderers. In all he played 12 league games that season, the first of his three goals coming in October in a home draw with Sheffield United. A fine strike in a 5-1 win over Derby County in March 1895 was a rare high as the Anfield club were relegated. In September of that year, he left for Nottingham Forest.

Kerr's brief stay with Forest was unremarkable, only playing one league match. And, during the close-season when he was back in Scotland, there was a tragedy on the evening of 24 July 1896. The events were described in the *Arbroath Herald* the following week, 'Neil Kerr, the old Cowlair-Rangers-Liverpool player, and who in years gone by has played on Gayfield Park, was on Saturday morning last the sole survivor of a very sad yachting accident on the Clyde. Kerr and two companions had been cruising about the Firth during the Glasgow Fair holidays, and on Friday opening the party found a yacht drifting at Large.

'About midnight Mr. Kerr and his companions – one of them Archibald Petrie, being the son of the owner of the yacht – resolved to take the vessel to safe quarters under the lee of the Bute Island.

When about mid-channel, Kerr, who was repairing a lamp, discovered that water was coming rapidly and gave alarm. In the excitement that followed the boat was accidentally upset by one of the party, and the unfortunate three men were thrown into the water. Kerr was apparently the only efficient swimmer and managed to give the others an oar each and urged them to do the best they could for themselves.

'The unfortunate men, however, were unable to hold on to the oars long and soon sank. Kerr pluckily made for a light visible from the Bute shore, and, after swimming for more than an hour, landed in a very exhausted condition and raise the alarm. A search party immediately put out, and the lifeless bodies of the two men were found washed upon the shore. Kerr soon came round, but he was naturally in a very distressed state of mind.'

This tragedy ended Kerr's career in England, and some weeks later he joined Falkirk. Despite his heavy heart, the return north proved good for his football, and he rediscovered his appetite for the game and his scoring form. His 16 goals in 31 games attracted the interest of his old club, and in September 1897 he returned to Rangers. But he was seen more as a back-up than a first team regular, adding just four appearances and one goal to his original total.

Whether it was a simple lack of form, or whether the accident of 1896 had never truly left him, we do not know. Kerr played no more senior football after 1897/98, even though still only in his 20s. His story ended on a tragic note when in early December 1901 several newspapers reported that he had died at his home, aged just 30.

- Ever present in Rangers' first title win
- Scored in Rangers' first league match
- Scored Rangers' second league hat-trick
- Scored and man of the match in the first cup final win over Celtic
- The only survivor of a terrible boating accident

62 ROBERT CAMPBELL

The Rangers captain and director who played for Celtic

ROBERT GORDON Campbell was born in Ellon in Aberdeenshire on 27 January 1883. A keen footballer who turned out for several local amateur sides, Campbell moved to Glasgow in the early 20th century where he briefly played for Junior team Rutherglen

Glencairn. His senior career started in 1904 with Queen's Park, where his fine skills combined with astute positional play and physical strength alerted several professional clubs. His debut for Queen's Park wasn't the happiest one, a 5-0 thrashing from Rangers at Ibrox on 22 October 1904, but things improved greatly the following weekend when he scored his first, and only, goal for the Spiders in a deserved 1-1 draw with Celtic. He then made the right-back position his own, making 25 starts in 1904/05 before joining the professional ranks in the close-season.

The move probably surprised Campbell's closest friends as the devout Wesleyan Methodist was transferred to Celtic in June 1905. He made his Celtic debut in August and gave a nervous display in a 3-1 win over Motherwell. He was given the nickname 'Baby' by his team-mates who likened his nervy start to that of a baby elephant. In all, Campbell was at right-back in 11 Celtic league appearances, losing only twice. One of those defeats was at Ibrox in October 1905, his first appearance in the biggest derby match in the country.

At Ibrox, Rangers were having a defensive crisis. The right-back position had been brilliantly filled for so long by the great Nicol Smith, but since his tragic and untimely passing in January 1905 the club were still searching for an adequate replacement. By coincidence, one of the players they had briefly fielded there was an Ayrshireman also called Robert Campbell, but by January 1906 several players had failed to impress or had suffered injury, and manager William Wilton was fielding forward Johnny Walker as an emergency defender. Wilton approached Celtic with a £350 offer for Campbell, and the player was delighted when Celtic accepted the fee. Many inside Parkhead were unhappy with Campbell's very public religious beliefs, although he was popular with both his team-mates and the supporters. He became the first direct permanent transfer between the clubs.

Campbell made his debut in Royal Blue on 20 January 1906, with 8,000 fans at Ibrox to see a convincing 4-0 win over Port Glasgow. He quickly became a fan favourite, possibly helped by his willingness to swap Parkhead for Ibrox but no doubt also thanks to a series of solid performances. By now he was known as R.G. Campbell, which identified him as different from others in the game at the time who shared his name.

This first season at Rangers had two special highlights, even though there was disappointment in failing to win the league or Scottish Cup. On 5 May Campbell played against his former club for the first time and enjoyed a thrilling 5-3 win at Parkhead in the semi-final of the Charity Cup. Then a week later he won his first medal when two goals by Jimmy Speirs helped beat his other old club, Queen's Park, 3-2 in the final.

Campbell was a mainstay of the team again the following season, but not in the way expected. A benefit match against Morton in November 1906 saw him played at centre-forward due to injuries, and incredibly he scored every goal in a 7-0 win. Wilton quickly reconsidered his defensive options and Campbell started in a new attacking role. Despite still being selected sometimes as a full-back, Campbell ended the season with 12 goals. He scored his first competitive goals for Rangers with a brace in a 2-2 draw away to Partick on 2 January 1907, followed by successive hat-tricks against Clyde and Port Glasgow in March, and rounded the season off in memorable fashion by scoring the only goal in the Charity Cup Final against Celtic in May.

Season 1907/08 was his most prolific with 32 goals in 39 competitive starts, including four hat-tricks. Despite his prolific scoring, this was a period where Celtic dominated and he had no medals to show for his efforts that year. The following season Campbell's versatility was often utilised by the manager. He found himself playing centre-back on several occasions and was so successful that many fans judged this to be where he seemed best suited. A career split between defending against speedy wingers and finding space against tough tackling centre-backs had given Campbell excellent game appreciation, and his reading of the play was a major factor in his success in the middle of the defence. He still scored 17 times that season, though. Campbell started the Scottish Cup Final against Celtic on 10 April 1909 back up front but failed to score in a 2-2 draw. He lost his place for the replay, new signing Willie Reid taking over, so he wasn't on the pitch when fans rioted when they discovered there was to be no extra time after another draw.

Reid was to become the regular centre-forward for many years, his scoring exploits becoming legendary, so Campbell's remaining Rangers career was back in defence. He and George Law shared the right-back slot for most of 1909/10, with Campbell only making 15 starts. He was more of a regular the next season, now sometimes at left-back, as Rangers mounted a real title challenge. The goals of Reid, alongside the brilliant wing play of Billy Hogg, were crucial in a first title in nine years. And in May 1911, Campbell won a third Charity Cup when two Reid goals defeated Celtic.

Campbell's remaining Rangers career saw plenty of highs. He won his first Glasgow Cup in 1911, and added further winners' medals in 1912 and 1913. The league title was retained then won for a third year in a row, and by now he was a regular captain of the side. On 19 August 1912, 5,000 fans attended his benefit match when a goal by future Everton hero Bobby Parker helped defeat Celtic 2-1.

He went full circle, becoming the right-back again, and scored his last Rangers goal from the penalty spot against Aberdeen in the Inter-City league in October 1912. His final season at the club in 1913/14 was a disappointing one, losing the title to Celtic and again failing in the Scottish Cup. He would never play in another final after that 1909 drawn match; like many great Rangers players of the time he endured the Scottish Cup jinx. Campbell lined up for the final time for Rangers on 1 April 1914, a forgettable 4-1 away loss to Falkirk. After 246 games, he left in the close-season to join Kilmarnock.

His football career drifted to a close in Ayrshire with brief spells at both Kilmarnock and Ayr before war took priority and he helped in the home efforts while younger men headed for the front.

But that wasn't the last of Robert Gordon Campbell at Ibrox. A regular attendee as a supporter and a staunch friend of many club officials, he was invited to join the board of directors in 1926, an honour he instantly and gratefully accepted. As a director he finally watched the 25-year Scottish Cup hoodoo ended in 1928. He enjoyed a period of Bill Struth-inspired domestic dominance on the pitch, and celebrated the opening of the magnificent new Main Stand. And he proudly sat in the boardroom as part of the biggest and best football club in Britain.

Campbell passed away on 31 May 1942 aged just 59. He is not remembered as one of the true Rangers greats, but he is remembered for a unique Rangers life.

- Signed directly from Celtic
- 246 appearances and 66 goals
- 3 league titles
- 3 Glasgow Cups
- 3 Charity Cups
- Became a Rangers director

63   ROBERT MCCOLL

The Rangers centre-forward with the high street name

ROBERT SMYTH McColl was born in the Glasgow district of St Rollox on 13 April 1876, the son of a superintendent in the Glasgow city cleansing department. A very talented footballer, he started his career as a centre-forward with the now defunct Benmore club in the Mount Florida area, before being signed in early 1894 by Queen's Park when aged just 18.

His debut for the famous amateurs came in a Charity Cup tie against Rangers at Hampden on 28 April 1894, and he played a fine match in a 2-0 victory. Two weeks later he played in the final against Celtic at Ibrox, but couldn't prevent the Parkhead men taking the trophy with a 2-1 win. Queen's Park had refused to join the Scottish League as they felt it threatened their amateur status, so McColl was limited to cup games and friendlies to show what he could do. And what he could do was score goals. He scored against Celtic in a Glasgow Cup defeat in his first full season, and in his time with Queen's Park he scored in the competition against every other significant Glasgow club. In 1898/99 he hit a first-round hat-trick to beat Partick, and played in the winning team in the final when Queen's Park shocked the 'Invincibles' of Rangers 1-0. The closest he came to a Charity Cup success came in 1896 when he was unlucky not to score in a heartbreaking extra-time defeat to Celtic.

In the Scottish Cup, McColl enjoyed a run all the way to the final in 1899/1900. After scoring in comfortable early-round wins over Leith and Abercorn, he hit the winning goals in both the quarter-final against Dundee and the semi-final against Hearts to take Queen's Park into a final against Celtic, which remains their most recent appearance in the national showpiece. He played well in a classic final but Celtic won 4-3. McColl scored at a rate of around two goals in every three games in his time with the Spiders, and despite never playing a top-level league match, he had attracted the attention of the Scotland team selectors from relatively early in his career.

He made a much-anticipated Scotland debut on 21 March 1896 against Wales in Dundee, and impressed all who watched the 4-0 win. Thanks to his international exploits, McColl became the hottest property in Scottish football over the next few years. He scored twice against Ireland in the opening 25 minutes in Belfast the following week before adding another against them in his both his next appearances in 1897 and 1898. Then in 1899 he hit six goals in the space of a week, with hat-tricks against Wales and Ireland in thumping victories. He couldn't find the net against England, however, in the last game of the Home International Championship that season, but his most famous match for his country was still to come.

In 1900, Scotland welcomed England to Parkhead for the annual fixture, with the SFA president and former prime minister Lord Roseberry in attendance. In tribute, the Scots wore his racing colours of yellow and pink, and in their unusual jerseys they gave England a hammering. McColl scored in the very first minute, and when he scored again after 25 minutes it put Scotland 3-0 in front. With the wonderful Rangers half-back Neilly Gibson pulling the strings, McColl completed his hat-trick before half-time. The final score of 4-1 perhaps flattered the English, and McColl's third Scotland hat-trick in a year made him a national hero and front-page news. In all, McColl played 13 times for his country, and he scored 13 goals, strangely never scoring for Scotland again in the four matches he started after that famous day. He did score for the Scottish League against the English League at Ibrox in 1901, however.

In 1901, McColl decided to leave Hampden and turn professional. It was a mark of the fame he then carried, that reports told of up to 50 clubs on both side of the border looking to sign him. It helped as well that with his amateur status it meant that any club signing him had no need to pay a transfer fee. Liverpool thought they had captured his signature after a phone call between the player and chairman Tom Watson, but he eventually decided the right club for him was Newcastle United, who were competing for honours and who had a significant number of Scots in their playing squad. They agreed to pay the player the huge sum of £5 per week.

McColl made an instant impression, scoring on his debut on 9 November 1901 against Manchester City, then the only goal the following Saturday to defeat defending champions Liverpool. His first season was badly interrupted by injury, but he and the fans were happy with his first professional season, ending in four goals in 12 starts, including one in a big FA Cup tie against Sheffield United. He was given the nickname 'The Prince of Centre-Forwards' on the terraces, undoubtedly helped by a memorable winner against arch-rivals Sunderland in season 1902/03 that ultimately prevented the Roker men winning the league.

His team-mates had a different name for him, however, calling him 'Toffee Bob'. This was because in late 1901, McColl invested a large part of his £300 signing-on fee from

Newcastle into his brother Tom's confectionary business, which consisted of three shops. The wily Tom decided to cash in on his brother's fame, renaming the shops as 'RS McColl'. The shops did a roaring trade, and the company expanded quickly, opening shops in Glasgow and beyond, becoming newsagents and often ice-cream parlours as well as selling sweets. By 1935, the RS McColl empire consisted 180 shops and employed around 300 people, and it was sold to Cadbury's but retaining the popular name. Many high streets across the country still have an RS McColl shop to this day.

Although popular at St James' Park, McColl struggled to settle in England. He played for one more season at Newcastle, scoring six times to help Newcastle to a fourth-place finish. After 20 goals in 67 competitive appearances, McColl returned to Scotland in September 1904, signing for Rangers for a fee of £400.

This was a Rangers team going through a significant rebuilding, with several of the players who had carried the club to unprecedented successes at the turn of the century now moving on. Ironically, his debut came at Hampden against Queen's Park in the league, the amateurs having been admitted into the league structure just as McColl was leaving them. In a potent-looking strike force beside R.C. Hamilton, he enjoyed a 4-0 win. He scored his first Rangers goal the following weekend, an important one as they scraped past Hibs with a 2-1 victory. In all, he started 12 league games in 1904/05, hitting the net seven times. The league season ended with the Old Firm clubs level on points at the top, meaning a play-off match was required. McColl started it but crucially Hamilton was out injured, and Celtic won 2-1. He also came up agonisingly short in the Scottish Cup, playing in both final matches against Third Lanark, the replay being a 3-1 defeat. Overall, he started in 26 matches across the various competitions during the season, and his 15 goals included a first against Celtic in Royal Blue, coming in an end-of-season Glasgow League win. This seemed poor consolation for another runners-up medal to the same opposition earlier in the season in the Glasgow Cup.

His first season ended with no winners' medals, and he failed to collect any in 1905/06 either. He hit six goals in 13 league appearances as Rangers finished a disappointing fourth. McColl was to suffer a season-ending injury in a Glasgow League defeat to Third Lanark in March, meaning he missed out on the only silverware won that season as Rangers lifted the Charity Cup by beating Celtic in the semi-final then Queen's Park in the final.

By the start of 1906/07, the 31-year-old McColl no longer enjoyed the professional game, and looked to his first club to enquire whether he could revert to amateur status and return to Hampden. He played a last game in Rangers colours on 22 September 1906 in a 2-0 loss to Dundee, giving him an Ibrox career record of 22 goals in 44 competitive starts in all competitions. The Queen's Park committee were by now considering his application to return, and there was heated debate within the club whether they could or should admit a former professional. It took the casting vote of the club president to agree to McColl's return. His second Queen's Park debut came on 2 November 1907, and the opposition at Hampden in a First Division match was none other than Rangers.

A much larger than usual attendance of 20,000 were in Hampden to see the game, with the *Glasgow Herald* stating this was 'due to the reappearance of RS McColl in the colours of the club with which his name will ever be fondly associated'. He didn't disappoint his adoring fans, scoring the second goal as Rangers were beaten 3-1 after having taken an early lead through George Livingstone. McColl played for the club for a further three years, his farewell being typically memorable when he scored nine goals in his last three games for the club, including six against Port Glasgow in his penultimate appearance. At the age of 34 he retired, his overall Queen's Park record reading 112 goals from 180 competitive games.

Despite his age, McColl joined the Royal Army Service Corps in the Great War, where he reached the rank of sergeant. After the war, he was well known for his generosity to friends, none more than the players who had starred with him in 1900 in the famous 4-1 win over England. In the 1920s he decided to pay for the transport, accommodation and tickets for all his team-mates every second year when the match was played down south, meaning those Scotland heroes enjoyed regular reunions.

Robert Smyth McColl died on 25 November 1959 in Cathcart, aged 83. While his Rangers career would never qualify him for the club Hall of Fame, he was a superstar of the game in his day, and he was inducted into the Scotland Hall of Fame in 2011. He is buried in Cathcart Cemetery, his gravestone within a stone's throw of that of the man who signed him from Rangers, the great William Wilton.

A household name in life and death.

- 22 goals in 44 Rangers appearances
- A national hero for Scotland
- Wanted by 50 clubs when turning professional
- High Street shops bear his name

64   SANDY NEWBIGGING

The oldest former player at the club's centenary celebrations

ALEX NEWBIGGING was born in Larkhall, Lanarkshire in 1876. A keen young footballer, he mostly enjoyed the position of goalkeeper where he attracted the attention of local Junior team Lanark Athletic, and he signed for them aged 18.

Such was his excellent form that Newbigging was capped by Scotland within a year at junior international level, playing in a 3-1 over Ireland in Belfast. It seemed inevitable he would graduate to the senior game, and he signed for Abercorn of the Second Division for 1897/98. This would be the start of a nomadic career for Newbigging, who never seemed to truly nail down a starting berth at a succession of clubs. He spent three seasons with Abercorn, one of them finishing bottom of the lower league, before a brief return to the Junior game with Lanark United, then a first move down south when he signed for Queen's Park Rangers of the Southern League in 1900.

He was mainly the backup keeper to Henry Clutterbuck, and made no appearances in their league starting line-up during his only season at the club. So, it came a something of a surprise in 1901 when he moved on to Nottingham Forest of England's First Division. He was again brought in as an understudy, this time to future England goalkeeper Harry Linacre. His Forest debut came away to Stoke City in October 1901 and he performed well in a hard-fought 1-1 draw. There was no doubt, though, that Linacre was the club's first choice, and over four seasons in Nottingham, Newbigging only started seven league games. One of those was at outside-right, when in 1902 only nine outfield players reported to the ground for a home game against Sunderland, forcing the manager to select Newbigging to make up the numbers.

In 1905 he returned to the Southern League with Reading, where he did feature on a more regular basis, but his stay there was a brief one as he was contacted by Rangers in the summer of 1906 and he returned to Scotland to join up with the Ibrox side.

This was a period where Rangers had struggled both on and off the park. The terrible tragedy in 1902 that saw 25 fans lose their life at Ibrox during a Scotland v England international match had seen the club sell players and cut costs in order to both rebuild the ground and to offer financial support to the families. Celtic had taken advantage of this, and were the dominant team in the country when Newbigging joined. Tom Sinclair had finished the previous season as the regular goalkeeper, but William Wilton decided to give the new man his chance as 1906/07 got under way.

Newbigging made his debut at Ibrox on 18 August 1906 against Falkirk in a season-opening 2-2 draw featuring goals by Alec Smith and Jimmy Speirs, and then remained firmly first choice for the entire season, starting all 34 league matches. It was a campaign dogged by inconsistency. The Glasgow Cup run was brief, Queen's Park winning the first-round tie after a replay. By the turn of the year the league challenge looked to have been fatally damaged after defeats to Dundee, Partick, Celtic, Motherwell and Hamilton. On 1 January 1907 Newbigging started for the second time against Celtic, and a huge 65,000 crowd at Ibrox went home delighted after a well-deserved 2-1 win. But typically of the season, points were then immediately dropped in the next two games against Partick and Morton, and Rangers could only finish the season in third as Celtic retained their title. The Scottish Cup bid also came to end at their hands at the quarter-final stage, Newbigging powerless to prevent a 3-0 home defeat.

But Rangers were to keep their best until last in the Charity Cup. Newbigging played in the early round wins, keeping clean sheets against both Partick and Third Lanark, before he lined up on 18 May against Celtic in the final. The near-40,000 crowd at Cathkin Park expected another Celtic triumph but holders Rangers were determined to keep the trophy at Ibrox. Future Ibrox board member R.G. Campbell scored a fine goal just before half-time, and the second half saw a magnificent rearguard display from Rangers with Newbigging and his defenders thwarting everything thrown at them. When the final whistle sounded, the underdogs had triumphed and Newbigging had his first winners' medal.

But if this victory was seen as a springboard for future success, it sadly proved to be a false dawn and 1907/08 was a forgettable season. With Newbigging still the undisputed number one goalkeeper, the league fixtures started well with only one point dropped in the first six, but a poor October saw the campaign start to unravel. A shock home defeat by Airdrie in the league was followed by Glasgow Cup Final defeat by Celtic after a replay. As the league started to look increasingly unlikely, it was even more painful to be knocked out of the Scottish Cup by Celtic in the second round. On 25 April, Rangers ended their league campaign at Ibrox with a previously postponed match against Celtic. The visitors were a point ahead at the top of the table with still a further game to play, meaning a win guaranteed them the title. In a highly physical and gruelling battle, future Rangers star Alec Bennett scored the only goal in the 35th minute past the despairing dive of Newbigging to give the visitors their triumph.

This would turn out to be the last Rangers appearance for Newbigging, and what a low to end on. Wilton had secured the services of experienced Scottish international goalkeeper Harry Rennie, and he would start the next match the club played. In total, Newbigging had been the Rangers goalkeeper in 75 competitive matches, winning that one cherished medal in the Charity Cup.

Newbigging then went back to his nomadic goalkeeping career. He left Ibrox to return to Reading, where he again stayed for just the one season. From there, he joined recent Southern League recruits Coventry City, again mainly as a backup to their regular goalkeeper Robert Evans. He did start eight times for them in 1909/10 before heading north to finish his playing career at Inverness Thistle.

Overall, other than those two seasons playing regular football in the biggest games in Scotland, it was an unremarkable career that would likely never be fondly remembered if it wasn't for Rangers' centenary celebrations in 1973. At the time, officials were of the impression that the Gallant Pioneers had started the club in 1873, which we now know to be a year later than actual. In 1973 Rangers celebrated their 100th birthday with a series of events, one of which was a special challenge match against long-time English friends Arsenal. The club looked to invite as many ex-players as they could, and the oldest living former player who took part in the parade of former stars was none other than Sandy Newbigging, who was now the grand old age of 97. He led the parade of around 200 ex-players, was introduced to the capacity Ibrox crowd by general manager Willie Waddell, and even remained sprightly enough to take a half-time penalty. The expression 'Once a Ranger, always a Ranger' never seemed more appropriate.

Newbigging passed away three years later in his 100th year.

- Scotland junior international
- A man of many clubs
- Cup winner against Celtic
- The oldest player given pride of place at the club's 100th birthday party

65 SANDY TAIT

The 'terrible' full-back who won the English FA Cup as a non-league player

THE TINY Ayrshire village of Glenbuck is famous as the birthplace of legendary Liverpool manager Bill Shankly. But it also produced an amazing number of other future professional footballers. This is the story of one of them.

Alexander Gilchrist Tait, known as Sandy, was born there on 3 December 1871. He had no fewer than 12 brothers and sisters, and on leaving school he did what many young Glenbuck men did when he found work down the mines. While playing as a defender for the local Glenbuck Athletic, he was a pit boy, a job that involved guiding pit ponies to and from the coal face. Still a part-time player, he had a brief spell at Ayr then three years at the Royal Albert club in Larkhall with limited success, before his big footballing break came along in 1891.

Joint Scottish champions Rangers had suffered a defensive crisis with previous regulars unavailable and approached Royal Albert to sign Tait on loan. The player needed little persuasion, and Tait wore the Royal Blue for the first time against Vale of Leven on 12 September 1891 in a debut to remember as Rangers cruised to an impressive 6-1 victory. Tait's Rangers career lasted for only a few months, the loanee starting seven games at left-back with a record of four wins, one draw and two defeats. By far the worst display was his final appearance when visitors Clyde embarrassed the Rangers support with a 5-1 hammering. His loan spell came to an end and his brief Rangers career was over.

In early 1892, Tait joined Lanarkshire League side Motherwell, who didn't join the national league setup until the creation of the new Second Division the following year. Tait enjoyed a sustained run in the Motherwell team, playing in either full-back position. He started in 17 of their 18 matches in their maiden league season, appearing 21 times overall. Motherwell finished a creditable fourth.

In late 1894, Tait made the move south to join Preston North End in the English First Division. Seen mainly as a backup, his debut came on 23 March 1895 at right-back in a 3-1 victory over Nottingham Forest. He started two more league games as Preston finished fourth. Season 1895/96 saw the tough-tackling Tait earn a regular place in the Preston team, his 26 starts being split between both full-back positions. A ferocious but fair competitor, Tait cut an intimidating figure with his massive handlebar moustache as he launched himself into tackles. This earned him the nickname 'Terrible Tait', perhaps unfairly as he was also a very sporting and fair opponent and was never booked in his entire career. On 23 November 1895, Preston goalkeeper John Wright suffered a fractured wrist in a game at Small Heath, with Tait playing the whole second half in goal. Unfortunately, he conceded three times in a 5-2 defeat.

Tait remained at Preston until 1899, racking up 76 league appearances for the Lancashire team. It was in the summer of 1899 that Tait moved to the club where he would most be remembered, when he left the First Division and moved to the capital and to Tottenham

Hotspur of the Southern League. He made his debut on the opening day of the 1899/1900 season against Millwall and didn't miss a match as Spurs won the Southern League title. But it was in the following season that Tait would help make history.

Ironically, it all started against his former club Preston, when Spurs were drawn at home against them in the first round of the FA Cup. After a hard-fought draw it seemed that their run would a short one, but the non-league Londoners pulled off a famous upset at Deepdale by winning 4-2. Tait played in every round as Spurs kept on winning. Bury and Reading were defeated, although the latter tie was highly controversial as Tait appeared to stop a goalbound shot on the line with his hand in the first drawn match, Reading denied a clear penalty seen by everyone except the referee. Spurs won the replay 3-0 to compound the injustice. West Brom awaited in the semi-finals, with Tait and his team-mates now sure that their name was on the trophy. A convincing 4-0 win meant the Southern League club then had the chance to become the first non-league team to lift England's biggest cup competition against Sheffield United.

An incredible 114,000 fans packed the Crystal Palace to see the final, which ended in a thrilling 2-2 draw. Also incredibly, Tait wasn't the only native of Glenbuck in the Tottenham team, with both goals scored by another villager, Sandy Brown. The replay took place on 27 April 1901 at Burnden Park, Bolton, but in front of a very much smaller crowd of 20,470 who were present to see football history as Spurs ran out 3-1 winners, to this day the only time the FA Cup was won by a non-league team. Brown scored the third and clinching goal to become the first player to score in every round of the tournament and fellow son of Glenbuck Tait joined him in collecting a winners' medal.

Tait remained a crucial part of the Spurs team for most of that decade. He made 349 appearances and even scored the occasional goal, 12 in total. In later years he became club captain and took on a player-coach role. He applied for the manager's position but was unsuccessful and left to join Leyton Orient in 1908 where he did become manager for a short spell. His football career ended at Croydon Common in 1911.

Tait enlisted in the 2nd Labour Battalion of the Royal Engineers during the Great War, rising to the rank of corporal. There is a tale told from his army days that one morning on parade the inspecting officer, stopped, looked very closely into Sandy's face and then turned to the junior officer with him and said, 'Good grief, for a moment I thought that was the great Sandy Tait.' While serving in France on Christmas Day he also famously was visited by his son, the younger Tait walking 20 miles from where he was stationed so he could wish his father a happy Christmas. Tait saw out the war, and remained in London until passing away in 1949 aged 77.

- Only briefly a Ranger
- A history maker in the FA Cup
- Long-serving Spurs captain
- Served in the Great War
- Not so 'Terrible' at all

66 TOM HYSLOP

The Rangers and Scotland star who played under a false name

BRYCE THOMAS Scouller was born in the Ayrshire town of Auchinleck on 20 August 1871. The family moved to the Renfrewshire village of Elderslie when he was young, and it was there that he started his football career with the town's amateur side. It would be a career that would see him play at the highest level in Scotland and England, but it was carved out using a false name he created for himself as he kept his true identity secret from the football authorities.

Scouller joined the Argyll and Sutherland Highlanders in 1888 aged just 16, and he next appeared in military records two years later when he joined the 2nd Battalion Scots Guards, based near Windsor Castle, under a new name. He was now Thomas Hyslop, this new identity a combination of his own middle name and his mother's maiden name. He represented the battalion's football team as a powerful centre-forward noted for a ferocious shot, and helped them to some success by winning the Army Cup and playing in the FA Cup.

His physical strength and goalscoring record attracted the attention of professional clubs, and he played a trial for Millwall without army permission, leading to a disciplinary hearing and an extension to his army service contract. By doing this, the army gave themselves a strong negotiating position with any football club desperate for his services. In January 1894 the mighty Sunderland bought out his contract by paying £18.

Sunderland were challenging for the title at the time, although they ended as runners-up, and 'Hyslop' had to wait for a regular run in the first team. His debut came in a home 1-0 win over Everton the following month, but he only made six appearances before the end of the campaign, hitting the net three time. His first goal was on 17 March against Nottingham Forest and he also scored later that month in a 3-1 friendly win at Parkhead over Celtic, a team who would become his great rivals shortly.

While still not a first choice, Hyslop hit the net a further seven times in 12 starts in 1894/95 to help Sunderland win the First Division, sometimes playing alongside fellow Scotsman Jimmy Millar. He played for the first time at Ibrox on 3 September in a 1-1 friendly draw, and hit a first professional hat-trick in a 3-0 league win over Burnley. Still unable to command a regular place, Hyslop grew increasingly frustrated at being in and out of the team, and Sunderland agreed to transfer him to First Division strugglers Stoke in February 1895. They looked doomed to relegation on his arrival, but Hyslop hit a debut hat-trick against Derby County and inspired their survival by scoring four more goals in an unbeaten run over the last six matches to survive by a single point.

Hyslop was Stoke's main man, and he enjoyed a hugely successful 1895/96 with them. He hit 21 goals in 30 league and cup appearances, the team ending the season in a much healthier sixth place. As well as another league hat-trick, reported as three 'cannonball shots' against West Brom, he hit four in a cup win over Burnley, and scored Stoke's first league penalty goal on 14 March 1896, ironically against former club Sunderland who were thrashed 5-0.

Now known as 'Long Tom' due to his height and a habit of scoring goals from distance, Hyslop's Stoke exploits attracted the attention of the Scotland team selectors, who had recently changed their selection policy to include Scottish players based in England. He was picked to play against England at Parkhead on 4 April 1896, and helped the team to a famous 2-1 win. And it wasn't just the Scottish selectors who had noticed his impressive form, as Hyslop was now also on the radar of Rangers manager William Wilton. Shortly after that international debut, and with the English season now over, Rangers made their move.

The season in Scotland had one last game to play, the Charity Cup Final between Rangers and the league champions Celtic, who had handed out two league hammerings to their rivals already in the season. It was a Rangers debut to forget as Hyslop was drafted into the team to try to reverse the trend, but instead he struggled to fit into the style of play and endured a chastening 6-1 humiliation.

Rangers were determined that this would be an experience not to be repeated, and the manager recruited wisely in the close-season, including Renton goalkeeper Matt Dickie and Hyslop's former Sunderland partner Jimmy Millar. Things would be much improved in 1896/97. The league campaign was to end in a close third-place finish, despite Hyslop hitting ten goals in 17 starts, including a league debut goal on the opening day against St Mirren and four at Clyde. But it was in the cup competitions that Hyslop and Rangers had great success.

His double helped beat Third Lanark in the opening round of the Glasgow Cup, which ended in Hyslop starting in the 2-1 win over Celtic in the final, earning him a first significant medal as a professional player as well as exacting revenge for that horrendous debut. His goals were also a feature of a successful Scottish Cup run. Hyslop scored in the early rounds against Partick and Dundee before hitting the net in the semi-final win against Morton and scoring Rangers' second goal in the final, where Dumbarton were swept aside 5-1. His season would end in a third final, and a third winners' medal, as he scored again in a 6-1 hammering of Third Lanark in the Charity Cup Final.

As well as winning three medals in his first Ibrox season, Hyslop was recalled to the Scotland team alongside debutant Millar for the clash with England at the Crystal Palace in London in April 1897. Hyslop headed home a first-half equaliser from club-mate Nicol Smith's cross before Millar grabbed a late winner as the Scots won 2-1. These two victories over England would be Hyslop's only international appearances.

The arrival of the legendary centre-forward R.C. Hamilton in 1897 meant that competition for the forward positions became intense, and often the manager had to choose between Millar and Hyslop for one place. Hyslop was picked for 13 of the 18 league matches and showed his scoring power by scoring 13 times, including two hat-tricks. He scored his first, and only, competitive Old Firm goal in a 3-1 win over Celtic in the Glasgow Cup semi-final, but picked up an injury that forced him to miss the final win over Queen's Park. After a spell out of the team where he missed the entire Scottish Cup run, he was back in the starting 11 for the final, picking up a second win in the competition when Kilmarnock were defeated 2-0.

Hyslop was, by now, seen as more of a backup player. His bustling and aggressive style didn't fit the stylish approach now being adopted by the Rangers team, and although he was still lightning quick (as shown by him winning the 220-yard race for professional footballers at the Rangers Sports), manager Wilton decided to allow him to return on loan to former club Stoke. His second spell there was a disaster, failing to score at all, and he was back at Ibrox again in May 1899. This was a Rangers team who had just won the league without dropping a point, his chances of a regular place were remote.

He did score twice in a Glasgow League match against Queen's Park shortly after his return, and scored three goals in the opening league games of 1899/1900, but he was soon back in the reserves. He scored his last Rangers goal in a 4-4 Inter-City League match against Third Lanark on 25 April 1900, then played his last match for the club in a Charity Cup tie against the same opponents. After 48 goals in 70 Rangers starts, Hyslop was transferred to Partick Thistle in July 1900.

His time there was brief, lasting less than a full season with 24 appearances and ten goals. In March 1900, he decided to abandon football and rejoin the army, joining the Scottish Yeomanry under his real name of Bryce Scouller, and seeing active service in the Boer War. On his return to Scotland in 1902 he played for lesser clubs Dundee Wanderers, Johnstone and Abercorn before realising time had caught up with him, retiring from football in 1906 at the age of 35.

His football career may have been over, but the story of Bryce Scouller/Tom Hyslop still had further twists. He emigrated to America in 1906, using the Hyslop pseudonym, settling in Philadelphia where he worked as a carpet weaver. But the lure of the army proved too strong when the world was swept into conflict a decade later, and he travelled to Canada in 1917 where he gave a false age to be able to join the Canadian Expeditionary Force under a third name of Thomas Scouller. He was stationed in Europe as a reservist during the remainder of the Great War.

After the conflict, he decided to abandon North America, and in 1922 returned to Renfrewshire, and from there he was a regular attendee at Ibrox to watch his old club who were again dominating Scottish football. He took ill in early 1936, and died in the Paisley Royal Alexandria Infirmary on 21 April, aged 64.

- 48 goals in 70 appearances
- 2 Scottish Cups
- Scored for Scotland against England
- Served in the armed forces on four occasions in two different conflicts
- Still listed in the record books under a false name

67 TOM MCKILLOP

The Rangers title winner who became a first Scot to play in Mexico

TOM MCKILLOP was born in Dreghorn, Ayrshire, on 27 October 1917, one of twin boys. Sadly, his brother William did not survive, so he grew up as youngest of four siblings. His football career started with his local team Dreghorn Juniors, where he was good enough to become a regular in their defence at just 16 years old. His performances alerted senior clubs, and in 1935 he was signed by Bill Struth for Rangers.

The great Davie Meiklejohn was now in the twilight of his career, and Struth had high hopes the Ayrshire youngster possessed all the qualities to one day become a similar fixture in the team, so it wasn't long before he was given his debut. With a Glasgow Cup Final against Celtic the following week, Struth decided to rest his first-choice centre-half Jimmy Simpson on 5 October 1935 in an Ibrox league game against Dunfermline, pitching the 17-year-old into the first team in the centre of the defence but with the experience of Meiklejohn guiding him. Rangers cruised to a 6-2 victory, McKillop doing well enough to earn praise but still well short of being a genuine challenger for a regular place. Struth's team selections paid off when Rangers then won 2-0 in the Old Firm final. Young McKillop only made one more start in 1935/36, in a draw against Queen's Park. He spent most of the season in the reserves, learning his trade in the most successful squad in the country. Rangers gave up their title to Celtic and the legendary Meiklejohn retired as a Scottish Cup winner.

Season 1936/37 was to be when McKillop put that learning to good use. He started one game in August, but it was in December that Struth turned to him after a combination of mixed results and injuries, and he grabbed it. His first two starts back in the defence saw convincing wins over Falkirk and Hibs, and Struth kept faith in the 19-year-old for the new year derby. In front of almost 95,000 at Ibrox a half-back line of McKillop, Simpson and Brown shut out the Celtic attack as an Alex Venters strike won the points. McKillop was a virtual ever present from then on, scoring his first goal in a 4-1 win at Fir Park and earning his first league medal with 17 starts as Rangers romped to their 23rd title.

Season 1937/38 saw McKillop play in 29 league games but Rangers were blighted by inconsistency, finishing a disappointing third. He did win a Glasgow Cup medal, however, playing in the final win over Third Lanark. He also become a Scottish international when selected against Holland in May 1938, his only cap.

The following season started badly but ended in triumph. An early season visit to Parkhead saw McKillop line up alongside a young centre-half called Willie Woodburn in a horrendous 6-2 defeat, but he gained revenge at the turn of the year when he played in the famous 2-1 win in front of the all-time Ibrox attendance of over 118,000. The season ended with a second league medal as Rangers coasted 11 points clear.

The final league game of 1938/39 against Aberdeen was to be the last 'official' match of McKillop's Rangers career. He then missed the start of the following season, which saw the league halted after a handful of games as war was declared. He played 34 games under the temporary format put in place in 1939/40, winning the Glasgow Cup Final against Queen's Park, the War Emergency Cup Final against Dundee United (in front of 90,000 at Hampden), and the Western League championship. He also had the distinction of playing in the same Rangers team as Stanley Matthews, when the legendary English winger made a guest appearance in Royal Blue at Ibrox against Morton on 30 March 1940 at Ibrox in front of 20,000 spectators.

Later in 1940, McKillop enlisted in the army, which meant a few guest appearances in Royal Blue, but these stopped when he was stationed down south. In between his active service, he guested for several English teams, with most appearances for little Cowes FC, the nearest club to him when he was stationed on the Isle of Wight. He captained them for a season, and such was the impact he made that when he was moved to new surroundings the fans and officials raised £7 10s in a collection.

After the war, he made two last Rangers appearances in December 1945, his 124th and final game being a 3-0 win at Falkirk at right-back in a defence featuring Jock Shaw, Willie Woodburn and Scot Symon.

In May 1946, William Raeside, the Scottish coach of Mexican top-division club Asturias FC, had come back home to recruit players. The three he targeted were approaching the end of their careers and were all able to negotiate free transfers. Jackie Milne was player-manager of Dumbarton after a successful career with Blackburn Rovers, Arsenal and Middlesbrough. Jimmy Hickie was an experienced defender with Clyde, who had played in their Scottish Cup Final win in 1939. And the third was Tom McKillop.

The players had to negotiate their release from their clubs first, and once that was agreed, passports were secured and the trio flew from Prestwick airport to Mexico via New York in June. They were given little time to acclimatise to their new surroundings, all three thrown straight into the Asturias team in a cup tie. Raeside had hoped his three Scots would improve the team's mid-table league position, but despite their efforts Asturias ended season 1946/47 in ninth, which was where they were in the table when McKillop arrived.

The players lodged with a Scottish couple in the Lomas district of Mexico City, and enjoyed Mexican cuisine and hospitality very much. The city was expanding, and food readily available unlike in post-war Britain where rationing was still a part of everyday life. The football itself was very different from the game back home, with several matches halted due to mass fighting among players, and the standard of refereeing was distinctly low.

Despite this, all three spoke of thoroughly enjoying their Mexican adventure, and they looked forward to a more successful second season. The dream quickly turned sour, however, as the club's American and Spanish owners abruptly withdrew their support prior to the new season starting, leaving the players abandoned and a long way from home. McKillop, Milne and Hickie returned to Scotland less than a year after their departure.

There was to be one more football adventure before McKillop hung up his boots. On returning to the UK, after a brief spell back in Scotland, he accepted a contract from Welsh club Rhyl. Although not greatly successful, he enjoyed the town so much that after retiring he remained a resident, and even returned there briefly as manager.

If being a title-winning Rangers player, a war veteran, one of the first Scots to play in Mexico and a manager in Wales wasn't enough, McKillop had one more claim to fame. His daughter Liz, who was born in Kilwinning in 1947 but raised in Wales, became one of the top civil servants in Britain. She worked closely with Margaret Thatcher in the 1980s, playing an important role in government communications during the Falklands War. She then moved to the Scottish Office where she helped create the government response to the Dunblane shootings, before resigning soon after the 1997 election when uneasy at the direction of the new Labour regime.

Tom McKillop died in Bromley in February 1984, aged 66.

Another ex-Ranger with a unique life story.

- Over 120 appearances for Rangers across a ten-year period
- 2 league titles
- Played in front of the record Ibrox crowd
- Served in World War Two
- One of the first Scots to play in Mexico
- A player and manager in Wales

68   TOM SINCLAIR

The goalkeeper who won cup finals with Rangers and Celtic, and the English league title – all in the same season

BORN IN 1880, Tom Sinclair started his football career in the Junior game with Rutherglen Glencairn in 1900. He quickly caught the eye with a series of excellent displays in a successful team, Glencairn winning both the Glasgow Junior League and the Scottish Junior Cup in 1902. Among his team-mates were future Scottish international Jimmy McMenemy and a man who would go on to represent Celtic, Rangers and Scotland, the 'Artful Dodger' Alec Bennett.

Like McMenemy and Bennett, it wasn't long before the offer of senior professional football was made to Sinclair, and he signed for Greenock Morton in 1903. Sinclair helped Morton to a respectable 11th place in season 1903/04, his displays catching the eye of Rangers manager William Wilton who was looking for a successor to the ageing long-time regular custodian Matt Dickie, and he made the move to Ibrox in the summer of 1904.

After an indifferent start to the season with another new goalkeeper, Willie Allan, as first choice, Wilton gave Sinclair his debut against Dundee at Ibrox on 29 October 1904, a match won 2-1 with a decisive goal by the legendary centre-forward R.S. McColl. Sinclair then established himself as the regular last line of defence for the rest of the season. Unfortunately, despite some excellent performances and memorable results, it would be a season of heartbreak at Ibrox. First, after a magnificent Scottish Cup semi-final 2-0 win over Celtic (a match abandoned due to Celtic fans rioting), Sinclair tasted defeat in the final in a replay defeat to Third Lanark. Then, even more depressing, he was in goal for the league championship play-off defeat to Celtic after both clubs ended the season on the same points.

Sinclair kept his number one status in 1905/06, the highlight being his first winners' medal at the club when he played in the May 1906 victory over Queen's Park in the Charity Cup Final. Overall, however, this was not a successful time for Rangers after their dominance at the beginning of the 20th century, and Wilton was unhappy with the number of goals being conceded, which was preventing the club returning to the top. That Charity Cup Final was to be the last top-team appearance for Sinclair after 73 games. He started 1906/07 in the reserves, with new number one Sandy Newbigging signing from Reading and claiming the jersey.

However, that 1906/07 season would turn out to be the one that gave Tom Sinclair his unique place in history. It all started on 16 August 1906 when Rangers played a benefit match against Celtic at Ibrox for great servant Finlay Speedie. With Newbigging in goal, Rangers won 4-2 and Speedie scored twice. But during the match, Celtic's regular keeper Davie Adams ripped a large gash in his hand while making a save thanks to a nail protruding from a goalpost. As a goodwill gesture to take responsibility for this nasty accident, Rangers agreed to loan Sinclair to Celtic for as long as Adams was unable to play. Any doubts the Celtic fans then had on relying on a Rangers goalkeeper were quickly dispelled as Sinclair, perhaps with a point to prove, gave several outstanding performances. He played nine games in the loan spell and incredibly kept a clean sheet in the first eight of them. After six league wins and two successful Glasgow Cup ties without conceding, Sinclair played his last game for Celtic in the Glasgow Cup Final against Third Lanark. The match was played at the home of his parent club, and 40,000 saw him collect a winners' medal in a 3-2 victory.

With Adams then fit again, Sinclair returned to Rangers. It can only be guessed how popular he now was among his team-mates or the support, but despite his form while wearing Celtic colours he remained in the reserves.

He did play in the majority of the second-string matches, and these included a win in the Second XI Cup final, which meant he had won a cup winners' medal for both halves of the Glasgow divide in the same season. Incredibly, he then added the English league title before the campaign had ended.

In March 1907, Newcastle United were top of the English First Division when they suffered a huge blow with an injury to their long-serving goalkeeper Jimmy Lawrence. Needing experienced short-term backup, they signed Sinclair from Rangers and he made his debut against Stoke City shortly afterwards. He played three times for Newcastle before

Lawrence reclaimed the starting berth, but those three games were of great importance with wins over Stoke, Bristol City and Blackburn and only one goal conceded. The Magpies won their second title by three points, and although Sinclair didn't play enough games for a medal, he certainly played his part in the success.

Sinclair stayed at Newcastle until 1912 but only played a total of eight first-team matches, Lawrence becoming a club legend with an amazing 18-year career. Sinclair's final game was against Arsenal in January 1912 before he returned north to join Dumbarton Harp in a very brief spell ahead of a move to Dunfermline.

His stay at East End Park lasted for four years but was interrupted by war, and Sinclair enlisted in the army. He guested for Dunfermline and Kilmarnock during the conflict before drifting out the game after 14 years a professional.

Little is known of his life after the war. He passed away in the West Dunbartonshire town of Bonhill in 1968, aged 87.

- A short Rangers career with just one winners' medal
- Temporary move to Celtic
- An understudy to a Newcastle legend
- But won competitions with all three teams in the same season

69   TOM WYLLIE

The former Ranger who scored the first Merseyside derby goal

TOM WYLLIE was born in the Ayrshire village of Maybole on 5 April 1870. After a brief spell with his local Junior team as a right-sided forward, he joined Rangers as an 18-year-old in the summer of 1888.

His competitive debut was a memorable one as Wyllie was among the scorers as Rangers defeated Partick Thistle in the first round of the Scottish Cup. These were the days just before league football, so the season contained many friendly and minor competition matches, but young Wyllie made enough of an impression to quickly become a regular in the most important games. He scored two Glasgow Cup hat-tricks in his first season in blue, in huge wins over United Abstainers and Pollokshaws Athletic. He added another Scottish Cup goal too but it wasn't enough to prevent a second-round exit to Clyde in a replay. The least said about his Glasgow Cup exit in late October 1888 the better. Wyllie was part of the first Rangers 11 to play Celtic in one of the main competitions of the time, and lost 6-1.

In March 1890 he was selected to play for Scotland for the first and only time, scoring in a 4-1 win over Ireland in Belfast. He stayed at Rangers until late 1890, playing in the first Rangers team to play a Scottish league match, a 5-2 win over Hearts on 16 August 1890. After starting in four of the first five league games, he made his last Rangers appearance on 22 November, scoring one of the goals in an amazing comeback from three down against

Third Lanark in the Glasgow Cup to snatch a draw. Despite being a Rangers regular, Wyllie decided to head to England and signed for First Division leaders Everton.

His Everton career started well with a 1-0 win over Wolverhampton Wanderers on his debut, and shortly afterwards he hammered in four goals in a 6-2 rout of Derby County. But after only four starts he picked up an injury, and failed to regain his place as the Merseyside club went on to win the title. With Rangers also winning the league in 1891, it meant he had played four times for both the Scottish and English champions in the same season, but neither was enough to earn a medal.

Wyllie regained his place in the Everton team the following season, scoring once in 18 league starts. The summer of 1892 saw boardroom unrest, resulting in Everton president John Houlding leaving to form a new club to play at Everton's Anfield ground – Liverpool FC. Among the players recruited was Tom Wyllie. Houlding had hoped that Liverpool would be admitted to the Football League, but this was rejected so they began life in the Lancashire League. On 1 September 1892 Liverpool played their first match, a friendly against Rotherham Town, the Midland League champions. Wyllie scored twice in a 7-1 win. Two days later, Wyllie was on the right wing for Liverpool's first competitive game, 300 fans at Anfield witnessing an 8-0 thrashing of Higher Walton. Liverpool went on to win the Lancashire League in their first season with Wyllie scoring ten times in 22 starts.

Liverpool also reached the final of the Liverpool Senior Cup, and were to face Everton on 22 April 1893. This was the first meeting of the teams since the acrimonious split the previous summer, albeit Everton played their second string 'Combination' team in the tournament. Everton were going for a fourth successive Liverpool Senior Cup triumph and were hot favourites. In front of an excited crowd of 10,000 at Hawthorne Road in Bootle, the famous Merseyside derby was born. Liverpool showed their more illustrious opponents little respect and had created several chances before the fixture's first goal. After 35 minutes, a free kick found John Miller who played a clever pass to Wyllie in space, the former Ranger beating goalkeeper Williams with a fierce low shot. It was to be the only goal of the game, although Everton were furious in the closing minutes when they claimed a Liverpool defender punched a corner clear and were denied a clear penalty. Such was their fury, their players surrounded the officials at full time and it was decided not to present the cup on the day. An Everton protest on the grounds of 'the general incompetence of the referee' was rejected by the Liverpool FA, and the cup was presented prior to Liverpool's next game three days later.

Liverpool were admitted to the Football League but Wyllie decided to stay in the Lancashire League that summer, switching to Bury. They finished runners-up, but were elected to join the Second Division. Wyllie was an ever present, scoring seven goals as they roared to the title by a nine-point margin. As were the rules at the time, they then played a 'test match' against the bottom club from the First Division to decide who would play in the top division the next season. At Ewood Park in Blackburn on 27 April 1895, Bury played Wyllie's former club Liverpool, who had ended the season in last place. Bury won 1-0.

Wyllie played two seasons for Bury in the top league, leaving in 1897 after 81 appearances and 18 goals. He moved to Bristol City of the Southern League, where he enjoyed a short career before retiring.

After football, he opened a newsagent in the Bedminster district of Bristol. He and his wife Mary had three sons, and by the 1911 census his occupation had changed to 'insurance agent'. At some point he moved back north, relocating to Maxwell Road in Glasgow, where he died of cancer at the age of 73 on 28 July 1943. His death certificate stated his occupation as a retired clothing manufacturer agent.

- Played in the first Rangers v Celtic game in a main competition
- Played in Rangers' first league game
- Played in a Scottish and English league-winning campaign in the same season
- Played in Liverpool's first match
- Scored the first Merseyside derby goal

70 WILLIAM CHALMERS

The future Juventus manager signed by Bill Struth

WILLIAM CHALMERS was born in Bellshill, Lanarkshire on 24 July 1907, and like many Scottish teenagers of the time his football career started in the Junior game, playing inside-forward with Bellshill Athletic. It wasn't long before the talented youngster moved on, joining the famous amateurs of Queen's Park in December 1922 at the age of just 15.

He made his debut at Hampden on 9 December, playing at centre-forward in a 3-0 Second Division win over Lochgelly United, with his first senior goal coming along in just his third start in a 5-0 home win over Broxburn. It took a few months for him to settle into the team on a regular basis, when he played an important part in Queen's Park clinching the title, and promotion back to the top flight, scoring a hat-trick against East Fife and a double against Lochgelly in the run-in. His first season at Hampden ended in a first appearance in a major final, when he started in the 4-0 Charity Cup Final loss to newly crowned Scottish champions Rangers.

Chalmers would then be a virtual ever present in the Queen's Park team in the First Division in 1923/24, making a real impression in the top flight when scoring in four successive starts around the turn of the year in games against Motherwell, Third Lanark, Kilmarnock and Hearts. He didn't hit the net in three further appearances against Bill Struth's Rangers, all defeats in league and Glasgow Cup, but his quick and direct play impressed the Ibrox boss. He played for Queen's Park for the last time against Ayr United on the last day of the league season in late April 1924, a draw securing safety from relegation. That summer, after 54 competitive first team appearances and 16 goals, Chalmers moved across the city to join Rangers.

The forward line at Ibrox was the most potent in the country, and Chalmers knew he would have a fight to command a regular place. His debut came against Falkirk at Ibrox on 18 October, the 11th league fixture of the season, replacing the injured Tommy Cairns at inside-left. He showed up well in a comfortable 3-1 win and retained his place in the team for the Old Firm fixture the following Saturday at Parkhead. Rangers had crushed their old rivals 4-1 in the Glasgow Cup Final a few weeks earlier, and were confident of another win despite missing skipper Cairns this time. Their confidence was well-founded, as Chalmers enjoyed a 1-0 win in his first taste of the derby fixture thanks to a goal by Alan Morton.

Chalmers made 12 league starts overall in 1924/25, scoring twice. His first Rangers goal came against Partick at Ibrox in November, and he also scored a double in a Scottish Cup win against lowly Montrose. After helping the team to the title in his first season, Chalmers was expected to become a big player, and although he again started the following season in the reserves, he was in the team for the visit of Celtic in the league on 17 October 1925. He scored the only goal of the match, briefly making himself a hero to the Rangers support. But that was the last goal he scored in a Royal Blue shirt and he soon lost his place again as his inconsistency made it hard for the manager to prefer him over the well-established stars at his disposal. Chalmers then suffered a broken leg in 1926, which effectively ended his time at Rangers, making just one comeback appearance on 29 October 1927 in a defeat to old club Queen's Park. In early 1928, after an Ibrox career that saw him score seven goals in just 26 appearances across four years, Chalmers was sold to Newcastle United for £2,500.

He scored on his debut against Leicester City, the only highlight in a dismal 5-1 loss. Chalmers went on to score in his next two starts as well, and hit the next seven times in his first 12 Newcastle outings. Despite the impressive statistics, his performances were again wildly inconsistent, and he found himself in and out the side. His old Rangers team-mate Andy Cunningham became manager in early 1930 but he was unable to inspire Chalmers into a more sustained level of performance. Eventually, Cunningham decided to move the player on, and after 13 goals in 42 appearances, Chalmers was sold to Grimsby Town in 1931 for a fee of £1,000.

His career then was spent in the lower reaches of English football, playing for Bury and Notts County before becoming player-manager of Aldershot Town in 1938. His time there lasted until well into the Second World War, scoring 33 goals in 93 starts. Many of his Aldershot team-mates were players from all over the UK who were stationed at the nearby barracks, until in 1943 he retired from playing the game and left the club.

Chalmers then moved to the now defunct Welsh club Ebbw Vale. His exact position with them is undocumented, although it seems likely he was team manager. Whatever his role, Chalmers received a phone call to his Welsh home in the early weeks of 1948 that would change his life. The caller was none other than the president of the world-famous Juventus, Gianni Agnelli, and he was offering Chalmers the job of manager. Until his last days, Agnelli never explained why he decided Chalmers was the man for the job. The former Ranger had no knowledge of Italian football or the language, only featuring once in a match against Italian opposition, scoring in a 1-0 friendly win for Newcastle over Inter Milan in 1929. Whatever the reasoning, Chalmers was announced as the new Juventus manager on 17 February 1948.

The big challenge facing Chalmers was the dominance of his city rivals, Torino, who were on the verge of a fourth successive title, and Chalmers started well with a debut win over AC Milan. In the close-season, Chalmers made the big-money signing of Tottenham inside-forward Johnny Jordan, who became the first British player to play in the Italian top flight. And 1948/49 started well with Juventus winning four of their opening five matches, including a handsome 4-0 victory over Lazio in the opener. The sixth fixture was the big one, the derby with Torino.

Chalmers' team played well against the champions but they squandered chances before falling to a late sucker-punch goal. That 1-0 defeat proved to be a turning point both in the season and in the managerial career of Chalmers. His team lost their next three matches, falling well behind in the title race, and the supporters started to turn on their British boss. His methods did leave him open to criticism, players talking of his obsession with physical fitness that he took to such extremes that he forced the players to exercise in the aisles of the trains that transported them to matches. By the time the second derby of the season arrived, Juventus were miles off the pace set by their local rivals, and a 3-1 Torino win basically sealed his fate.

Chalmers did complete the season, his side ending in fourth place, but by then football seemed less important as the Torino team were all killed in a tragic plane crash when flying to Portugal to play a friendly against Benfica. They had a commanding lead in the table at the time, and were declared champions with four matches remaining, these fixtures completed by youth teams.

Chalmers left Juventus after just that one full season, with a match record of just 24 wins in 48 matches, and he remains the only Juventus manager in their history with a 100 per cent losing record against Torino when taking charge of more than one derby.

He returned to the UK and spent a single season as a coach back at one of his former clubs, Bury. Chalmers then disappeared from the game and lived out the rest of his days away from the limelight. He died on 16 July 1980 at the age of 72.

- Teenage sensation signed by Rangers
- Ibrox career ended by injury
- Played under Andy Cunningham at Newcastle
- Made surprise move to Italy to manage Juventus
- Lasted just one season in Serie A

71   WILLIAM YUILLE

The little-known Rangers player whose grandson is a Barcelona Bear

WILLIAM YUILLE made his Rangers debut at inside-left at Hamilton Accies in a league match on 12 December 1908. He scored in a thumping 7-0 win but was a reserve player for all of his short Rangers career, only making 16 senior starts in two years.

His best day in Royal Blue came later in that debut season, on 13 March 1909, when he was picked to face Celtic at Parkhead in a vital match in the league run-in as regular inside-left Willie McPherson was injured. Yuille scored Rangers' first goal in a 3-2 win, but it unfortunately didn't stop the Parkhead team retaining their title.

Yuille made just six starts in 1909/10, his only goals being a double in a home win against Airdrie in March. He tasted further defeat in May when starting in a Charity Cup loss to a Clyde team who were trained by future Rangers manager Bill Struth.

He played once more against Celtic, again at Parkhead, in October 1910 and Rangers' 1-0 win meant he had a 100 per cent record in Scotland's greatest fixture. Yuille's last Rangers appearance was a 1-0 defeat away to Aberdeen on 3 December 1910. In his 16 appearances, he scored five times.

Little is known about him after he left Ibrox. A very religious man, he decided to quit football and to 'come apart' from the world in order to concentrate on his faith. He was a member of the Plymouth Bretheren, and he brought up his daughter Annie in this strictly devout lifestyle.

In the 1930s, Annie met Thomas McLean and they were married. Annie and Tom then went on to have three sons: James Yuille McLean, William McLean, Tommy McLean.

Yuille never won any medals in his short Rangers career. His eldest grandson, Jim, is the most famous manager in the history of Dundee United. Willie McLean was also an excellent manager at clubs such as Motherwell, Raith Rovers and Ayr United.

His youngest grandson Tommy played 459 times for Rangers, scoring 59 goals. He won three league titles (plus another with Kilmarnock), four Scottish Cups, three League Cups and is a club immortal by winning the 1972 European Cup Winners' Cup. He was also briefly Rangers' caretaker manager before embarking on a highly successful club managerial career that saw him lift the Scottish Cup with Motherwell.

In an interview with *The Scotsman* in 2014, Tommy described his grandfather as 'an auld bugger who was very strict', and being the reason why his own father gave up playing football. Luckily, he had no such influence on his grandchildren.

Unlike his grandson, William Yuille will never make the Hall of Fame. But his legacy is known to us all.

- A brief Rangers career with a perfect record in Old Firm matches
- Gave up football
- A life of strict religious beliefs
- A very famous footballing family

72 WILLIE REID

The greatest Rangers goalscorer not in the Hall of Fame

THROUGHOUT THE club's history, Rangers fans have watched some truly outstanding goalscorers. The likes of R.C. Hamilton, Jimmy Fleming, Jimmy Smith, Sam English, Willie Thornton, Jim Forrest, Derek Johnstone and Ally McCoist are all legendary names with their names proudly in the Hall of Fame. But there is one magnificent goalscorer who does not yet have his name beside theirs, despite a goalscoring record better than most. His name is Willie Reid.

William Reid was born in Baillieston, Glasgow, on 3 May 1884. His first club was the local team Baillieston Thistle, where he quickly attracted Morton's attention as a goalscoring centre-forward. The youngster then learned his trade at Greenock, being eased into the side, and spent two seasons there. He hit 11 league goals, helping Greenock maintain their top flight status, before a strange and very short stint at Third Lanark. He joined them in April 1906 and made his debut in the Scottish Cup Final on 28 April against Hearts at Ibrox. He was unable to prevent a 1-0 defeat, and never played for the club again, being transferred to Motherwell shortly afterwards.

It was during his time at Fir Park that Reid started to build a reputation as one of the country's deadliest finishers. He scored a shock winner at Ibrox in December 1906 as the Lanarkshire team held on for a 1-0 victory. His 32 league goals in less than two full seasons helped the club to two safe top-ten finishes, and he earned a transfer in early 1908 to Portsmouth of the English Southern League. He continued his scoring form on the south coast, including a hat-trick at Birmingham in the FA Cup, and in April 1908 Rangers manager William Wilton persuaded the centre-forward to return north and join up at Ibrox.

Since the great R.C. Hamilton had left the club, Rangers were desperate to find his successor to lead the forward line. They were going through a painful trophy drought, made worse by great rivals Celtic dominating the Scottish game, Wilton hoping that Reid could be the prolific marksman the team needed. And he joined the club just as the team were preparing to face Celtic in the Scottish Cup Final replay, meaning a debut in the biggest match in the country. He replaced future club director Bob Campbell up front but his debut ended up being removed from the records as fans of both teams rioted at the end of a 1-1 draw when they realised there would be no extra time, with the SFA abandoning the tournament and the trophy withheld. Reid hadn't scored, and he failed to hit the target in two more matches before the season ended. The Rangers fans had no reason to think they had found a new goalscoring hero, but they were soon to realise that Reid was the centre-forward they had been waiting for.

Rangers strengthened further during the summer, with English stars Billy Hogg and Herbert Lock arriving, but the pre-season optimism was to prove to be premature as the league challenge fizzled out. Reid scored a decent but unremarkable 14 times in his first full season in Royal Blue, notching three doubles and one hat-trick against St Mirren. He won no honours in 1909/10, but eight goals in his last seven starts suggested he had now found his feet at Ibrox.

The following season saw Reid become the most feared marksman in Scotland with an incredible 48 goals in just 42 competitive games, 38 of these in the league. He scored four goals against both Hearts and Motherwell, and a hat-trick against Hibs, and hit the net in 25 different league games out of the 33 he started. His goals were a massive reason why Rangers finally reclaimed the title nine years since they were last champions. He also started to enjoy the Old Firm fixture. He scored the third goal in a 3-1 Glasgow Cup Final win over the Parkhead men, hit a crucial goal in the New Year fixture that earned a 1-1 draw, then rounded off a memorable season by scoring both goals in a 2-1 Charity Cup Final success. Rangers had won three of the four available major honours, Reid only missing out in the Scottish Cup after a defeat by holders Dundee.

Reid was the division's top scorer in 1910/11, and he also became a Scotland international, playing in all three of the Home International matches. He scored his first Scotland goal in March 1911 against Ireland, and ended his career with four goals from nine caps, the highlight being the clinching third in a 3-1 win over England in 1914 at Hampden which was watched by over 105,000 people. Reid also represented the Scottish League on eight occasions, scoring in four different matches against the English League, and hitting a hat-trick against the Irish.

Rangers retained their title in 1911/12, and Reid was again the top scorer in the top flight. He hit 39 goals in the campaign, 33 of them in the league, featuring four-goal hauls against Third Lanark and Hamilton in addition to three more hat-tricks. One of those trebles came in the Glasgow Cup semi-final against Queen's Park, and he claimed a second winners' medal in the competition when a Billy Hogg goal beat Partick. The excellent Clyde team of the time knocked Rangers out of both the Scottish and Charity Cups, meaning Reid would be one of so many great Rangers players who would never win the national competition.

A league title hat-trick was then completed in 1912/13, Reid again the club top scorer. His eight goals in the first eight matches set the tone and the title was won by four points from Celtic. He enjoyed his most prolific season against them, scoring twice in the league at Parkhead, twice more in a 3-2 Charity Cup loss, and a hat-trick at Ibrox in the minor Inter-City League competition. He didn't score in an amazing 3-1 Glasgow Cup Final win over the great rivals, Rangers coming back from a goal down at half-time with just ten players after John Robertson suffered a nasty injury. In the second half, Rangers adopted an innovative 'one man at the back' strategy to constantly catch the Celtic forwards offside, then took advantage of their confusion with goals by Hogg, Smith and Bennett.

Celtic prevented a fourth successive Rangers title in 1913/14, but it was through no fault of Reid. He hit another 24 league goals over the season, including nine in the first nine fixtures, but two painful Old Firm defeats plus unusual inconsistency saw the Parkhead men deservedly win back the flag. He did win another Glasgow Cup, scoring the winner in the semi-final against Clyde before hitting a double in the final against Third Lanark.

This would be the last season before Europe was plunged into the horrors of war, Reid remaining a registered Rangers player for the duration of the conflict. He scored 29 goals in 1914/15 then 26 goals the next season, neither seeing Rangers win a trophy despite his deadly finishing. Reid had now finished top scorer at the club for six consecutive seasons, but he would not get a chance to make that seven as he had enlisted with the 52nd Division of the Royal Field Artillery, and would be called up for active service in 1916.

Gunner William Reid served his country for over two years at home and abroad, playing just once for Rangers in that time when home on leave. Typically, he scored both goals in a 2-1 win over Hamilton on 8 December 1917.

When the war ended and Reid returned to civilian life in 1919, he was almost 35 years old. Rangers had narrowly lost their league title the previous season, and manager Wilton was determined to bring the trophy back in 1919/20. Reid was no longer his first choice at centre-forward, but the veteran goal-grabber was still a great option for him, and Reid scored eight goals in just nine starts to help Rangers win the championship. His 260th and final appearance for the club came on 10 April 1920, just short of his 36th birthday.

Reid scored 224 goals for Rangers in those 260 starts, and to this day there are only six players who have ever scored more goals for the club. His goals to games average is behind only Jimmy Smith and Jim Forrest of players with 100 or more appearances, and he won four league titles.

But Reid still wasn't finished and in the summer of 1920 he accepted an offer from Scottish Cup runners-up Albion Rovers to become their player-manager. He continued the playing side of the role for two seasons, and scored 36 league goals for them in the top flight. After he hung up his boots to concentrate on the managerial role, Reid had amassed a total of 270 goals in the top division of Scottish football, which is still the fourth highest of any player in the history of league competition in Scotland. From his tally, 188 were scored for Rangers.

Reid remained at Albion Rovers until 1929, then returned to the game as manager of Dundee United two years later. He was unable to keep them in the First Division and was badly hampered by serious financial problems at the club. He left in March 1934, ending his association with senior football.

Reid lived until the age of 81, passing away at his home in Baillieston on 1 May 1966.

He was one of the greatest goalscorers in Scottish football history and a man who was instrumental in Rangers winning three successive titles after a long wait. Who knows how many goals he might have scored if he hadn't given up three years of his career to serve his country?

He is not, as yet, inducted in the Rangers Hall of Fame, and that surely is an oversight that must be put right at some point in the future.

The name of William Reid should be legendary.

- One of the greatest ever Rangers goalscorers
- 224 goals in 260 appearances
- 4 league titles
- Great War veteran

ARSENAL FOOTBALL CLUB 1949

LEFT TO RIGHT - BACK ROW :- L.SCOTT, W.BARNES, T.PLATT, G.SWINDIN, L.SMITH, H.DANIEL. MIDDLE ROW :- A.FORBES, A.FIELDS, L.COMPTON, A.MACAULAY, D.COMPTON, T.VALLANCE, FRONT ROW :- I.McPHERSON, T.LOGIE, D.LISHMAN, P.GORING, D.ROPER, H.LEWIS, F.COX.

Arsenal in 1949, featuring Ian McPherson and Archie Macauley.

Everton, league champions 1939, with Torry Gillick and Alex Stevenson.

EVERTON F.C. 1939 - DIVISION 1 CHAMPIONS

LEFT TO RIGHT - BACK ROW :- LAWTON, T.G.JONES, SAGAR, COOK (Trainer), MERCER, GREENHALGH. FRONT ROW :- W.COOK, GILLICK, BENTHAM, THOMSON, STEVENSON, BOYES.

Andrew McCreadie, Jimmy Millar and Tom Hyslop at Sunderland in season 1894/95. (Courtesy of Paul Days at Ryehill Football)

The Albert Gudmundsson statue in Reykjavik.

England international Billy Hogg of Sunderland FC. (Courtesy of Paul Days at Ryehill Football)

Bolton Wanderers, FA Cup winners in 1923, featuring Jack Smith.

Bradford City, FA Cup winners in 1911, with Jimmy Speirs (captain) and David Taylor.

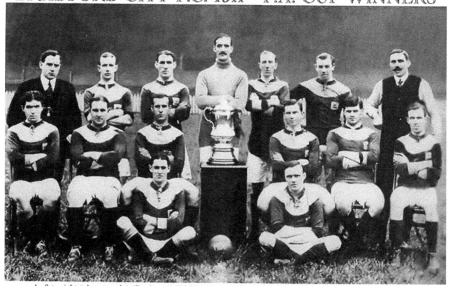

BRADFORD CITY F.C. 1911 - F.A. CUP WINNERS

Left to right (players only) (Back row) TORRANCE, O'ROURKE, MELLORS, MCDONALD, DEVINE (Middle row) (Reserve), CAMPBELL, SPIERS, ROBINSON, TAYLOR, THOMPSON (Front row) LOGAN (Reserve)

Chelsea player and first-ever manager Jacky Robertson. (Courtesy of The Founders Trail)

Liverpool in 1905/06, including future World War One casualty David Murray.

LIVERPOOL F.C. 1906 - DIVISION I CHAMPIONS

Left to right (Back row) CONNELL (trainer), HEWITT, WILSON, S.HARDY, PARRY, DOIG, DUNLOP, J.HARDY
(Middle row) ROBINSON, GORMAN, MURRAY, HUGHES, RAISBECK, COX, FLEMING, RAYBOULD, WEST
(Front row) GODDARD, LATHAM, CARLIN

USA National Cup champions New York Nationals in 1928 with Geordie Henderson front row second from right.

Everton, league winners in 1915, with captain Jimmy Galt (fourth player, second row) and top scorer Bobby Parker, (on ground bottom left).

R.S. McColl in his Queens Park days. (Courtesy of The Founders Trail)

The Scotland team to play England in 1881. George Gillespie sits right of Andrew Watson, the first black internationalist. Rangers pioneer Tom Vallance is in the back row.

SCOTLAND FOOTBALL TEAM 1881

Liverpool's first-ever title-winning team in 1901, with Johnny Walker kneeling bottom left.

William Chalmers, manager of Juventus.

Tom McKillop coaching local schoolchildren in Rhyl.
(Courtesy of Colin Jones at Rhyl Life)

Non-league Tottenham Hotspur won the FA Cup in 1901 with 'Terrible' Sandy Tait in the team.

TOTTENHAM HOTSPUR F.C. - F.A.CUP WINNERS 1901

PLAYERS ONLY - LEFT TO RIGHT - BACK ROW :- ERENTZ, CLAWLEY, TAIT. MIDDLE ROW :-
CAMERON, MORRIS, HUGHES, JONES, KIRWAN. FRONT ROW :- SMITH, BROWN, COPELAND.

THE RESTORATION OF RANGERS GRAVES PROJECT

HALF OF the author proceeds from this book will be donated to this wonderful cause, which lovingly restores or replaces headstones and adds plaques to the final resting place of significant names from the history of Rangers FC. Some of the players and managers featured in this book have had their graves restored due to this fantastic work, as well as supporters killed in the tragedies that have occurred at Ibrox.

The link below gives more details of the work carried out by these unpaid volunteers, as well as details on how to donate to their fund should you wish to do so.

https://www.thefounderstrail.co.uk/post/the-restoration-of-rangers-graves-project-how-you-can-help